NORTHERN
NEW SPAIN

Cover Illustration: This 1851 drawing by John Russell Bart-
lett shows the plaza at El Paso del Norte outwardly little
changed in nearly 200 years. The Franciscan mission of
Guadalupe, founded in 1659, was constructed between 1662
and 1668; the bell tower was added about 1800.

The Documentary Relations of the Southwest

This volume is one in a series entitled The Documentary
Relations of the Southwest, *which includes three major categories:*

The Jesuit Relations of the Southwest,
The Franciscan Relations of the Southwest,
The Civil-Military Relations of the Southwest.

*These three divisions reflect the primary sources of docu-
ments for Southwestern history and ethnohistory. By their
very nature they provide geographical, chronological, and
topical control for the rich and complex resources in Southwestern studies.*

NORTHERN NEW SPAIN
A Research Guide

Thomas C. Barnes
Thomas H. Naylor
Charles W. Polzer

THE UNIVERSITY OF ARIZONA PRESS
TUCSON, ARIZONA

About the Authors . . .

THOMAS C. BARNES came to Tucson in 1973 with a graduate degree in Western American and Latin American history from Utah State University. His interest in the West and the Southwest began with courses taught by Charles S. Peterson and John Francis Bannon, S.J. Barnes was appointed a research associate with the Documentary Relations of the Southwest in 1975.

THOMAS H. NAYLOR in 1976 received the Herbert E. Bolton Prize in Spanish Borderlands History. He earned graduate degrees in both history and anthropology from the University of Arizona, was appointed associate editor with the Documentary Relations of the Southwest project in 1975. His publications and research have spanned such topics as archaeology, dendrochronology, colonial ethnohistory, the Mexican Revolution, and Mormon colonization in northern Mexico.

CHARLES W. POLZER, ethnohistorian at the Arizona State Museum since 1972, is well known as a specialist in Spanish colonial history, particularly the Jesuit missions. In 1974, with a staff of historians and anthropologists, Polzer began directing the editing of basic documents from U.S., Mexican, and European archives as part of the Documentary Relations of the Southwest project at the University of Arizona.

The University of Arizona Press
www.uapress.arizona.edu

© 1981 by The Arizona Board of Regents
All rights reserved. Published 1981
Century Collection edition 2016

Printed in the United States of America
21 20 19 18 17 16   7 6 5 4 3 2

ISBN-13: 978-0-8165-0709-2 (cloth)
ISBN-13: 978-0-8165-3517-0 (paper)

This book was set in 10/12 Linotype Melior.

Library of Congress Cataloging-in-Publication Data
Barnes, Thomas Charles, 1946–
      Northern New Spain.

      Bibliography: p.
      1. Southwest, New—History—To 1848—Sources—
Bibliography. 2. Southwest, New—History—To 1848—
Archival resources. 3. Mexico—History—To 1810—Sources—
Bibliography. 4. Mexico—History—To 1810—Archival
resources. I. Naylor, Thomas H., joint author. II. Polzer, Charles
W., joint author. III. Title.
Z1251.S8B37   [F799]   016.979   80-24860

♾ This paper meets the requirements of ANSI/NISO Z39.48-1992
(Permanence of Paper).

CONTENTS

ACKNOWLEDGMENTS

Northern New Spain: A Research Guide owes many debts of gratitude to persons who have worked hard on its compilation. A pilot volume first appeared as the *Documentary Relations of the Southwest Project Manual* which received wide circulation. Many scholars around the world added their comments to the contents of the *Manual.* Influenced by these suggestions, the authors of the *Guide* have produced the present work in the hope that it will aid in deepening our knowledge of the history and anthropology of the greater Southwest.

Although the *Guide* represents the hard work of many persons, special credit is due Thomas Barnes who reviewed and expanded the bulk of the material included. Thomas Naylor investigated and compiled the ethnological and geographical sections of the *Guide.* Robert Erskine prepared the calligraphy and maps that appear throughout the volume. The material concerning the DRSW computer bibliography is the work of Fritz Jandrey. Thanks are due J. Bankston for his help in compiling the section on colonial weights and measures, and to John Kessell, Ursula Lamb, and Michael Meyer for reviewing portions of the manuscript. Thomas E. Sheridan critically reviewed the manuscript; María Segawa patiently typed the tedious lists. And finally the authors owe Carmen Villa Prezelski credit for constancy in performing the scores of unnoticed and unheralded tasks that make a publication possible.

The authors of the *Guide* are particularly indebted to the National Endowment for the Humanities and the National Historical Publications and Records Commission because their financial support for the Documentary Relations of the Southwest project at the Arizona State Museum ultimately made this *Guide* possible. Although the *Guide* was not a direct goal of the DRSW project, its compilation resulted from the research requirements of the project itself. Publication of this *Guide* should make the research capabilities of the DRSW an even more valuable tool in the expansion of Spanish colonial studies in the Southwest.

Behind all the work accomplished in this publication and in the DRSW project has been the quiet, solid support of the University of Arizona and the Arizona State Museum. Raymond H. Thompson, Museum Director, deserves special mention for his encouragement in this entire effort from research through publication. The University of Arizona Press is also to be thanked for effecting publication; its editor Marie Webner patiently guided the book to a speedy completion.

CHARLES W. POLZER, S.J.
General Editor
Documentary Relations of the Southwest

PREFACE

Researchers and students who probe the mysteries of Spanish colonial times need background information that is not always conveniently found. This research guide was first conceived to fulfill multiple needs of the research team of the Documentary Relations of the Southwest (DRSW) project at the Arizona State Museum. In performing research tasks, it became evident that reference material was scattered throughout scores of books and monographs. A single complete source book was simply not available. If the research team could benefit from a guide, so would the potential user of the project findings. Hence, the editors of the DRSW project compiled this guide. Admittedly, there is nothing new about its contents. What is new, however, is the scope and format of information included under one cover.

The controlling idea of the guide is to provide the user with simple discussions on basic topics: for instance, types of documents, political and social organization, paleography, and special terms. Useful lists and tables are provided so that the user can be assisted in identifying and correlating information encountered in archival research. In no way does this guide pretend to be exhaustive or definitive; comprehensive reference works must be consulted for that level of information. Yet, the investigator needs some standardization in orthography and nomenclature. As presented here, the material has been standardized for the DRSW project. The welter of treatises and monographs on weights, measures, money, legal processes, and paleography required careful analysis to extract relevant equivalents for northern New Spain throughout its different periods of growth.

Included in the guide are somewhat lengthy descriptions of the DRSW computer bibliography. When the book was first designed, it focused on the special needs of the DRSW research group. Then, as the information file grew in size and availability, it became increasingly apparent that any user of the computerized file would need a guide to explain the intricacies of the data bank. The project directors decided to combine the "manual" and "source book" aspects into one research guide. This book now serves those multiple purposes.

We have entitled the book *Northern New Spain: A Research Guide.* The territory under study comprises all of northern Mexico in colonial times. The reader will note that throughout the text mention is made of the "Southwest," especially in regard to the Documentary Relations of the Southwest project. If this book were entitled "A Handbook to Spanish Colonial Studies of the Southwest," it would contain an intrinsic contradiction because there was no "Southwest" in Spanish colonial times. Modern usage in the United States has introduced an anachronism because, by extension, the "Southwest" is rapidly becoming the name by which the larger region is identified.

Traditionally, the region of northern New Spain has been known as "El Norte." For whatever romantic reasons in the age of discovery and colonization, the "North" held a fascination every bit as strong as the later "Northwest Passage" for the Anglo-Americans. Mexicans still refer to the tier of northern states as "El Norte," although a vast part of the former colonial territory has now become part of the United States by conquest and purchase. The people of the United States customarily call the ceded territory the "Southwest." And in the language of the present the two politically separate sectors have often been called the "greater Southwest." Students and scholars have long recognized that this extensive geographical zone is a region of analogous cultures. Whether "southwesterner" or "norteño," whether North American or Mexican, the region possesses distinct cultural features that lend meaning to the designation "Southwest" or "El Norte." The meaning connotes more than a compass direction from earlier colonial centers. A final descriptive definition has not yet been given to this region. But it has its own distinctive character recognized by people on both sides of the present border. As far as this research guide is concerned, it cannot and does not enter into the difficult political issues that confuse our contemporary understanding of the region. It seeks only to accept its historical and cultural origins.

For the purpose of this research guide, northern New Spain and the greater Southwest are coextensive. Perhaps the geographic limits set down by the editors of the guide are somewhat broader than generally held by scholars in the field. But neither culture nor climate always respect lines drawn by men. The geographic region encompassed in this guide is bordered on the south by the 22nd parallel of north latitude, and on the north by the 38th. The eastern limit is the 94th meridian of west longitude; the western limit, the 123rd. This vast region encloses within the United States parts of California, Nevada, Utah, Colorado, Kansas, Oklahoma, and Texas, and all of Arizona and New Mexico. In Mexico it includes parts of Aguascalientes, Jalisco, Nayarit, San Luis Potosí, and Zacatecas, and all of Coahuila, Chihuahua, Durango, Nuevo León, Sinaloa, Sonora, Tamaulipas, and Baja California Norte and Sur. Such an extensive part of the North American continent ought to have a distinctive name, but neither usage nor history has given us one. Perhaps someday, as this region becomes better understood for its similarities and diversities, it will have one.

The user of this research guide will immediately note that there is no priority arrangement of chapters. The editors have grouped the information under headings that appear useful; explanations frequently precede discrete blocks of data. There has been no attempt to synthesize either information or explanation. Some chapters will be found very useful and others less so depending on the particular need of the individual user. The guide begins with a detailed discussion of the Documentary Relations of the Southwest Master Index. For those who have access to this file, the explanation will be indispensable; for those who may never use the file, the chapter may still have value as contributing to research design. What we are saying, quite simply, is that *Northern New Spain* provides under one cover an assortment of ideas and information that we have found valuable, if not indispensable.

THOMAS C. BARNES
THOMAS H. NAYLOR
CHARLES W. POLZER

THE DOCUMENTARY RELATIONS
OF THE SOUTHWEST

The Documentary Relations of the Southwest (DRSW) is a multiple volume series of documents pertaining to the ethnohistory, cultural heritage, and humanities of the American Southwest. The DRSW project recognizes the increasing need for more complete and accurate ethnohistorical data, particularly as that information expands knowledge about desert ecology and material culture. The DRSW contains information on Indian ethnohistory, Spanish colonial expansion, Spanish and Mexican social history, and general Indo-Hispanic culture. In order to develop a sound documentary basis for expanded research and study the DRSW is locating, selecting, editing, annotating, and publishing a series of volumes relating the culture of Indian, Spanish, and Mexican peoples during the epoch of colonial expansion and early national emergence in the greater Southwest.

The DRSW goal is the publication of significant and informative documents — not merely the collection, preservation, and cataloging of archival material. A significant number of documents, some of which are included in the publication process and some not, has been accumulated in the DRSW Computer Access Bibliography, thus permitting further research and study beyond the level offered by the published volumes. Until a general body of documents is available to the academic community and the general public, broader studies in southwestern culture will remain difficult or impossible. The gathering and cataloging of information is useful to a small number of scholars, but the information contained in such documents remains inaccessible to scholars of other disciplines who lack the requisite skills of language and interpretation. The intention of the project is to create a series of volumes that will assist educational efforts below the graduate level as well as acquaint scholars of varied disciplines with the useful nature of vastly unknown archival resources. Moreover, the DRSW provides a sound basis and desirable balance for the rising consciousness and interest of various American ethnic groups in their own ethnohistory.

The Documentary Relations of the Southwest took its name in imitation of the Jesuit Relations of North America, a landmark work resulting from the translation of missionary records. Unfortunately, the impression has been given that no other substantial body of documents pertaining to American ethnohistory was extant. The contrary is the case. There is much more information extant and accessible than in the Jesuit Relations. These documents are for the most part in Spanish and housed in Spanish and Mexican archives. Unlike the Jesuit Relations of North America, which were largely taken from published sources, these documents are unpublished and scattered over the world. Painstaking work is required to correlate the material and make it available for publication. Throughout the last century these documents have been variously consulted and occasionally published without the least intimation that vast stores of information remain untouched.

The Documentary Relations of the Southwest appear as volumes in three sections or series. The first section is the Jesuit Relations of the Southwest; the second is the Franciscan Relations of the Southwest; and the third is the Civil-Military Relations of the Southwest. The reason for this division was the natural ordering of the documents by their source and present storage. The religious documents are by far the best organized and most detailed; they serve as a control source for the organization of the civil-military papers which are voluminous and more disorganized. To anyone who has paid careful attention to the Jesuit Relations of North America, it is immediately evident that the documents are very sketchily "religious" but profoundly descriptive. In other words, although two of the announced series of volumes refer to religious orders, the content of these series is only peripherally ecclesiastical and essentially ethnohistorical.

PROJECT METHODOLOGY

The members of the DRSW research team were instructed from the outset to review selectively the material found in archival collections. Each researcher consulted the catalogs of a collection before beginning actual work. When a catalog indicated that there was reasonable hope of finding ethnohistorical material on the Southwest in a given collection, the researcher consulted the material in whole blocks to determine whether the catalogs were correct and whether other information might be useful. Whenever a document showed promise of being sufficiently informative for possible inclusion in the final published series, a review was made and a précis written. The information garnered by the researchers in these cases was also processed for inclusion in the computer access bibliography which will be described in greater detail below. Thus a large Master Index has been built up for the entire project. The Index includes all documents summarized by the research team, although it was evident from the beginning that not all the documents consulted and selected would be published. Many of the unpublished documents, however, are referenced in annotating the documents chosen for publication. The intent of the DRSW publication program is not to publish all documents selected but to select documents that are useful and representative in a way that will aid persons in expanding their research.

The problem of selectivity always presents some difficulty. Probably no system of selection will be ideal for each person consulting the DRSW material. But it is well for the user of the DRSW publications and bibliographical file to realize that broad principles were employed in choosing the various documents. No researcher approached the archival material with specific research questions or categories in mind. Each team member was instructed

"to let the documents speak for themselves." To the degree possible each researcher tried to see a broad range of topics and categories that would be useful to many academic disciplines. When a document was selected for inclusion in the file, it had to possess a recognizable level of ethnohistorical richness. No document had to contain large amounts of information, but each document had to contain significant information even if it applied to only one category under consideration in the DRSW project. Ultimately the selection process had to admit some degree of arbitrary inclusion or exclusion; the guarantee of objectivity had to be the insight and preparation of the research team member.

Generally considered, the methodology of the DRSW project holds in view the broad purposes for which the information will be employed. The researchers were therefore presented with some problems in resolving their choices. The broad scope of the selection process remains an objection for many, but these objections are usually rooted in a desire for a narrow and specific principle of selectivity suited to a single research need. The DRSW information file could not include all particulars in the documents; the file will, however, direct a researcher to the location of data.

DRSW COMPUTER ACCESS
BIBLIOGRAPHY

The Documentary Relations of the Southwest project has developed, as an integral research tool, a computer access bibliography of primary documents. This bibliography is named the DRSW Master Index because the complete listing of documents is entered into the computer file in a way that permits selective retrieval of information through indexing. The computer file uses the SELGEM system of computer programming developed by the Smithsonian Institution for information management. These programs have been adapted and refined by the DRSW project for its particular needs, thus allowing organization and manipulation of extensive archival material for use by a variety of disciplines.

Three computer files form the heart of the system. The first and most comprehensive is the DRSW Master Index of primary documents. This file contains bibliographic data on each document selected and analyzed by the DRSW research group. Since the information is serially entered, there is no particular prearrangement. A full discussion of the entry process and data retrieval follows below.

The second computer file in the system is called the Biofile. Essentially this is a biographical dictionary. Names of persons who are significantly mentioned in *published* works on southwestern history are serially entered in this file. Hence each person acquires a Biofile identification number. This file is periodically merged with the Persons Index from the DRSW Master Index, and the information contained in primary document sources is then added to the accumulated information taken from published sources. Birth, marriage, and death dates are recorded; occupations and family history are listed. With this kind of information accumulation Biofile is then capable of generating finder-lists of major and minor officials and other prominent people. It makes possible the standardization of spelling for personal names without disturbing the original forms in the documents.

The third computer file is the Geofile. Like Biofile, this data bank is a separate research tool with valuable interlinks to the DRSW Master Index. The welter of place names encountered in the DRSW Master Index required a thoroughly independent control device to distinguish between places of the same name and to standardize the orthography. Consequently, the best available series of maps drawn at a scale of 1 : 250,000 were chosen as the base for Geofile. In a few instances the cartographic information on these maps is in error, but the topographic rendering is reliable because the entire series was based on comprehensive aerial photography. In creating the Geofile all the maps in the series were inspected; each fifteen-minute quadrant was assigned a specific designation based on an archaeological grid system used in the Arizona State Museum. This procedure rendered the Geofile compatible with extensive archaeological survey files in the Southwest. Every place name or major topographical feature in each quadrant was registered and ultimately assigned an identification number by the data entry process. To distinguish between place names and geographical features, parenthetical descriptions were tagged to topographical features, e.g. (peak) or (river) or (canyon). The computerized file that has resulted from this procedure allows all the information contained in the DRSW Master Index to be arranged geographically as well as to be distinguished when similar names occur in the indexes. Computer printed maps that relate the kind and density of information contained in the Master Index can be generated with minimal difficulty. A more detailed explanation of the quadrant system used in the Geofile can be found in the section that presents the general locator maps.

These three files — the DRSW Master Index, Biofile, and Geofile — illustrate how vast amounts of information on the greater Southwest can be made available in a variety of formats. The information is basic to many scientific and humanistic disciplines.

DRSW MASTER INDEX

The data entry process for the DRSW Master Index of primary documents begins with the selection of a document for its ethnohistorical value. The definition of "ethnohistory" for this purpose is extremely broad inasmuch as it encompasses history, anthropology, linguistics, and environmental sciences. When a researcher has determined that a document meets the criteria of selection, the information is recorded directly on a computer terminal or on a printed DRSW document form. A sample of the printed form can be seen on pages 7–8. When an investigator has completed a survey of the documents in a particular section of an archive, the completed forms are sent on to the computer section of the DRSW project where they are edited for data entry. At this time the document is assigned a serial number, and hereafter the complete entry is described as a "serial entry." In the case when the documents consulted have been analyzed on microforms at the central research office, the data are entered directly on local terminals; the computer section edits this material on special data processing equipment.

Each document entered into the bibliography is assigned a serial number either by the data processor program or by the computer editor. The editorial section reviews the information categories for accuracy and completeness. At this time "key words" are assigned by the editors after comparing information in the title, summary, and categories with the DRSW Thesaurus, a specialized vocabulary of finder-terms described below. If the original entry is defective in any way, the editor returns the entry for clarification or amplification. When a sufficient number of serial entries have accumulated, they are submitted for processing by the computer that enters and stores the serials on a master tape. Usually at this time a printout is made of the newly added material, and this printout is then proofed against the original entries or forms.

Periodically the master serial file is processed by the computer in order to generate new sortings, listings, and indexes. A major updating of the bibliographic file thus occurs about every four to six months depending on the quantity of serial additions. The periodic printouts contain a sequential listing of all serial entries, each of which contains the complete information file pertaining to that serial. This master-file printout numbers thousands of pages and is usable only with the accompanying indexes that derive from the information categories. Indexes are available for persons, places, ethnic groups, general subjects, key words, and archival references. Each index is primarily arranged by alphabet, and within this alphabetic arrangement similar entries occur chronologically. The cumulative index gives the serial number of the document, the author, and a portion of the document's title. The user then needs only to consult the master-file printout for more complete information. If the user has a cassette or disk form of the indexes or master file, the information sought can be locally processed and selectively retrieved.

Special searches and bibliographic listings can be generated from the master file. For example, a special search can provide a bibliography of primary documents dealing with Spanish/Apache conflicts in Chihuahua between 1700 and 1750. These specialized bibliographies can undergo several selective searches and can be arranged in a variety of formats depending on the request.

Because individual documents are written with wide variation in spelling, especially for persons and places, additions and revisions of the master file are a continuing process. As the master file expands, the assignment of key words also undergoes refinement. These changes and additions are retroactive, so that the entire master file is updated. Users of the DRSW master file who are engaged in specific research have often provided more detailed analysis of documents than is provided by the original entry. This information is added to the extant entries so that the overall process of analysis and use enriches the master file. Unlike a simple locator file, the DRSW master file is constantly expanding and is enriching previous work at the same time it continues to add new entries.

To provide more accuracy and precision in the use of the DRSW Master Index and in its updating and refinement, the DRSW Thesaurus has been created. Researchers often define terms differently. The Thesaurus or key-word dictionary is designed to minimize differences in definition and to allow more precise definition in the revision of material already entered in the Master Index. Maintained as a separate file in dictionary form, the Thesaurus distinguishes words and synonyms which are and are not used in the categorization of subject areas. Consequently, the Thesaurus is constructed around "broad terms," which are further defined and broken down by "narrow terms." Cross-referencing of either a broad or narrow term is made possible by the inclusion of definitions for these terms and notes that put terms in perspective in relation to other subjects or terms. Persons with special research topics can, by using the Thesaurus, determine definitions, synonyms, and term relationships used by the DRSW computer editors in assigning key words. Thus the dictionary refers the researcher to the key words closest in meaning to the topic in question. For example, a person interested in "blacksmiths" would be directed to look under the term "metal working industries" in the key-word index. Someone interested in "education" would find six subdivisions of that term.

There are two methods of documentary entry. One is by direct storage on a data processor terminal. The other, and older, is by the completion of a DRSW document form. The two methods use identical categories; thus, the explanation that follows about each category is valid for either method. A typical document follows on pages 5 and 6; data taken from it appear on the sample DRSW form on pages 7 and 8. Explanations for each category are listed on pages 9 and 10.

Serial No. _____

030 From-By:To BALTHASAR HORTIZ —to— CAPITÁN DOMINGO de APRESA FALCÓN

Title-Description VENTA DE ESCLAVOS

040 Place SAN JOSEPH DEL PARRAL   Date of writing 14 FEBRERO 1676 Pages 2

Type: (Letter) Informe Relacion Residencia Auto Peticion Other VENTA

Form: (Original) (Signed) Copy Transcription Other _____

Date of contents 1676   Date of certification _____
(DCT)   (DCN)

170 Consulted at: UN. of Az. ARCHIVO Hidalgo del Cat. no. _____ Pages 2
PARRAL

Film No. 318   Reel No. 1676 A   Frame No. 550-551

171 Primary Location: ARCHIVO HIDALGO del PARRAL   Pages 2

172 Other Location: _____ Pages _____

173 Other Location: _____ Pages _____

111 Publication Reference _____

150 Misc. Notes _____

300 Language of Document SPANISH

294 DRSW Info.   Agriculture   Architecture   Biography   (Economics)   (Ethnography)

Catagories   Exploration Geography   History (Legal) Linguistics   Maritime Military

Mining Missions Political Religious (Social-Organization) Technology

295 Key Words _____

155 Classif.   SJ   OFM   (CM)   (DRSW)   JHI

201 Ethnic Groups NEGRO

160 Precis Balthasar Hortiz sells to Domingo de Apresa Falcón his two Negro slaves, Vicente age 20, and Pascual age 20, for 900 pesos de oro común. Both slaves originally purchased by Joseph Hortiz, Balthasar's brother, from Capitán Juan Molino Lago Marín in Veracruz.

_____ J. Smith 6-7-78
                          Investigator Date

022 Persons Balthasar Hortiz
Domingo de Apresa Falcón (capitán)
Vicente (slave)
Pascual (slave)
Joseph Hortiz
Juan Molina Lago Marín (capitán)
Martín Leal
Domingo de la Fuente
Miguel de Aranda (escribano)

281 Places San Joseph del Parral
Mexico (city)
Veracruz

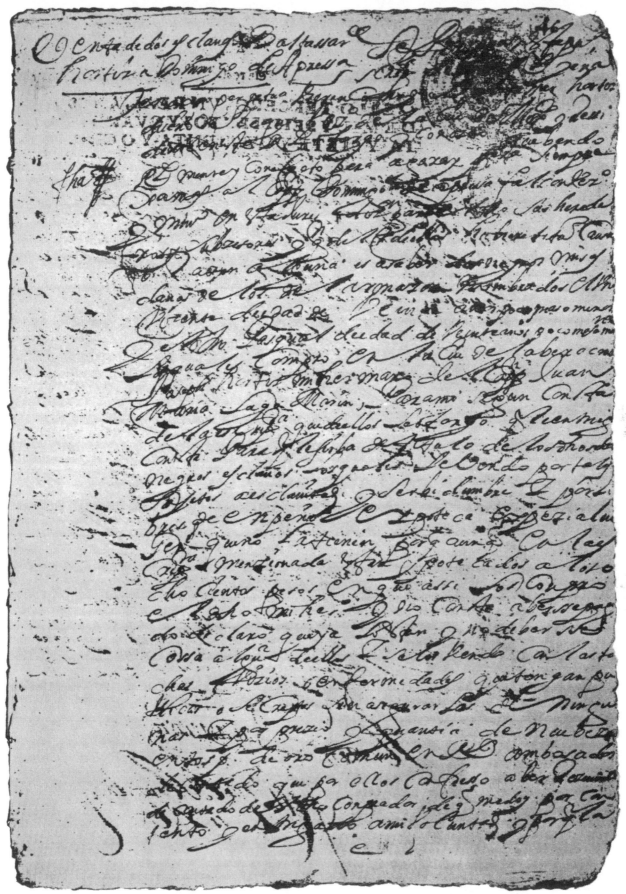

This is a faithful reproduction of a frontier document from the Archivo del Hidalgo de Parral. Legibility is frequently a serious problem owing to discoloration of the paper, oxidation of the chemicals in the ink, and deterioration of the page.

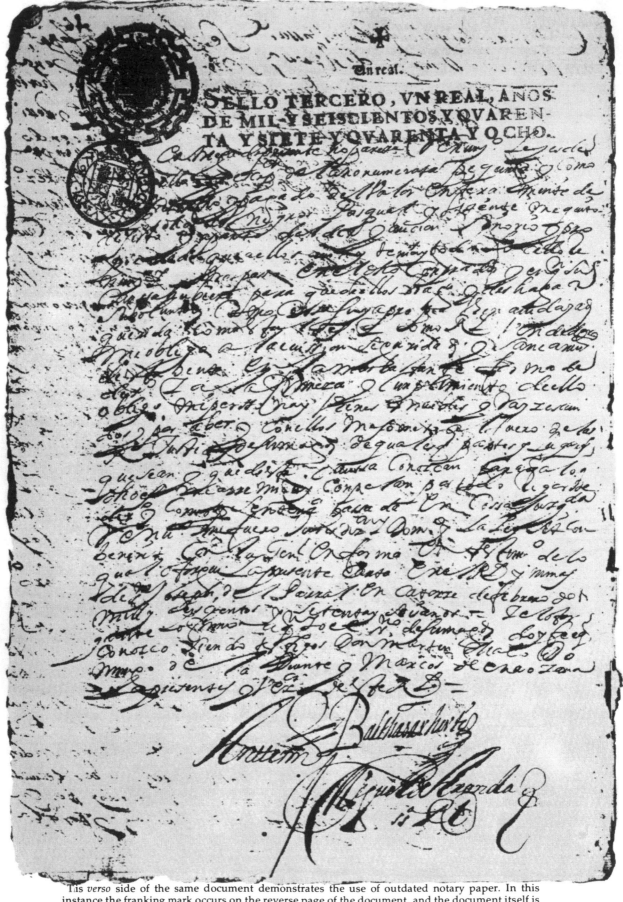

This *verso* side of the same document demonstrates the use of outdated notary paper. In this instance the franking mark occurs on the reverse page of the document, and the document itself is dated thirty years later than the official seal (1647 vs. 1677).

EXPLANATION OF CATEGORIES — DRSW DOCUMENT FORM

Category 30
Author, recipient, and title of document. If there is no author, three asterisks (***) appear instead. If there is no actual title, the investigator supplies one that is brief and descriptive.

Category 40
Place and date of origin of document. The date of the document's contents as well as any date of certification is written here. The length is also recorded.

Category 170–173
Location of consultation and availability. Category 170 records the place where the document was read with the particular archival or library classification number. Category 171 gives the primary location of the document. Categories 172 and 173 list other secondary locations where the document or a copy can be consulted. If the document has been published, this information can be found in Category 111.

Category 150
Investigator's notes. Information that is significant but not included under other categories is recorded here. Any comments about the document's physical condition, difficulty of location, or dubiousness will be herein entered.

Category 300
The language in which the document is written.

Category 294
General Information Categories. These describe the document in the broadest terms. If the document falls outside these categories, more specific descriptions will be found in Category 160 (précis), Category 150 (notes), or Category 295 (key words). Specific subjects not covered in other categories are identified by the computer editor and entered in Category 295.

Category 155
DRSW publishing classification. This indicates the probable series in which the document may be used, i.e., Jesuit (S.J.), Franciscan (O.F.M.), or Civil-Military (CM) Relations.

Category 201
Ethnic groups. All ethnic groups mentioned in the documents—Indian tribes, bands, racial or national terms, and non-Spanish European groups—are included.

Category 160
Investigator's summary. This is a general outline and précis of the document's contents.

Category 022
Persons. This includes the names of persons mentioned in the document whether religious, military, civilian, or native. The author of the document is also listed here.

Category 281
Places. All place names mentioned in the document, including the place of origin of the document, are recorded here.

If the researcher is using the printed DRSW document form these parts are filled in and passed on to the computer editors who assign key words and then submit the forms in batches for data entry and processing. The completed information appears in the Master Index under an assigned, sequential serial number. The listing begins with the serial number and each serial is followed by the various information categories identified by code numbers. Below are explanations of category entries in the DRSW Master Index. Note that the numbered information categories do not correspond exactly with the information categories on the document form because not all the categories are included on the form. Throughout the editing process more numbered categories are assigned and often appear in the DRSW Master Index printout.

EXPLANATION OF CATEGORIES — DRSW MASTER INDEX

Category 021
Author(s) of the document. Name is listed with last name first, then first name, and title, if any. If the document is a court case, death certificate, or similar document, the name of the subject person is used instead of the official writing the document. When the author is unknown, three asterisks (***) are used as an indication that the omission of a name was intentional and not the result of an error.

Category 022
Personal names. The names of persons mentioned in a document are recorded here, including those in Category 021. When the document is a tax list, census, petition, or the like, the names are *not* entered; such documents are described in the categories for précis, title, and key words. The names are entered in the standard format of last name first, first name, and title in parentheses. Titles of respect are not recorded unless for clarification. Titles for religious have been standardized as "Padre," "Fray," or "Hermano." The individual religious orders are distinguished by abbreviation "S.J." for the Society of Jesus, "O.F.M." for the Franciscans.

Category 023
Personal names. This is an extension of 022 when available computer filing space is exhausted.

Category 024
Personal names — standardized. Names occurring in Categories 021, 022, and 023 are spelled exactly as they occur in the document. This category gives the corrected or preferred name and spelling as reflected in Biofile.

Category 030
Title. Often included are the names of the author and recipient of a document when appropriate. If no title occurs in the document, the investigator assigns a brief descriptive title.

Category 040
Documentation. This records the place where the document was written, the type of document (e.g., *auto, informe*), the form in which it was read (e.g., original, copy), and the dates. The first date is that of composition. The second is the date range of the contents. The third is the date of certification, which refers to an official registration. For example, a document written on January 1, 1700 (first date), might deal with an expedition with inclusive dates of June to August, 1699 (second date), that was officially certified in May, 1703 (third date). When an entry gives no dates, the initials "N.D." are used. When no place of writing is known, the initials "N.P." are used.

Category 111 and Category 112
Refer to publication of the document or a work about the document.

Category 150
Notes on the document. Refers to physical condition, legibility, marginal notes by other persons, references to related materials, and aids to easier location of the document.

Category 155
Classifies the document according to publishing goals of the DRSW project.

Category 160 and Category 161
Précis. Investigator's general description of the contents of the document, concluding with the investigator's name and the date of his reading.

Category 170
Location of the document actually consulted by the investigator. This may be an original, a copy, or a microform.

Category 171
Primary location of the original document.

Category 172 and Category 173
Other locations of other original-copies, copies, or microforms.

Category 180
Bibliography. All entries are given the code CP-1 for this project, thus allowing this file to be merged with other files at a later time. If the entry is copied or located in any other bibliography, the notation is recorded here.

Category 201
Ethnic groups. All ethnic groups mentioned in the documents are recorded here, including non-Spanish Europeans. Language use is noted in other categories.

Category 202
Ethnic groups — standardized. As with personal names an place names, many variants occur in ethnic names. The original spelling is registered in Category 201; this category gives the names as standardized by contemporary usage, if established.

Category 250
This is a "computer" date that is taken from Category 040. If the date of content is known, this is the date used here. Otherwise the date is the date of the writing of the document. This entry is an eight-digit number. The first four digits indicate the year; the next two, the month; and the final two, the day. Thus, August 10, 1645, would appear as 16450810. If the date is unknown, eight zeros are used. If the month or day is unknown, this will be recorded with zeros accordingly.

Category 281 and Category 282
Place names. All place names mentioned in the document are recorded, followed by titles or descriptions in parentheses: e.g., Fronteras (pueblo), Fronteras (ciudad), Fronteras (presidio).

Category 283
Place Names — standardized. Here are recorded the contemporary name with standardized spelling for the place mentioned in Category 281. Because place names have many historical variations, the actual place has been assigned a locator number from Geofile and a standardized spelling given to the place.

Category 294
General Subject Categories. DRSW data entry forms contain nearly a score of broad terms by which the investigators classify the documentary contents. These classifications enable the sorting and indexing of documents by general subjects.

Category 295
Key Words. These are specific terms relating to the content of a document. If information falls outside the broad classifications of Category 294, it is individually recorded here. Key words are frequently assigned by the computer editor from information furnished by the investigator. The DRSW Thesaurus is built from terms employed in this category. Many key words relate to Category 294 as species to genus.

Category 298
Sources. The word "archive" appears here in anticipation of the merger of this file with other files containing published works. Thus, the primary nature of the information is preserved and permits future sorting by "primary" and "secondary" criteria.

Category 300
Language. This is the language in which the document is written.

These are the complete categories employed in the DRSW Master File at this writing. Other categories can be added to the system and retroactively assigned to the total number of serials if occasion warrants.

The sample serial entry below was compiled from an analysis of the document reproduced on pages 5–6. Data taken from that document are shown on pages 7–8. After editing and computer processing, the information can be presented in several formats, one of which appears below.

On the following pages are sample entries from specific indices that illustrate a few of the other possible formats in which data can be retrieved and arranged.

SAMPLE SERIAL ENTRY — DRSW MASTER INDEX

Serial	Category	Line	Data
00001297	021	01	Hortiz, Balthasar
	022	01	Hortiz, Balthasar/Apresa Falcón, Domingo de (capitán)/
		02	Hortiz, Joseph/Molina Lago Marín, Juan (capitán)/
		03	Leal, Martín/Puente, Domingo de la/Aranda, Miguel de
		04	(escribano)
	023	01	
	024	01	Ortiz, Baltasar/Ortiz, José
	030	01	Venta de esclavos
	040	01	San Joseph del Parral. February 14, 1676. Carta
		02	de venta. Orig. Sgnd. MF. 2 pp.
	111	01	Historia Mexicana, Vol. 24, pp. 121–122.
	112	01	
	150	01	
	155	01	CM
	160	01	Balthasar Hortiz sells to Domingo de Apresa Falcón
		02	his two negro slaves, Vicente and Pasqual, both
		03	20 years of age, for 900 pesos de oro común. Both
		04	slaves previously purchased by Joseph Hortiz,
		05	Balthasar's brother, from capitán Juan Molino Lago
		06	Marín in Veracruz. (J. Smith) (1978)
	161	01	
	170	01	AZU. Archivo Hidalgo del Parral. MF. 318. Reel
		02	1676A. Fr. 0550–0551.
	171	01	Archivo del Parral
	172	01	University of Texas, Austin. Microfilm.
	173	01	
	180	01	CP-1
	201	01	Negro
	202	01	
	250	01	16760214
	281	01	San Joseph del Parral/México (city)/Veracruz
	282	01	
	283	01	
	294	01	economics/ethnography/legal/social-organization
	295	01	slaves (sale)/prices/commerce/labor force
	298	01	Archives
	300	01	Spanish

Examples of Subject Indices Derived From Information in the Master Index

Example from key-word index, composed of categories 295 (key words—in this case, "slaves"), 250 (date), 021 (author), and 030 (title).

Serial	Subject term	Date	Author	Title
01793	slaves (sale)	1660/08/01	Madera, Antonio	Venta de esclavo
**01297	slaves (sale)	1676/02/14	Ortiz, Baltasar	Venta de esclavos
02669	slaves (sale)	1711/01/06	Velarde, Luis	Venta de esclavo
03243	slaves (sale)	1758/12/21	García, Juan	Venta de esclavos

Example from general-subject index, composed of categories 294 (general information—in this case, "economics"), 250 (date), 021 (author), and 030 (title).

Serial	Subject term	Date	Author	Title
04819	economics	1799/09/16	Bringas, Diego	Inventario de la hacienda
02475	economics	1671/03/05	García, José	Petición sobre unos solares
02078	economics	1692/10/08	Muñoz, Pedro	Manifestaciones de plata
**01297	economics	1676/02/14	Ortiz, Baltasar	Venta de esclavos

Example from persons index, composed of categories 022 (persons), 250 (date), 021 (author) and 030 (title).

Serial	Subject term	Date	Author	Title
00913	Casas, Juan de	1744/12/16	Casas, Juan de	Juan de Casas. Venta de tienda
00167	Estrada, Pedro	1648/11/02	Valdez, Luis de	La residencia que se trata
**01297	Ortiz, Baltasar	1676/02/14	Ortíz, Baltasar	Venta de esclavos
02675	Reyes, Carlos	1716/03/21	Reyes, Carlos	Carta de dote para

In the examples above, information from the document, the document form and the serial entry in the Master Index on the preceding pages is noted with two asterisks. Many other combinations of information can be retrieved in index form. Thus, a printout could be produced consisting only of information in the Master Index concerning Baltasar Ortiz. Or, all slave sales could be made available.

The computer aspect of the DRSW thus begins with the completion of the document information form and ends with a researcher being able to extract general or specific information from the Master Index of Documents. The possibilities for information retrieval are many, and the savings in time and money normally spent on research are great.

Some of the numbered information categories in each serial entry in the Master Index are designed to be searched for specific subjects or terms (all categories could be designed in this manner) and thus represent the indexing capabilities of the computer. At present, the following categories are so designed: 021 (authors), 022 (persons), 024 (personal name standardization), 111 (publication reference), 170 (location of document consulted), 171 (primary location of document), 172 (other locations of document), 155 (project publication classification), 180 (bibliography), 201 (ethnic groups), 202 (ethnic group standardization), 250 (dates), 281 (place names), 283 (place name standardization), 294 (general information categories), 295 (key words), 298 (sources), and 300 (language).

The indexing capability of the computer becomes pertinent when an individual wishes to locate information on specific topics. Separate indices can be printed from any of the search categories. These indices can be provided for a single category or any combination of categories. Each entry in such an index contains information from the category requested and is identified by the serial number under which it appears in the Master Index. If an investigator decided certain entries in a specific index would be valuable for his work, he would then refer to the entry serial number which would guide him to the more complete entry in the Master Index. From that point, categories 170–173 of the entry in the Master would refer him to the location of the actual document or copies of it.

TYPES AND STRUCTURES OF DOCUMENTS

Significant portions of many documents, especially of administrative, civil, or military origin, are taken up with form and formalities. No matter how one goes about it, reading colonial documents is a slow process. However, when one knows the different parts of a document and what kinds of information these parts typically contain, the time spent in searching for specific data is substantially reduced.

The key to distinguishing important material from routine form is practice. Once the investigator has learned to read the documents, he becomes familiar enough with routine formalities to employ certain shortcuts. Indeed, the form of the document itself provides assistance for rapidly identifying the location of routine and nonroutine information. Knowing the type of document under scrutiny and the customary structure or sequence of presentation is the point of departure for efficient analysis.

Perhaps the most useful aid in determining the contents of a document are the notations placed in the margin by the scribe who wrote it or by the official who later reviewed it. Unfortunately not all documents have such marginal notes. These notations often indicate the specific nature of information contained in the body of the document; occasionally they merely record decisions made. Knowing what such marginal notes mean and how to use them comes solely from practice and experience. There is no strict standard to be followed, only a particular style to be understood.

A general pattern for documents of administrative, civil, ecclesiastical, and military origin has been assumed, and the discussion that follows gives an explanation of the structure of some of the more common types. It must be stressed, however, that despite their regularity many documents will vary according to the individual whims of authors and scribes.

ADMINISTRATIVE DOCUMENTS

RESIDENCIAS

Regarding documents of administrative origin, the *residencia* is among the most complex. The residencia is an official review of a person who has just completed a term of office. The first part of these lengthy documents concerns the instigator of the review. The higher his status, the longer this part of the document; all titles of nobility, honor, and office must be listed. A careful reading, however, will often find the author mentioned in the first half-page. The next part of the residencia mentions the official authorization or order for the review. Included in this part is the person to be investigated, his official capacity, and the designation of a *juez de residencia* (the judge). The third section of the document usually contains the order, given by the judge, to set the review in motion. The three or four entries immediately following describe and acknowledge the powers and duties of the judge and the naming of other necessary officials, such as the *escribano* or *notario*. Generally, the document then deals with an official notification or publication which informs the citizens of a district that a residencia will be held.

Once all parties necessary for the conduct of a residencia have been designated, the review process itself is detailed. A short note confirms the time, place, and the manner in which the investigation will be conducted. A set of questions to be asked is devised and listed. If there are no further complications in the review, the next part, in which the questions are answered by each witness, is usually the longest in the document. Each witness is identified, and his replies to the series of questions are recorded. These questions and answers, which form the heart of the document, frequently contain the most sensitive information.

The questions concluded, the judge then indicates that he is proceeding to examine all records and account books of the official involved. When he has finished this inspection, the judge normally states that the official examination is completed. He notes the results of the investigation and sends these together with his own recommendations to the governor or appropriate official for final determination. Frequently at this point a *petición* is filed by the examinee, who attempts to explain certain parts of the residencia that he feels have not properly or accurately portrayed his actions.

In an ordinary residencia the last section of the document records the decision of a higher authority, often the governor of a province. This is sometimes accompanied by his opinion on the conduct of the residencia. If the case is not routine, there may be a lengthy presentation including statements from various persons commenting on answers to official questions. These comments may be followed by replies of the official under investigation. As the residencia grows, the process can be greatly prolonged, thus adding its own historical perspective as the parties involved support their arguments with even older evidence.

The final section of the residencia is the order directing that the findings be sent on to the Council of the Indies. If there are appeals outstanding at this time, the council may or may not take them into consideration. The final section of a residencia is usually a certification of completion, signed by the judge, his scribe, and the person investigated.

If one is interested only in the principal parties, such as the judge or the official investigators, the search can be easily narrowed down to the first three or four pages. If one is looking for the final judgment, this will probably be found in the last quarter of the document. The task will be noticeably easier if marginal notes have been added.

VISITAS

Another common and informative type of administrative document is the *visita*. There are many kinds of visitas ranging from a governor's annual inspection of a province's stores, bakeries, butcher shops, mines, haciendas, and presidios, to a general inspection of a large region carried out by an official appointed in Spain. Because of the investigatory nature of a visita, these documents frequently contain important material.

A visita is usually arranged in three general parts. The first is the order for the investigation. This statement identifies the person authorizing the inspection, denotes the geographic area and object of the inspection, and names the person responsible for the actual review. The central portion of the document records the remarks of the *visitador* as he conducts the inspection. This is usually the longest part of the document and contains the most detailed information. The final section of the visita concludes with a summary of the inspection and possibly some opinions of the official in charge. There is also the usual formality of confirmation, that is, that the inspection did indeed occur as witnessed by concerned parties. These three sections are occasionally followed by an official report from the visitador; in many cases this is lacking because the visita may have been concluded at a place other than where the inspection was made.

INFORMES AND RELACIONES

Spanish administrative documents also include the broader ranging *informe* and *relación*. There is only a vague distinction between these two types of documents; both were primarily written to convey information. The informe, however, ordinarily constitutes an official report on a matter of immedi-

ate importance, often serving as the basis for a juridical decision. On the other hand, the *relación* was lengthier, more general, and less formal. It often related information on topics of no immediate bearing on administrative issues, serving as a background report or position paper. Both kinds of documents present summaries and syntheses as written by civil or ecclesiastical personnel who were immediately involved with the subject. Because of the nature of the author's involvement, these documents often provide some of the richest sources of information on frontier life, especially concerning mission practice, Indian problems, military campaigns, and details of civil administration.

MILITARY DOCUMENTS

From the military standpoint, particularly in regions dealing with hostile Indians, the *autos de guerra* (order of war) constitute the most important documents. These documents are frequently lengthy and complex because of the number of people involved, the variety of information presented, and extensive time periods covered in a single report. Because of these variations, only a most general description can be presented here.

An auto de guerra opens with a description of the event that necessitated military action by the Spaniards. This report may take the form of an official statement or it may be simply a letter from a citizen or soldier that sets down the character of the problem. After this initial declaration there are generally reports of preliminary actions taken by individuals, local militia, or presidial patrols.

The next section of the document usually is identified by orders from the governor which announce a military response to some threatening situation. He may have decided to act on his own authority or he may have called a *junta de guerra* to assist and support his decision. Whatever decision was reached is recorded, and a statement of the issuance of orders, acknowledged by the recipient, follows. The standard procedure is for the governor to issue a war command and for the presidial commanders to acknowledge it.

If presidial troops were required to take the field against hostile Indians, the next part of the document normally relates the field diaries of the commanders. Here a wide variety of information is encountered. In addition, this section of the document may well contain letters or statements of citizens affected by Indian hostilities or military engagements.

Once the military action has concluded and the field reports filed, the official ordering the action summarizes the incident. This summary is often accompanied by final assessments from the commanders and the participants. Such documents in their entirety can become distressingly long. Thus, it should be noted that there are two or three places in the document where the most useful information is commonly found: first, that part of the auto that contains the journals or field diaries of the military commanders; second, the summary of the action as recorded in the junta de guerra; and third, the summaries at the end of the auto which contain the final conclusions of the officials involved.

CIVIL DOCUMENTS

Civil documents cover a wide range of topics. They are as routine as any papers found in a county courthouse. Ordinarily they involve actions, transactions, or disputes over the performance of services or the exchange of property — including sales of slaves, livestock, real estate, mines, and movable goods. Although filled with legal formalities, these civil documents are excellent sources of economic and ethnohistorical information.

Most civil documents are short and self-explanatory. They fall into broad categories of petitions, claims, proceedings, judicial procedures, and decrees. Each one expresses a nuance of difference. The *petición* may come from one person or a group who seeks an authoritative response to some request. The *demanda* is the filing of a claim pursuant to a contract or previous judgment; it connotes some controversy in law or justice. The *expediente* is a simple executive order that does not involve litigation in the performance of some action. A *diligencia* is an order or action taken by one in the position of responsibility. With regard to the internal contents of these civil instruments there is little difference and no need to discuss their structure. When they are incorporated into more complex legal instruments, it is beneficial to distinguish between their individual purposes. In this way they may apply to administrative, civil, or even criminal proceedings.

Other documents found in civil archives have more precise legal definitions and accordingly serve specific purposes, such as the *denuncio* which establishes a mining claim. Since these documents are legal instruments, they have definite formal structures which determine where certain kinds of information are located. A knowledge of these formal structures aids in extracting useful information with efficiency.

WILLS

Perhaps the most important civil documents in terms of the extent and variety of information are those dealing with inheritances. Usually only wealthy or prominent citizens filed wills for the distribution of their estates, and consequently the documents are lengthy and detailed. They contain descriptions of property, price structures, credit relationships, and insights into the material culture of the times. Most of these papers include lengthy inventories and minute descriptions of properties with monetary appraisals. Household goods, tools and articles of clothing, as well as slaves, livestock and real estate holdings are enumerated.

TESTAMENTOS (TESTAMENTARIAS)

Testamentarías are the executions of the estates of deceased persons. Such documents begin with a *testamento,* or last will and testament of the individual, in which this person affirms the legitimacy of his parentage, describes his illness, commends himself to God, and enumerates his legal children and beneficiaries. The testator then itemizes and describes his possessions. And finally, the testator names his *albacea* or *testamentario* (executor).

Following the section written or dictated by the deceased, the inventory or inventories of his estate are appended, each item of which is appraised according to its value in pesos. If the estate includes slaves, the racial origin, age, and value in pesos is given; occasionally, the parentage or place of origin of the slave is recorded. After the inventory there appears a list of outstanding debts and credits.

Whenever a prominent citizen died without leaving a will, his estate was declared *intestado* (intestate). Legal proceedings often resulted from this situation in which an heir would be named and an inventory and appraisal of the estate would be ordered. These inventories are similar in detail to those found in the testamentarías.

VENTAS DE ESCLAVO AND CARTAS DE LIBERTAD

Other common civil documents are those that deal with the sale, purchase, or manumission of slaves. A slave sale is called a *venta de esclavo,* and a manumission, a *carta de libertad*. Ventas de esclavos follow the same general format as other bills of sale. Most are short — one or two pages in length. The bill of sale begins with a paragraph briefly describing the buyer and the seller involved in the transaction; this statement includes the place of residence, occupations, and titles. Midway through the document the slave or slaves are described. Racial origin, age, sex, and price are almost always included. Occasionally birthplaces, parentage, conjugal relationships, and offspring are recorded. The place and date of sale are usually found in the last ten lines of the document.

The *carta de libertad* is also brief. The owner delineates the slave's legal history, including former owners, and establishes his legal title to the slave. Then he describes his reasons for setting the slave free. Often slaves purchased their own freedom.

TITULOS AND PETICIONES

Another large category of civil documents deals with land and mines. *Títulos,* or land titles, comprise collections of brief documents describing the land in question, noting its location, extent, and boundaries, and registering ownership with the proper colonial authorities. The first part of the document usually states the title as registered by the owner; herein is contained most of the essential information about the property itself. The final sections are administrative or procedural and written by officials.

Occasionally títulos involve petitions for actual land grants. In these cases a *petición* for the land appears first among the papers. In the petición the applicant sets forth a need for the land, asserts that his being granted title will not conflict with the interest of other parties, and records prior use and occupation often by the petitioner himself. Most títulos also describe topography and water sources.

DENUNCIOS

These documents are mining claims. Also quite brief, the denuncio begins with the description of the mine as filed by the claimant. This part states that the mine in question has either been abandoned or left unworked for the requisite period of time. Following this claim are often the counterclaims of present or previous owners challenging the denuncio. Frequently the testimony of neutral parties is included, together with pertinent procedural or administrative directives of officials.

REGISTROS

These are brief documents registering mines with appropriate colonial officials. In form and function, a registro is similar to a denuncio with the emphasis on the simple recording of ownership.

PODERES

The *poder* is equivalent to a power of attorney. It involves one person giving another the legal authority to act on his behalf for the purposes of buying and selling. These two parties are identified in the first paragraph. There follows a description of the legal power bestowed, usually in terms of the transaction to be carried out. Finally, the document records the place and date of the transfer of power and a statement that the transfer was confirmed by a witness.

ECCLESIASTICAL DOCUMENTS

LETTERS

Aside from documents of ecclesiastical courts or the Inquisition, these types of documents are simple in form. The majority of such documents are letters written by or to clergy at various levels of church administration. They normally report on the spiritual and temporal affairs of missions and colleges. Most letters contain both types of information, a characteristic that immerses ethnohistorical data in discourse on religious matters.

Letters customarily begin with the addressees' names and titles; this is often prefaced by abbreviated phrases of respect, such as "My Most Reverend

Father Procurator Juan Ortiz, the Peace of Christ." The text is concluded with traditional forms of respect and good wishes. This final part can be extensively abbreviated. The place and date of the letter are among the last items written. The author's name and rubric appear last.

In colonial times the conservation of paper was a primary consideration. Hence letters were carefully folded to protect the interior writing in much the same fashion as a modern airletter. Often a writer after reaching the bottom of a page would write sideways along the remaining margins. Occasionally the margins contain notes or corrections. These added remarks are frequently preceded by a cross (+) indicating the phrase is to be inserted where the cross appears in the text. It is not uncommon to encounter a letter with such additions or corrections together with marginal summations by the recipient or later reviewer; the difference in handwriting can distinguish between them.

PADRONES

Because the church constituted a major but separate part of colonial administration, there are many kinds of quasi-civil documents that appear in ecclesiastical archives or ecclesiastical sections of civil archives. The missionary was often required to take the *padrón* (census) of a native town; that document may appear in church archives. The padrón was taken on a relatively regular basis. But the quality of information varies widely, from a mere head count to a detailed register of names and ethnic origins. Such padrones also helped to certify marriages and freedom to marry.

INFORMES

Under the general category of *informes* occur a diversity of official reports. These may involve civil or military matters inasmuch as they might contain recommendations for the conduct of cultural or presidial affairs. This same general category can include the *visita general,* a report on the state of a mission district or a vicariate. In the case of the missions administered by religious orders, these general visitations were usually annual. They contain information touching on the spiritual welfare of native communities as well as temporal matters dealing with agriculture, commerce, and construction. Hence they are an excellent source for social and economic history.

PETICIONES

Occasionally a *petición* will be found among ecclesiastical documents. These petitions were generally submitted to civil or military officials by certain people under a priest's jurisdiction. More often than not they were made during a crisis when normal channels of redress were inoperative.

DIEZMOS

In handling ecclesiastical documents one should remember that they reflect the structure and practices of the colonial church. The secular church was directly controlled by the established hierarchy of bishops who had obligations toward the welfare of the people. Accordingly, they had the power to tax for the conduct of ecclesiastical affairs. The collection of these taxes generated a vast amount of documentation, especially in the case of *diezmos* (tithes). Mission communities were exempt, but not all the activities of the religious orders were free from taxation. The diezmo can serve as an excellent source of economic information as long as it is remembered that many exemptions were in effect. An *expediente* of any diezmo contains the usual information about the powers of the bishop to extract such payment and a description of the properties and products affected by the tithe.

INQUISITION DOCUMENTS

The documents of the Inquisition have long been a rich source of information. This ecclesiastical court functioned on the frontier but not as extensively as in central New Spain; hence, a longer analysis of these documents is not included here. It is sufficient to say that the structure and form of Inquisition documents follow much the same style as juridical papers in the civil courts. Judges, witnesses, and testimony are merely different in name and content.

REPORTS TO RELIGIOUS ORDERS (CARTAS ANNUAS)

A widely used source of information has been the archives of the religious orders, especially the Jesuits and the Franciscans. It is helpful to review the administrative character of the orders to understand the kinds of records that were generated. In the case of the Society of Jesus (Jesuits), there was a strong tradition of filing annual reports. These ultimately appeared as the *Cartas Annuas* or annual summary reports sent to the Jesuit General in Rome. These reports contained information on the state of the provinces, the colleges, houses, and missions — including both spiritual and temporal affairs. These summaries were drawn from information sent in by missionaries and workers all over the province. The first level of information was compiled in an expediente called the *Puntas de Annua*, or annual notes from individual participants in the apostolates. These field reports, and the summaries made from them, contain valuable information on population, architecture, agriculture, subsistence patterns, ethnic composition, religious customs, and economic transactions of missions and colleges. They are one of the richest sources of information on early Indian acculturation throughout New Spain.

INFORMACIOS AND LIBROS DE REGISTRO

The last kinds of ecclesiastical documents that merit mention deal with personnel affairs. Special reports were filed about the suitability of religious for promotion to orders or to positions of authority. These documents, called *informacios*, were confidential statements about the legitimacy of parentage for a priest-to-be, or about the personal life of a man taking vows. The *informacio ad gubernandum* specifically dealt with a man's suitability to govern others. Such documents are characteristically brief and self-explanatory.

Many civil archives preserve the *libros de registro* from the early missions and parishes. These books record those baptized (*Libro de Bautismos*), those married (*Libro de Matrimonios*), and the deceased (*Libro de Difuntos*). As such these books are indispensable sources for social history.

PALEOGRAPHY

The purpose of this discussion on paleography is to make the reading of Spanish colonial documents somewhat easier. It must be conceded, however, that persistent practice is the only method that will assure any degree of competence.

Colonial documents — whether written by an ecclesiastical or civilian scribe, frontier notary, anxious priest, or semiliterate rancher — can be difficult to read. There are some general guidelines which may help in getting started. Most important to determine are the author and recipient of the document. Once this is done, the overall picture of the document becomes clearer; at least one knows who is writing to whom. If the document contains marginal notes, and if they are legible, they usually provide a more detailed outline of contents than a mere title. Initially it is better to peruse the entire document to ascertain the areas of particular visual difficulty. In some cases a document will appear at first to be nothing more than a maze of unintelligible scrawls; careful and painstaking reading alone will unravel it. Although a brief perusal of a document may reveal little about the contents, it serves the purpose of familiarizing the reader with the legible portions and the penmanship of the author. These spots often become the only reservoirs of reference to interpolate other sections of the writing.

After such a brief overview is made, the real work begins. If the document or parts of it elude interpretation, then each sentence, each word, and, many times, each letter require careful repetitive study. Throughout this process several techniques become invaluable in deciphering the writing. General rules of paleography hold true for most forms of handwriting, but one must be prepared for the individual disparities that occur frequently enough to frustrate even the most accomplished scholar. It is probably better to be cautiously doubtful than pedantically precise.

Most Spanish colonial documents lack punctuation, capitalization, and accentuation. Those that have them vary so widely in their standards of application that the reader is left helpless. It is a futile exercise to search for capital letters starting sentences or for periods ending them. Sentences as often as not begin and end without a break in the stroke of the author's pen. Many words are joined together. Some words may be written with the initial syllable attached to the previous word, or the last syllable appended to the following word. Added to this potpourri is the apparent lack of rules for hyphenation. A word can be broken almost in any fashion as the writer nears the margin of the page; the word is resumed on the next line, hopefully with no omissions. In many cases proper names lack capitalization. Common given names are frequently reduced to one or two letters, sometimes just a scrawl. Confusing combinations are endless. There are, however, a few things which can make reading such material easier.

When you begin, forget about the document's coherence and meaning. Once the document is deciphered, coherence and meaning emerge as the reward of careful analysis. Break each line down into words, or as many words as possible. If necessary, break words into individual letters. Words or letters encountered for the first time may be illegible, or at least unintelligible. When this occurs, search the page for clearer samples of better formed letters or similar words. Most authors had a style of sorts, and often words or letters can be identified by referring to other material written in the same hand. A difficult word in one context may be perfectly evident in another.

Colonial writing habits reveal an inherent tendency to use multiple forms for the same letter written by the same author in a single context. It is expected that a letter might vary from author to author. But many documents exhibit multiple variations in the formation of several letters by the same writer. For example, "s" will be shaped quite differently. Initial "s," terminal "s," and inclusive "s" will be interchanged in a cursive hand. At times the writer will use the older "f" shape for an "s." No one can write rules for breaking rules. Expect the unexpected.

In an age of industrial affluence we tend to discount the conservation of paper. Not so in the colonial era; paper was precious and hard to come by. The colonial copyist tended to conserve paper by writing in abbreviations. Then too, since documents were entirely handwritten until the very last years of the era, abbreviations saved time in an otherwise tedious task of writing and copying. Again, rules for abbreviations were unknown, not followed, or nonexistent — but abbreviations abound. The profusion and variety of nexuses, word and letter connections, the imperfect separation of words, the extraordinary abundance of strokes and flourishes, and simply poor penmanship leave the impression that almost everything was abbreviated. However, this was not the case.

There are several ways to identify abbreviations. A straight or curved line above a word or phrase usually indicates one. A period used at the end of two repeated consonants stands for a plural abbreviation: for example, MM. stands for *Madres,* or SS.MM. stands for *Sus Majestades.* Plurals are frequently noted with nothing more than doubled consonants without an ending period. Superscript letters at the end of the first or second syllable indicate an abbreviation. These superscript letters most often occur at the end of a word, but it is not uncommon to find them lodged in the middle of a long word. Some abbreviations were standard; others were inventions of an individual writer. Again, there is no substitute for familiarity with one author's style — a knowledge that derives only from experience.

A corollary to the phenomenon of abbreviation is the occurrence of linear scrawls. These cursive shapes can actually denote specific meaning once a reader deciphers an author's consistencies. Perhaps the most extreme example of this will be found in the notarial writing of the sixteenth century. There were conventions followed by trained writers, but each admitted to individual peculiarities and variations. For the nonprofessional reader the only avenue to solution is to grasp the meaning of the words preceding and following the linear enigma. More often than not the scrawl has merely replaced repetitive phrases or routine remarks easily interpolated from the context. Fortunately, the bulk of documents dealing with northern New Spain were not written in this notarial hand so reminiscent of cursive Arabic.

Double and triple consonants are a curiosity. "C, N, P, R, S, and T" are the most frequently encountered. This practice leads to varying degrees of frustration especially as one tries to decipher doubled letters in a poorly written word — for example, doubled "t's" in *ttesttamentto.*

Further problems in reading result from the fact that one and the same writer commonly transposed several letters. Modern readers are accustomed to stricter standardization, but the practice was quite acceptable in colonial paleography. "C" and "V" were often interchangeable, as were "B" and "V", "S, C, and Z," "Y and I," "J and X," "U and V," "J and G," — to name only some of the more common. *Vecino* may well be spelled *Bezino* in the same document.

Other orthographic variations include dropping the first letter of words, such as *ijo* for *hijo,* or sometimes disguising the initial letter as a nondescript scrawl. Some elisions also occur.

These orthographic variations are actually explainable. And the reason for these inconsistencies constitutes one of the best methods for decipherment of difficult words and passages. Most extant colonial documents were written by scribes or copyists who *listened to the text being dictated.* Behind the written Spanish word is usually the *spoken* word. A mere change in vocal emphasis is often reflected by a scribe's choice of consonants, just as a change in the speed of dictation often led to the employment of abbreviations. Many of the copyists lacked extensive education, with the result that they wrote down what they heard rather than what was orthographically preferred. Sometimes the copyist knew neither word nor correct grammatical form.

Because this vocal characteristic plays such a significant role in the recording of colonial documents, one of the most successful paleographic practices is to read the document aloud — at least to oneself. When a word or phrase is undecipherable for any of a variety of reasons, the reader should go back a line or two and read aloud with some speed and emphasis. It often happens that the ear then provides what the eye is unable to discern.

The table of abbreviations that follows is composed of examples taken from actual documents written in northern New Spain. The samples were traced from microfilm enlargements and they range over the entire colonial period. This table is designed to assist the reader in deciphering documents more easily and efficiently. Many paleographic guides are available to the serious researcher, and these are most useful. The value of the following table is its derivation from rustic frontier sources. Many of the legalistic and courtly forms encountered in peninsular documents are foreign to frontier practice.

Again, the only certain way to learn to read documents of the Spanish colonial period is patient practice. Whole courses in paleography pale before the cactus-thorn scratching of a frontier captain. Incorrect spelling, poor grammar, lack of punctuation, poor penmanship, faded ink, water stains, worm holes, and the author's inability to articulate can only be overcome with determination, persistence, and insight. And sometimes even that fails.

TABLE OF ABBREVIATIONS

Word	Abbreviation	Word	Abbreviation
agosto	*(handwritten)*	cinquenta	*(handwritten)*
Agustín (Augustín)	*(handwritten)*	ciudad	*(handwritten)*
alcalde	*(handwritten)*	colegio	*(handwritten)*
alférez	*(handwritten)*	communión	*(handwritten)*
alguacil	*(handwritten)*	compañía	*(handwritten)*
alguna	*(handwritten)*	Compañía de Jesús	*(handwritten)*
alguno	*(handwritten)*	confesión	*(handwritten)*
algunos	*(handwritten)*	conocimiento	*(handwritten)*
Alonso	*(handwritten)*	corriente	*(handwritten)*
año	*(handwritten)*	cruz	*(handwritten)*
ante, ante mí	*(handwritten)*	cumplimiento	*(handwritten)*
Antonia	*(handwritten)*	de	*(handwritten)*
Antonio	*(handwritten)*	de esta	*(handwritten)*
arrendamiento	*(handwritten)*	de estas	*(handwritten)*
arrobas	*(handwritten)*	de este	*(handwritten)*
audiencia	*(handwritten)*	de los	*(handwritten)*
aunque	*(handwritten)*	del	*(handwritten)*
bachiller	*(handwritten)*	demás	*(handwritten)*
Baptista	*(handwritten)*	derecho	*(handwritten)*
Bartolomé	*(handwritten)*	después	*(handwritten)*
beneficio	*(handwritten)*	dicha	*(handwritten)*
Bernardo	*(handwritten)*	dichas	*(handwritten)*
cavallero	*(handwritten)*	dicho	*(handwritten)*
cámara	*(handwritten)*	dichos	*(handwritten)*
cantidad	*(handwritten)*	diciembre	*(handwritten)*
capitán	*(handwritten)*	Diego	*(handwritten)*
capitán general	*(handwritten)*	dijeron	*(handwritten)*
Castillo	*(handwritten)*	diligencia(s)	*(handwritten)*
carta	*(handwritten)*	doctrina	*(handwritten)*
christiano	*(handwritten)*	Domingo	*(handwritten)*
Christo	*(handwritten)*	Doctor	*(handwritten)*
Cristóbal	*(handwritten)*	Don	*(handwritten)*

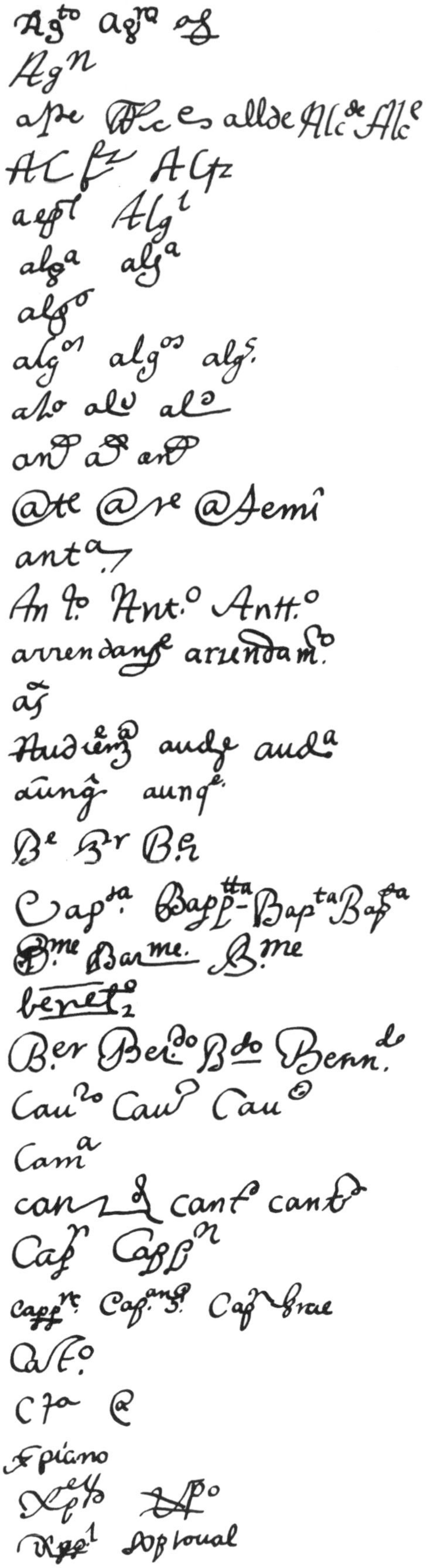

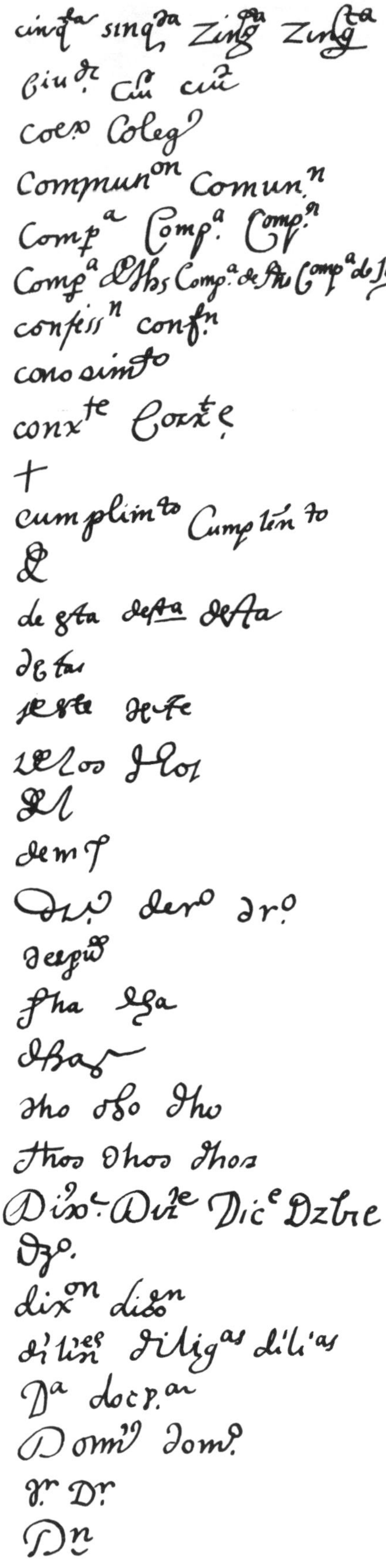

Doña		
Durango		
enero		
Enríquez		
escribano		
escripta (escriptura)		
escribano público		
esta		
estado		
estando		
este		
Estevan		
etcetera		
excelencia		
excellentísimo		
familias		
febrero		
fecho, fecha		
Fernández		
Fernando		
firmo		
fojas		
Francisca		
Francisco		
Fray		
fundación		
general		
Gerónimo		
gobernador		
González		
granos		
guerra		
Gutiérrez		

hacienda		
haciendas		
henero		
hermano		
Hernando		
iglesia(s)		
Ignacio		
instrumento		
Jesús		
Joseph		
Juan		
juramento		
jurisdición		
justicia		
legajo		
legítima		
legítimo		
libra		
licenciado		
Lorenzo		
llamado		
ministro		
magestad		
mando		
manera		
Manuel		
María		
marqués		
Martín		
Martínez		
marzo		
mayor		
memoria		

—mente		para
México		para que
mercader		parte
merced		partes
mi		plata
Miguel		pasado
minero		pedimiento
ministro		Pedro
misión		Pérez
misionero		persona
mismo		personas
necessario		peso
ninguno		petición
ningunos		Phelipe
nombre		pido
noticia		partida
noventa		poder
noviembre		porque
nuestra		posesión
nuestra reverencia		pregunta
Nuestra Señora		presente
nuestro		presentes
nuestro señor		primeramente
nueva		primero
obedecimiento		propia
obispos		provincia
obligación		provincial
octubre		pública
otorgante		público
Padre		pueblo
Padre rector		qual
Padre visitador		quanto
padres		quarenta
pagado		

que		señores	
que el		septiembre	
quenta		sete cientos	
quentas		siguiente	
quien		siguientes	
quienes		solamente	
real		su magestad	
reales		superior	
realmente		súplico	
receptor		testamento	
rectorado		testigo	
regidor		testimonio	
residencia		teniente, theniente	
residente		tipo	
reverencia		tobaco	
reverendo		tomines	
reverendo padre		ud.	
reverendísimo		vecinos	
reyno		vienes (bienes)	
Rodríguez		veinte	
sacramentos		vuestra reverencia	
Salvador		venta	
San		vicario	
Santa		voluntad	
Santo Cristo		Vuestra Reverencia	
santos		Xavier	
sargento, sargento mayor			
Sebastián			
secretario			
segundo			
seis cientos			
señor			
señora			

Bese la mano de vuestra reverencia su servidor

Bese la mano de vuestra reverencia su servidor

Bese la mano de Ud.,
sea fina hija que a veras le ama

**Humilde súbdito, y afecto siervo de vuestra reverencia
en Cristo Dómino**

[handwritten example]

A Diós guarde a vuestra reverencia muchos años

[handwritten example]

Nuestro Señor guarde a vuestra reverencia muchos años

[handwritten example]

Pido a Diós guarde a vuestra reverencia muchos años

[handwritten example]

Nuestro Señor le guarde muchos años

[handwritten example]

Bese la mano de vuestra reverencia

[handwritten example]

Mui afecto siervo y súbdito de vuestra reverencia

[handwritten example]

Hermano vuestro guarde diós a vuestra reverencia muchos años

[handwritten example]

**Mui afecto servidor y súbdito
de vuestra reverencia IHS**

[handwritten example]

**Diós nuestro señor guarde muchos años a
vuestra reverencia en cuyos Santos Sacrificios**

[handwritten example]

Bese los pies de vuestra reverencia

[handwritten example]

Bese la mano de vuestra reverencia

[handwritten example]

Mi amado Padre

[handwritten example]

Muy afecto siervo de vuestra reverencia

[handwritten example]

**Bese la mano de vuestra reverencia su mas afecto
y Seguro Servidor y Capitán**

[handwritten example]

Number	Handwritten
1/2	½
14,014	14 Vol4
19	19
20	20
38	Vo38
45	45
50,050	50 Vo50
138	138
198	198
208	208
543	543
1735	1)35
1539	1539
9 pesos	Voo9P
250 pesos	V250.P.
300 pesos	oV300-P-
332 pesos, 7 reales	V332P7
610 pesos, 4 reales	V61oP4
619 pesos, 5 reales	V619PS
1,365 pesos, 7 reales	1V365P.)
1,780 pesos	1V780-P-
6,445 pesos, 7 reales	6V445P.)
6,560 pesos	6V560.P-
10,044 pesos, 7 reales	10o44P7V
25,253 pesos, 6-1/2 reales	25V253p6V½
30,130 pesos, 4 reales	30V130P4V
1,1,2,2,2,3,3, 4,4,5,5,	11 221 33 44 55
6,6,7,8,8,9,9,	66 7 88 99

DOCUMENTARY COLLECTIONS

This discussion is designed solely to provide a brief description of documentary collections useful to the study of northern New Spain from the mid-sixteenth to the mid-nineteenth centuries. It is not all-inclusive. Rather, it concentrates on major sources in Mexico, Europe, and the United States, delineating particular archival strengths. Archives and libraries not mentioned will probably receive attention in various guides and aids listed at the end of this essay. The bibliography which follows this section was compiled in order to avoid confusion that might arise from a massive listing of documentary repositories and to permit investigation beyond the limits of this essay.

Knowing the contents of particular documentary collections before initiating research can save hours, even days, of wasted time and effort. It is important to make maximum use of archival guides, indexes, and calendars. In addition to such published sources, most archives and libraries have "in-house" indexes which are not available off the premises. Consulting accessible guides and descriptions permits the researcher to compare and contrast holdings in various collections.

Documentary repositories seem to change continually in location, name, methods of operation, and contents. Published sources of information are often not current. Therefore, it is recommended that pertinent periodical publications be consulted. In addition to standard scholarly journals which note this kind of evolution, major archives publish their own bulletins that keep scholars abreast of recent archival activity.

This part of the *Research Guide,* in conjunction with the sections on documentary types and structures and paleography, provides a base to begin the study of northern New Spain by way of primary source materials.

MEXICAN ARCHIVES

This discussion of Mexican archives is limited primarily to repositories containing information pertinent to northern New Spain for the years 1520–1820. Mainly owing to the unknown status of many small municipal and parochial archives, the listing is not complete. Nevertheless, this survey serves as a guide to numerous major holdings and points to smaller collections not discussed. Mexican archives are here divided into two broad categories: those located in Mexico City and those elsewhere in the country. Where applicable and possible, these two classifications are separated into civil and ecclesiastical divisions.

A few observations about the character of Mexican archives and repositories are in order. Because the colonization of New Spain resulted from closely linked efforts of the state, the military, and the Church, civil archives may well be rich in military or ecclesiastical material. Conversely, an ecclesiastical archive may contain information of a civil or military character. Material preserved today in the archives is as intertwined as was the colonization endeavor itself. At one time or another every town, parish, and province had an archive. Some archives have been lost owing to armed conflict, natural disasters, carelessness, and greed. Others have been merged with larger archives or have changed names. The holdings of some repositories end at a certain point in time and are not supplemented thereafter. Others are of more recent vintage, beginning with documentation from a certain date; this is especially true of state archives established after Mexico's independence. The process continues, and, because of the ever-changing nature of location, nomenclature, and administration, it is vital that available guides, indexes, and current information in pertinent periodicals be consulted before initiating research.

Names of most repositories are usually clear and practical in that they provide some idea of an archive's orientation. However, a few terms, commonly employed, deserve brief mention. Notarial archives are those preserving documents which passed before a notary. These documents are often labeled *protocolos*. This material is civil in character and concerns the everyday business of community life, such as buying and selling, notes of obligation, powers of attorney, testaments, and dowries. Archives of this type are often called *Archivos Notarías* or *Archivos (de) Protocolos*. In some instances they are closely related to or constitute a part of *Archivos del Registros Públicos de la Propiedad*. The term "register" is often used in reference to the holdings of an ecclesiastical archive. Registers of a parish archive are those books or records which contain data concerning births, baptisms, confirmations, marriages, and burials.

In the interest of clarity, the many guides and aids to various archives are listed at the end of this essay. They are arranged in the same manner as the essay; that is, those for Mexico City are noted first, followed by those pertinent to the various states.

Mexico City

Several archives in Mexico City preserve material relative to northern New Spain. The most important of these is the Archivo General de la Nación (AGN). Formerly located in the Palacio de Comunicaciones on Calle Tacuba (having been moved from the Palacio Nacional), the archive was transferred to the old federal prison (Lecumberri) in late 1980. Most studies of colonial Mexico risk serious omission unless the vast amount of material available in this repository is consulted. Although some holdings were destroyed by seventeenth-century riots and other materials have been stolen over the years, this archive is still the most complete depository of colonial material in the nation. Documentation in the AGN spans all of New Spain in time and subject matter. It is especially valuable for political and administrative material beginning in the eighteenth century, with the strength of its holdings increasing thereafter. Prior to the eighteenth century, documentation is less complete, and recourse to the Archivo General de Indias (AGI) in Seville may be necessary. By using available guides to the AGN and the AGI, it can be determined where research will be most fruitful.

Documents in the AGN have traditionally been divided or classified according to *ramos* (branches), each ramo being composed of *tomos* or *legajos*. Generally speaking, a tomo is a bound volume made up of *folios* (pages). A legajo is a loose bundle or volume of documents, the pages of which are called *fojas*. As the AGN progresses through its present program of reorganization, parts of this classification system will change. In order to further clarify the archival contents, new divisions labeled *unidades* (units or sections) are being created. Nevertheless, the basic unit remains the ramo, and an understanding of the ramos and their contents will continue to be applicable during and after the present restructuring. Those ramos or branches within the AGN which are the most productive for research directed to northern New Spain are the following: Californias, General de Parte, Historia, Jesuitas (cuentas), Jesuitas, Misiones, Provincias Internas, Real Hacienda, and Tierras. Other ramos do hold significant information. A full listing of the various ramos with a brief description of their contents as of 1977 is provided in the guide prepared by Miguel Civeira Taboada and María Elena Bribiesca, *Guía descriptiva de los ramos que constituyen el Archivo General de la Nación*.

In conjunction with the consolidation of archives at Lecumberri, the AGN has initiated a program of selective microfilming of Mexican documents in the Archivo General de Indias (AGI) (Seville). These selections will supplement records available in Mexico City with the ultimate goal of gathering all pertinent historical documents for the national archive center.

Residing in the same building with and historically very much a part of the AGN is the Archivo Histórico de Hacienda (AHH). The holdings of this archive cover approximately the same time period as those of the AGN and are almost an extension of every fiscally related section. Together, these two archives provide the greatest concentration of colonial documentation available for the study of northern New Spain. As the name implies, the AHH houses material relative to colonial and early national economic affairs. In addition to the vast amount of ordinary financial and commercial material therein, the archive is especially rich in the areas of Aduanas, Consulado de Comercio, Casas de Monedas, and Temporalidades. Held with the Temporalidades material is the Archivo de la Procurador de la Compañía de Jesús, a valuable collection, confiscated after the expulsion of the Jesuits in 1767. Moreover, this repository is a source of information for the Franciscan mission period of California.

The Biblioteca Nacional (BN), administered by the Universidad Nacional Autónoma de México (UNAM), preserves a variety of colonial documentation. However, it is strongest in literary material, particularly of the Jesuit and Franciscan orders. Of specific interest is the Archivo Franciscano, held in the rare books and manuscripts section of the library. This is one of two parts of the Franciscan archives which were housed in the Convento de San Francisco, Mexico City, during the nineteenth century. The other portion of this Franciscan documentation rests in the Museo Nacional. Composed of the Archive of the Holy Gospel Province and the Archive of the Commissaries General of New Spain, this historical record of the Franciscan order, like that of the Jesuits, provides general information on secular and religious matters. The role of these two orders in the exploration, settlement, and development of frontier areas makes the material especially worthwhile for the study of northern New Spain.

The Instituto Nacional de Antropología e Historia (INAH) has another repository preserving documentation pertinent to New Spain. The historical archive of the institute is strong in material from Mexico's northwest. The Centro de Documentación, a part of the institute, is a microfilm project which includes the filmed records of many local, civil, and parish archives. Before research is initiated in this film collection, a check should be made with the Academia Mexicana de Genealogía y Heráldica. The Academy's holdings, a joint effort on the part of the Mexican government and the Church of Jesus Christ of Latter-day Saints (Mormon), consists of microfilmed parish and civil archives for many parts of Mexico. This project, an enormous aid to researchers, is nearly complete at this writing. A microfilm copy of the documentation is also housed at the Genealogical Society of Utah in Salt Lake City. Preservation of these kinds of local historical records provides excellent research opportunities in social, economic, political, religious, demographic, and ethnographic subjects.

The Museo Nacional, administered by INAH and located in Chapultepec Park, holds, as mentioned above, the other portion of the Franciscan papers—called in this instance the Fondo Franciscano. Other collections of note in the Museo are the Colección Paso y Troncoso, Colección Gómez de Orozco, and the Colección Lancaster Jones, which deals with northern Mexico, especially California, Texas, and Sonora. Another collection of interest is the Aubin-Goupil Collection from the National Library of France (Paris), which the Museo has on microfilm. This material offers valuable information for the northern provinces of New Spain and the Indians of the same area.

Another source of some value in Mexico City is the Archivo Histórico Militar (Defensa). As would be expected, most of the material concerns military affairs and national defense. Holdings are strongest for the nineteenth century (post-independence); however, there is documentation for northern New Spain prior to that period. Military matters pertinent to New Mexico, the Provincias Internas, California, and Texas (1800-1845) are well represented. Documentation resulting from the role of the military establishment in the expulsion of the Jesuits is also found here. Owing to the fact that some of the holdings deal with national security matters, access to the archive is restricted, especially to foreigners. Prior arrangements are well advised. Some of the documentation in this archive is on microfilm at the Bancroft Library (University of California at Berkeley) and, therefore, more accessible. The archive is an excellent source for biographical studies because of the detailed nature of military records.

The Archivo General de Notarías (sometimes known as the Archivo Histórico de Notarías) of the federal district contains documentation for northern New Spain. Although not directly concerned with the northern region of the colony, many transactions notarized in Mexico City involved people and land of the northern frontier. This archive, together with local notarial archives, provides a more complete source for the study of general social, economic, demographic, and ethnographic local history.

Located in the geographic and meteorological section of the former Secretaría de Agricultura y Ganadería is the Mapoteca, a cartographic collection. This collection of maps, only recently organized, now contains some 60,000 pieces. Supplementing the maps of a historical character are the aerial and satellite photographs which provide in many instances the first accurate mapping of Mexico's hinterlands. Another source of reliable cartographic information is the series of modern color maps issued by the Mexican government agency DETENAL beginning in the 1970s. Although incomplete, maps covering a large percentage of the country (especially Mexico City northward) have already been published and are available to the public. These maps are based on aerial photography and are the most detailed and accurate available for Mexico. Especially valuable are the topographic, geologic, current land-use, and potential land-use sheets at a scale of 1 : 50,000. In addition, there are climatic and other topographic series at a scale of 1 : 250,000.

In contrast to the archives mentioned thus far—all of them government administered—is the Centro de Estudios de Historia de México. This archive is run privately by CONDUMEX, S.A., an electrical-industrial firm. Founded primarily to halt the loss of historical documents and to acquire them from any possible source, this repository preserves a variety of material spanning the whole of Mexican history. For northern New Spain, it is strongest for sixteenth-, seventeenth-, and eighteenth-century Nueva Galicia, natural resources, trade, and trade associations. Some of the documents acquired by the Centro have been donated to the state and deposited in the AGN. All documents housed in the Centro have been photocopied and are well cataloged.

Ecclesiastical archives supplement the public and private repositories and libraries in Mexico City. The most important of these are the Archivo del Cabildo de la Catedral de México and the Archivo del Sagrario Metropolitano. Much like the notarial archive of the federal district, these two centers do not deal directly with northern New Spain. However, their records of births, baptisms, confirmations, marriages, and burials (registers) are a necessary complement to local ecclesiastical archives in the northern area of the country. Local parish archives in the city preserving historical information in the form of registers are San Miguel Arcángel, Santa Catarina Mártir, Santa María la Redonda, Santa Veracruz, and San Sebastián. Other ecclesiastical depositories of note are the Congregación de San Felipe Neri, which served as an administrative center for some of the northern Jesuit missions, and the Convento de Santo Domingo, the colonial headquarters for the Dominican missions in Baja California.

Mexican States

Local archives in the Mexican states, in contrast to major repositories in Mexico City, are smaller, narrower in scope, and often less organized and preserved. The remainder of this discussion, which deals with archives in the Mexican states, focuses by necessity on state capitals. These cities were often provincial capitals or important urban centers during the colonial years, and consequently the major local archives are located in them. The presentation that follows is in alphabetical order.

Baja California. Much of the historical record for Baja California exists outside the peninsula in other Mexican or foreign depositories. However, this situation was altered in 1969 with the opening of the Archivo Histórico Pablo L. Martínez in La Paz, capital of Baja California Sur. The goal of the new repository was to consolidate documents from various public, private, and corporate collections on the peninsula as well as to acquire microform copies of relevant material held in archives and libraries in other parts of the world. This effort in conjunction with the work of the Instituto de Investigaciones Históricas (UNAM) and the Centro de Investigaciones Históricas of the Universidad Autónoma de Baja California should prove beneficial and convenient to scholars of the region.

In addition to the Archivo Histórico P.L.M. there are two important municipal archives with modest records of mining activity. In the south is that of the Real de San Antonio and in the north is the mining town of Santa Rosalía. Ecclesiastical records for the peninsula have been scattered throughout various U.S. and Mexican institutions; a correlation of these collections by Michael Mathes has been published in the *SMRC Newsletter,* Number 35, May 1977.

Chihuahua. With the exception of the municipal archive in Hidalgo del Parral, repositories with material relative to the history of northern New Spain in the state of Chihuahua are located mainly in the capital, Chihuahua City. The Archivo General del Estado (also known as the Archivo de la Secretaría de Gobierno) was the major repository for the colonial period. However, it burned down in 1941. A description of its former contents can be found in Bolton's *Guide.* The Archivo del Tribunal Supremo de Justicia contains local judicial records from the end of the eighteenth century through the first decades of the nineteenth. The Archivo de la Tesorería holds financial documentation beginning with the initial years of the nineteenth century. Like the Archivo del Tribunal, these records encompass New Mexico and Texas as well as Chihuahua.

There are three important municipal archives in the state. The most significant is the Archivo de Hidalgo del Parral. This archive, completely microfilmed and available at a number of libraries in the United States, contains a wide range of colonial material. Beginning in 1632, and running into the 1820s, it is the most important single source of information for what was colonial Nueva Vizcaya— today, the states of Chihuahua, Sonora, Sinaloa, Durango, and portions of Coahuila. Material pertinent to the north, northwest, and northeast is also well represented. Although Parral was not the official capital of the province of Nueva Vizcaya at any time, it did serve as the unofficial capital, being the residence of the provincial governor for over a hundred years. Combined with the archives of Durango (the official capital) and Guadalajara (the seat of the respective audiencia), the documentation at Parral is central to any study of northern New Spain. The municipal archive of Chihuahua City preserves material relative to colonial affairs for the surrounding area. Holdings begin in the eighteenth century and, like Parral, include information for New Mexico as well as Nueva Vizcaya. The same type of local information is found in the municipal archives of Ciudad Juárez (El Paso del Norte) and Valle de Allende. Initiated in the late seventeenth century, they cover the more northern and southeastern parts of the area, including Texas and Coahuila.

While civil archives, such as those discussed above, contain a wide variety of official documentation, local ecclesiastical archives provide biographic, demographic, ethnographic, and social records in their registers. Parish records preserved in Ciudad Juárez, Parral, Santa Bárbara, San Francisco del Oro, and Guadalupe (Ciudad Juárez) commence with the middle decades of the seventeenth century. For later years (especially the independence period), the Archivo de la Catedral de Chihuahua in Chihuahua City is useful.

Coahuila. Major archives in Coahuila are located in Saltillo, the capital. Like Parral, Saltillo was an important urban center in the colonial period. The Archivo General de Gobierno (del Estado) contains a diversity of colonial documentation beginning in the 1680s. Strongest in this collection is material for the last of the eighteenth century and the beginning of the nineteenth. Some judicial documentation can be located here, but most of it is in the Archivo Judicial (Archivo del Tribunal Superior de Justicia del Estado). This repository holds material from the 1670s, and in addition to its judicial character, preserves important civil, political, and administrative records. There is information relative to Texas as well as material on locally important political figures for the independence period. The Archivo General de Historia del Estado, begun in 1666, preserves a variety of colonial data.

Reaching back into the 1590s, the municipal archive of Saltillo serves as a source for general local history. Moreover, it contains some documentation for eighteenth-century colonization in Texas. The municipal archives of Monclova and Guerrero, housed in the Archivo General de Gobierno (del Estado), together with records from other state municipalities, are good local sources; documents in the Monclova collection date from 1675.

Ecclesiastical archives of Coahuila, much like those of Chihuahua, contain registers for the colonial period. The Archivo de la Catedral (Saltillo) and parish archives in San Esteban (Saltillo), Guerrero, and Santiago are important in this regard, with records beginning in the first years of the seventeenth century. Not to be overlooked is the parish archive of Parras de la Fuente, an invaluable source of ethnographic and native demographic information for the Bolsón de Mapimí during the seventeenth century. Eighteenth century Franciscan material is located in the Archivo de la Catedral.

Durango. Durango has several important collections. In the city of Durango, the Archivo General de Gobierno del Estado holds various civil and military data for New Spain and Nueva Vizcaya beginning in the 1580s. Used in conjunction with the archive at Parral, it becomes even more useful, providing a detailed picture of the colonial years. The Archivo Municipal, with documents also dating from the 1580s, is a valuable source for local history and the central-northern presidios. Records of the *cabildo* of Durango are located in the Archivo del Ayuntamiento. Various religious documents from the beginning of the seventeenth through the first part of the nineteenth century are preserved in the Archivo del Museo Regional. Important municipal archives are located in Nombre de Diós, Topia, Nazas, El Zape, and Santiago Papasquiaro.

The central ecclesiastical archive for the colonial period in Durango is the Archivo de la Catedral, which dates from the 1620s. It has a nearly complete set of the *Actas Capitulares* (from 1635) and documentation pertinent to the history of the episcopal see of Nueva Vizcaya. The Archivo del Sagrario contains registers dating from the end of the sixteenth century. Parochial archives in Durango and Nombre de Diós also possess registers dating from the 1660s and the 1690s, respectively.

Guanajuato. Although Guanajuato lies south of the area considered in this guide, its archives preserve information relative to northern New Spain. Serving as a frontier region for many years, it was traversed by many people whose destinations were farther north. In the city of Guanajuato under the administration of the Universidad de Guanajuato is the Archivo del Ayuntamiento de Guanajuato, with documentation of a regional character from 1611. This depository is one of the better local archives in the area with generous information on civil activities, land, mining, and local military and religious affairs. The notarial or protocol division of the archive contains records from the late 1600s to 1810. The Libros de Cabildo are nearly complete, part in this archive and part in the Archivo de Notarías. Mining information is concentrated in the Archivo de Registros de Minas, although some is included in the Archivo de Notarías and the Archivo del Ayuntamiento; this covers the latter portion of the sixteenth century and reaches into the twentieth century. The Archivo Histórico Municipal de León is one of the more complete and copious municipal archives in Mexico, with documentation beginning in 1580.

From the ecclesiastical perspective, the Archivo de la Notaría Parroquial del Sagrario de Guanajuato and the similar repository in Celaya possess registers from the 1630s and 1650s, respectively. The Archivo Franciscano de Celaya is the most complete Franciscan provincial archive extant. For the most part, its holdings cover the Franciscan province of San Pedro y San Pablo de Michoacán and the Colegios Apostólicos de Misiones de Santa Cruz de Querétaro.

Jalisco (Guadalajara). Next to the major archives of Mexico City and the archive at Parral, the state of Jalisco, and specifically its capital, Guadalajara, have archival sources with the most varied information concerning northern New Spain. The Archivo del Ayuntamiento contains the Libros de Cabildo from approximately 1607 to the present. This represents a wealth of municipal documentation concerning government, finance, commerce, education, land, and justice. The records of the Real Audiencia de Nueva Galicia are now distributed in several places. Part of the government affairs of the audiencia are in the Archivo de Instrumentos Públicos (1670s to the 1750s). Also located in this archive is the Archivo de Notarías, which preserves a great quantity of civil and notarial documentation beginning in the sixteenth century. The Archivo del Registro Público de la Propiedad is also incorporated in this archive. Its holdings include land titles and general land and water data from 1584 continuing into the nineteenth century. The Biblioteca Pública de Guadalajara (also referred to as the Biblioteca Nacional del Estado) is one of the most important repositories in Mexico. The Archivos Judiciales and Fiscales from the audiencia are kept here. Many smaller archives and libraries from Guadalajara and colonial Nueva Galicia have been absorbed by the Biblioteca, making it an important center for research. It contains a significant number of Franciscan documents, especially from the Colegio Seminario del Señor San José and from several convents. Furthermore, the Biblioteca holds many records of the Antigua Universidad de Guadalajara (from 1792), the Archivo de Gobierno del Estado de Jalisco (1850-1920), and the Archivo del Juzgado General de Bienes de Difuntos. In addition to the material concerning estates of deceased persons (1550-1810), it includes a variety of civil documentation. There is also a large manuscript collection.

The ecclesiastical archives of Guadalajara are rich in colonial material. The Archivo del Arzobispado contains records from the sixteenth century through the nineteenth century. This archive preserves registers dating from the seventeenth century, *padrones órdenes* (documents relating to the legitimacy and the purity of blood of priests), the establishment of *capellanías*, testaments and information concerning *cofradías*. Moreover, many of the parish archives of the state of Jalisco have been microfilmed and stored here. As might be expected, the business of governing the diocese is well documented and preserved here and in the Archivo del Cabildo Eclesiástico. A history of religious life and activities in northern New Spain would not be complete without either of these two collections. The latter archive preserves the Actas Capitulares from 1552 until the present as well as sources for the study of religious financial and governmental affairs. The Archivo de la Provincia Franciscana de Jalisco contains important religious material.

Nuevo León. For the eastern portion of northern New Spain, the archives of the state of Nuevo León, especially those located in the capital, Monterrey, provide the best documentary sources. Good regional material from the end of the eighteenth century is located in the Archivo del Estado. The Archivo del Ayuntamiento (El Archivo Municipal de Monterrey) has a greater diversity of material than the Archivo del Estado. This archive serves much as Parral does for the more central part of northern New Spain. Protocols and the registry of mines date from 1599 and 1598, respectively. Principal sections of the collection are on film at the Centro de Documentación of INAH in Mexico City. The Biblioteca del Instituto Tecnológico de Monterrey holds a variety of pertinent information, including the library of Salvador Ugarte, noted for its material on Indian languages. The Department of Agriculture through its division of Rural Communities, has documentation on land and water matters dating from 1596.

The ecclesiastical archives of Monterrey, the Archivo del Obispado, the Archivo del Cabildo Catedralicio, and the Archivo de la Parroquia del Sagrario all preserve documents, including registers, from the seventeenth century forward, but are rather sparse in content until the eighteenth century. Registers in the Sagrario date from the mid-seventeenth century.

Outside of Monterrey, the municipal archive of Linares is strong with records commencing in the late 1600s. The Archivo de la Secretaría del Gobierno del Arzobispado de Linares is useful for its religious information and its varied documentation on the northeast, including Texas and Louisiana. Other parish and civil archives of note are those in Cadereyta, Salinas Victoria, Montemorelos, General Terán, Sabinas Hidalgo, Villaldama, Villa de García, Bustamante, and Lampazos. Many of these collections date from the seventeenth century.

San Luis Potosí. San Luis Potosí, like Guanajuato, is on the southern fringe of northern New Spain. However, because of its strategic geographical location and the intense settlement and development there due to the rich mines, documentation preserved in the state's archives is important for areas to the north. Probably the richest of the state's

repositories is the Archivo Judicial (Archivo del Tribunal Superior de Justicia). Documents in this archive date from the end of the sixteenth century and include notarial records from 1595 to 1632 and *bienes de difuntos* from 1596 to 1621. Furthermore, papers from the *alcaldías* of San Luis (Potosí) and San Pedro de Guadalcázar are preserved here. For later years there is abundant information concerning the Provincias Internas (the eastern half) and the intendency of San Luis Potosí (Coahuila, Texas, Nuevo León, Tamaulipas, and San Luis Potosí). Data on other smaller colonial communities are located here. Complementing the Archivo Judicial is the Archivo General del Estado, with most of its contents best representing the period after the end of the eighteenth century. For the city of San Luis Potosí and the immediate area, the Archivo de Notarías y del Registro Público de la Propiedad is also of value, as is the Archivo del Ayuntamiento, which has documents from the end of the sixteenth century.

Outside the capital city, archives in Charcas, Río Verde, Pastora, Guadalcázar, Ciudad del Maíz, Alaquines, Catorce, and Venado possess documentation ranging back into the seventeenth century.

The Archivo de la Catedral (de Obispado) contains pertinent religious material for the large bishopric of San Luis Potosí beginning in the sixteenth century. Although this see was not created until the nineteenth century, the archive preserves early documentation for a large area, with registers initiated in the sixteenth century. Records of several smaller parishes are located here. Parochial archives in Charcas, San Luis Potosí, Ciudad del Maíz, Río Verde, Guadalcázar, and Pastora have registers dating from the seventeenth century. Although not an archive as such, the Biblioteca del Estado contains several valuable manuscripts of religious nature (mostly Franciscan) from the seventeenth and eighteenth centuries.

Sinaloa. Archival resources in Sinaloa are not as abundant as those of some other states. Owing to its political-administrative history, many records pertinent to Sinaloa's past reside in the archives of Sonora, Parral, and Guadalajara. However, the Archivo General de Notarías y del Registro Público de la Propiedad in Culiacán is essential for the reconstruction of local history in this western part of northern New Spain. The Archivo del Obispado (or Cabildo Eclesiástico) contains valuable material on religious activity in the area, including data on the missions and Indians of northwestern New Spain. The parish archives of Mocorito, Rosario, and El Fuerte provide significant information of a religious character.

Sonora. Archives in Sonora complement those of Sinaloa and Parral by providing necessary sources for the study of northwestern New Spain. In Hermosillo, the Archivo General del Gobierno (once called the Archivo Histórico del Estado de Sonora) preserves documentation from the last third of the eighteenth century, with information of a regional character concerning Indians, presidios, and missions. Registers of property and land preserved in this archive date from the mid-eighteenth century. Notarial records dating from the eighteenth century are located in the Archivo General de Notarías. Late civil and state records rest in the Archivo del Congreso del Estado (as is the case in most states). Judicial material beginning near the end of the eighteenth century is located in the Archivo Judicial del Estado de Sonora, which also has records from colonial and post-independence judicial districts outside Hermosillo.

Municipal archives outside Hermosillo have yet to be fully investigated. However, the Centro Regional del Noroeste (a regional branch of INAH) located in Hermosillo is surveying and gathering information about these smaller repositories with the goal of preserving and cataloging them.

The Archivo del Obispado (Hermosillo) has documents dating back to 1740 and is the best source for research in religious matters such as missions, conversion of Indians, and the secularization of the mission system. In addition, this archive has information relevant to Arizona and Alta California. Smaller ecclesiastical collections in the state such as the parish archives of Alamos, Arizpe, Altar, Guaymas, Moctezuma, Magdalena, and Navajoa have registers covering portions of the colonial period.

Zacatecas. In the same manner as San Luis Potosí, Zacatecas developed as a center of regional importance very early in the colonial era owing to its rich mines. As the frontier moved north, Zacatecas served as a crucial link in communication and supply to the newly opened frontier areas. In the capital the Archivo de Gobierno del Estado, with records beginning in the 1780s, provides valuable information on the colonial intendency. This archive is complemented by the Archivo de Notarías with records from the seventeenth and eighteenth centuries, and the Archivo Municipal with documentation of a more local character from the 1580s. The Biblioteca Pública del Estado has preserved some of the records and registers from the Convento de San Francisco de Zacatecas and also holds other Franciscan documentation.

Religious archives in Zacatecas are a necessary supplement to the civil repositories. The Archivo de la Catedral possesses records from 1742 and is augmented by the parish archives of Santo Domingo (Zacatecas), San José de la Isla, Ciudad García (Jeréz), Santa María de los Angeles Tlaltenango, and Ojocaliente. Many important Franciscan documents are located in the Biblioteca del Colegio de Guadalupe de Zacatecas, which was the apostolic college primarily responsible for northeastern New Spain. There are other sections of this college archive now in Guadalajara.

SPANISH ARCHIVES

As the most dominant empire of Europe, Spain managed its overseas colonies through a complex, well-recorded bureaucracy. And that bureaucracy generated extensive archival records which have become for modern times an incomparable source for the history of the New World. This brief section will deal with some of those archives as they pertain to northern New Spain. The first part deals with the Archivo General de Indias in Seville and the subsequent parts deal with archives in Madrid and outside Madrid.

Of all the archives and collections of interest to the student of colonial Mexican history, the Archivo General de Indias (AGI) (Sevilla) is the most extensive and promising. For the study of New Spain it is indispensable, a rich supplement to Mexico's important sources and often an archive of last resort. Established in the late eighteenth century to unite in one place the documentation concerning Spain's overseas possessions, the AGI became the repository for documents from (among others) the Council of the Indies (Consejo de las Indias), the Archivo General de Simancas, and the Casa de Contratación.

Seville

Because many documents originating in the overseas colonies were duplicated at least once, much of what rests in the Archivo General de la Nación (AGN) in Mexico City is also located in the AGI. This duplication has been a blessing for historians, as documents not available in one of these repositories may well be located in the other. Replication of this sort often extended to local sources, thereby producing three and sometimes four copies of a document. Thus documentation sought but not found in Parral or Durango is probably extant in Mexico City (AGN) or Seville (AGI).

Documents in the AGI are arranged by section. There are fourteen of these, composed of various volumes (*legajos*) numbered consecutively. Indexes, guides, or catalogs exist for all sections, some being more elaborate and developed than others. Following is a list of the sections with a brief description of their contents:

1. *Patronato.* Documents in this section range from the 1480s to the 1790s. A significant portion of the material concerns the early years of exploration and conquest in New Spain.

2. *Contaduría.* Material here is basically financial with documentation from the early years of the seventeenth century to the end of the eighteenth. Of interest for New Spain are the Papeles del Consejo de las Indias (1514–1760), Asientos de Negros (1541–1739), Papeles de la Casa de Contratación

(1520–1741), Consulados de Sevilla y Cádiz (1555–1760), and Reales Cajas de Nueva España (1521–1764.)

3. *Contratación.* The information from the Casa de la Contratación concerns maritime operations in the empire from 1492 to 1795. Data on the embarkation and debarkation of passengers is especially worthwhile, as are the classifications under which these travelers were listed—soldiers, colonial officials, negroes, and their destinations. The same is true for ships and cargos. This is the major source for Spanish colonial martime history and, combined with section two (Contaduría), provides the bulk of material for colonial financial history.

4. *Papeles de justicia.* Judicial records of the archive date from 1515 and run to 1644 and are divided in two parts within this section: (a) cases heard by the various audiencias in the New World and appealed to the Casa de la Contratación or the Consejo de las Indias; and (b) cases heard *in the first instance* by the Consejo de las Indias. This approximates a division of original and appellate jurisdiction. Both groups of documents are arranged by audiencia, facilitating access to particular areas and cases.

5. *Audiencias e Indiferente.* Nearly 19,000 volumes or legajos comprise this, the largest, section of the archive. Divided in two parts, Audiencias and Indiferente, the documentation is of a general political and administrative nature. Material in the Audiencia portion is classified by audiencia. In contrast, the Indiferente papers have no geographical orientation. Correspondence of an official character from the smallest administrative units to higher levels of the bureaucracy and royal orders to all levels of officialdom constitute a large part of this material, beginning in 1492 and ending in 1856.

6. *Escribanía de Cámara del Consejo de las Indias.* Section six is basically a continuation and supplement to section four (Papeles de justicia). Together, they contain documentation for a judicial history of the colonial era. Most of the material is organized geographically. The time span is 1525–1761.

7. *Secretaría del Juzgado de Arribadas de Cádiz, y Comisión Interventora de Hacienda Pública en Cádiz.* Documents begin in 1560 and continue through 1821. The papers of the Secretaría and Comisión concern maritime affairs relative to the port of Cádiz and thus complement the holdings described in section three.

8. *Papeles de Correos.* Arranged geographically and chronologically, these papers are divided as *correspondencia y expedientes, correos marítimos, cuentas documentadas,* and *diarios de navegación.* Most of this material originated in the last third of the eighteenth century and the first quarter of the nineteenth.

9. *Papeles de Estado.* These political and diplomatic documents range from 1686 to 1860, the heaviest concentration being toward the end of the colonial period. Classified by audiencia, they supplement material in section five (Audiencias e Indiferente).

10. *(Papeles de) Ministerio de Ultramar.* Geographically arranged, this documentation begins in 1605 and continues to 1868, covering civil and ecclesiastical government and miscellaneous topics.

11. *Papeles de Cuba.* Although this section deals primarily with the island, other areas bordering the Gulf of Mexico are represented. Documents date from the 1770s and terminate in the 1820s.

12. *Papeles de Cádiz.* Most documentation concerns the port of Cádiz with information dating from the early seventeenth century and continuing into the early nineteenth century.

13. *Títulos de Castilla.* Of value here in relation to New Spain are cases of people resident in the colonies who returned to Spain in quest of titles of nobility.

14. *Papeles de España.* Nearly all information in this section deals exclusively with Spain and is of limited utility for the study of the colonies.

Madrid

The Archivo Histórico Nacional (AHN), so designated in 1866, is not as its name implies, the national archive. The Archivo General de Simancas and the AGI serve in this capacity. The Archivo Histórico, like the AGI, is divided into sections:

1. *Clero secular y regular.* Of specific interest for New Spain are the numerous documents concerning the Jesuit order, specifically the Jesuit expulsion.

2. *Ordenes militares.* Perhaps the most valuable section of the archive in relation to New Spain. As the years passed, more and more men found their way into the Spanish military orders. As a result, this section preserves a wealth of genealogical and biographical data.

3. *Estado.* In addition to a variety of diplomatic information, this section contains material pertinent to Spanish-Anglo relations in the eighteenth and nineteenth centuries. Documentation concerning the wars for independence in the western hemisphere is well represented as is conflict between *criollos* and *peninsulares* in the colonies.

4. *Juros.* Finances relating to colonial Spanish America are treated in a variety of topics.

5. *Universidades y colegios.* This section documents higher education in the New World, especially for the sixteenth, seventeenth, and eighteenth centuries. Some of this information deals with Spanish officials who were not involved in the educational structure.

6. *Sigilografía.* Included here are collections of royal seals — of minor significance for New Spain.

7. *Inquisición (Consejo de la).* This section conserves the archive of the Consejo de la Suprema Inquisición del Santo Oficio. As such, it includes the inquisition records from the tribunal in Mexico

City (1572–1808). In addition to records of cases heard and tried before this tribunal, there exists a substantial amount of genealogical and biographical data.

8. *Consejos suprimidos.* Most of this material originates in the last half of the eighteenth century and the whole of the nineteenth. It is composed of communications between the higher levels of the colonial bureaucracy.

9. *Códices y cartularios.* This documentation is primarily concerned with Spanish history before the discovery of the New World and is of little utility for the study of Spain's colonies.

10. *Archivo de ultramar.* Much of this material is in general disorder; parts of it are found in the AGI. Little concerns New Spain.

11. *Diversos.* This section is a collection of letters, reports, and manuscripts dealing with the New World.

As is the case with the AGI, the map collection of this archive is excellent.

There are three major libraries in Madrid which preserve documentation in relation to the colonial history of northern Mexico. The Biblioteca Nacional, the Real Academia de la Historia, and the Biblioteca del Palacio Real preserve various pertinent manuscripts. Those in the Biblioteca Nacional fall under general geographic headings. Those classified in the Hispanic American section (under América en general and Nueva España) provide a wide variety of information from the sixteenth through the nineteenth centuries. In addition to the general type of documentation concerning New Spain, there is significant material relative to the eastern Spanish borderlands. Also worthy of attention is the Biblioteca's map collection.

Of special importance in the Real Academia de la Historia is the Colección Boturini or Memorias de Nueva España, a thirty-volume set of material compiled in New Spain and sent to the mother country during the tenure of Viceroy Revillagigedo (1789–1794). This material emanates from the eighteenth century; access to it is facilitated by the fact that much of it has been published. Another important section of the Academia pertains to the Jesuits, with emphasis on economic data. Its Colección Juan Bautista Muñoz is best known for documentation from the early chroniclers and on viceregal affairs.

In the Biblioteca del Palacio Real is a variety of information spanning the colonial era located in the sections "América en general" and "Nueva España." Together these three libraries ought not be overlooked in research dealing with the colonial years of northern Mexico.

Other collections in Madrid worthy of mention are the Archivo General del Ministerio de Hacienda (the holdings of which were nearly destroyed in the Spanish Civil War—fortunately, however, parts of the "Memorias de Nueva España" survived), the Museo de Ciencias Naturales (with data on scientific expeditions, including Humboldt's), and the Archivo de la Embajada de España cerca de la Santa Sede (a wide variety of ecclesiastical material).

Although documentation relative to military affairs in New Spain is well represented in the AGI and the Archivo General de Simancas, the utilization of Spain's military archives can prove worthwhile. The Biblioteca Central Militar of the Servicio Histórico Militar contains important and diversified material. Documentation begins in the sixteenth century and continues well into the nineteenth. General information on troops, payrolls, presidios, and military administration is abundant for all of Mexico. The northern borderlands, their settlement, and Spanish disputes with France and the United States are topics worth investigation in this repository. The Museo Naval is of major importance for the history of Spain's maritime activities. Like the Biblioteca Central Militar, it has an impressive map collection, as well as many manuscripts dealing with Spanish exploration and sea voyages in the New World. Spanish expansion into Alta California is represented by documentation concerning the de Anza overland expeditions and the travels of Fathers Domínguez and Escalante. The Servicio Geográfico del Ejército and the Archivo General de la Marina preserve records of Spanish maritime activities in the northern coastal areas of New Spain.

Other

Outside Madrid the most fruitful source for research is the Archivo General de Simancas. Previous to the establishment of the AGI this was the major repository in Spain. However, in the last years of the eighteenth century, documentation entitled "Papeles de América" was transferred to the AGI in Seville. Yet owing to lack of organization in the archive, many papers pertinent to New Spain were left behind, scattered throughout the archive's different sections. Of special note are documents indexed under section fifteen (Contaduría de Cruzada), which are economic in nature; section seventeen (Contaduría del Sueldo), which contains military documentation relative to New Spain; section twenty (Dirección General de Rentas), especially the portion labeled "Registro del comercio libre con América (1778–1795); and section twenty-one (Dirección General del Tesoro), which contains information relative to colonial offices and the people who held them. Because of the wide dissemination of documents pertinent to New Spain throughout the archive, it is likely that information exists which has yet to be discovered.

The library of the monastery in the Escorial contains manuscripts important to the study of the early years of New Spain. Because of the historical value of these papers, many have been published.

As do their counterparts in New Spain, the notarial archives of Spain provide data concerning various civil transactions. The records preserved in Seville, Cádiz, and Madrid are especially important, as many legalities were handled in these cities just prior to taking leave for the New World or upon return to Spain.

OTHER EUROPEAN ARCHIVES
Italy

For many reasons a significant amount of documentation concerning Mexico and northern New Spain has come to rest in European archives outside the Iberian Peninsula. Next to Spain, the archives of Italy have the most important collections, owing primarily to Rome's involvement in the religious aspect of colonial life in the New World. This brief review of Italian archives only mentions repositories with significant holdings of Mexican material; it is not all-inclusive. More detailed accounts of Italian sources are found in guides by Burrus, Fish, and Gómez Canedo noted at the end of this essay.

Archives of the Catholic Church are abundant in Mexican documentation. Both the Vatican Library and the National Library (Rome) possess Hispanic American material, most of it in manuscript form. Much of the information in the Vatican Library pertinent to North America and especially Jesuit activities is on mircofilm at St. Louis University (St. Louis, Missouri). In the National Library, material relative to Spanish America is located for the most part in the Fondo Gesuitico. The Vatican Archive with its numerous subdivisions is perhaps the most rewarding of all Italian collections for research in colonial Mexico. Two sections of this archive deserve mention. The Archive of the Secretary of Briefs preserves significant quantities of colonial religious information. The *prócessi* section of the Archivo Consistorial maintains documentation on the candidates for episcopal sees. This information is indexed alphabetically by bishopric, and thus material for colonial church history is easily located for the bishoprics of Durango (1630–1831), Guadalajara (1630–1831), México (1636–1839), Michoacán (1623–1831), Monterrey/Linares (1778–1843), and Sonora (1780–1837). Also of value is the Archive of the Secretary of State, which preserves material relevant to church-civil affairs, especially in the section of *nunciaturas*.

Established in 1623 to coordinate conversion in previously non-Christian areas of the world, the Sacred Congregation of the Propagation of the Faith generated numerous, sensitive documents recording contact with newly discovered regions and their inhabitants. The Archivio della S.C. di Propaganda Fide in Rome preserves this extensive documentation. Because the Propaganda Fide functioned as a link between the Papacy and the religious orders active in the western hemisphere, the archive has a large volume of communications between Rome and the higher superiors of the orders operating in New Spain.

The archives of various religious orders are scattered throughout Rome. Many of these are unique and rich in material concerning New Spain and the whole New World. The Archivum Romanum Societatis Iesu located at the Jesuit Curia is an indispensable source; its holdings deal with the activities of the Society throughout the world with material dating from 1540. The Fondo Gesuitico which was at one time the archive of the treasurer-general (Procurador General) is under the direct control of the Italian government; this archive is located in the Biblioteca Nazionale of Rome. It is particularly useful for the history of church finance and education. Sections of both these archives are available on microfilm at St. Louis University, St. Louis, Missouri.

Franciscan documentation is preserved in the Civezza Collection in the Archivum Generale O. F. M. Although documentation on the Franciscans is found in greater abundance in the Archivo General de la Nación (Mexico) and in the Real Academia de la Historia (Madrid), the Roman material is distinct in character. Only a small part of this material has been made available on microfilm.

The archives of the other major religious orders involved in the missionization of New Spain have been only minimally utilized, and relatively little is known about the extent and quality of documentation. Consultation of whatever materials might be made available would certainly be requisite for a full understanding of their role in New World acculturation.

There are several notable archives outside Rome. In Florence, the Archivio de Stato, the Biblioteca Nazionale Centrale, and the Biblioteca Mediceo-Laurenziana contain material on the Americas. The Biblioteca Comunale dell' Archiginnasio and the Biblioteca Universitaria in Bologna deserve mention, as they preserve various linguistic materials and numerous manuscripts left by Jesuit exiles from Mexico. In Milan, the Biblioteca Ambrosiana preserves travel accounts and scientific information relative to the New World, as does the Biblioteca Trivulziana. The Biblioteca Nazionale de Brera contains some linguistic and bibliographic material. The Biblioteca Nazionale de Turin has cartographic information. Also in Turin, the Biblioteca Civica and Archivio de Stato have documentation concerning the New World and Mexico.

Venice hosts the Archivio de Stato (diplomatic papers), the Biblioteca Nazionale de San Marco (travel and cartographic), and the Biblioteca e Museo Civico Corres (cartographic). In Genoa, the Archivio de Stato, the Palazzo del Comune, the Palazzo Bianco, the Societa Ligure de Storia Patria, and the Civica Biblioteca Berio have useful records pertinent to Columbus and early New World discoveries. The Archivio de Stato and the Biblioteca Estense in Modena contain material helpful in the study of native American languages. Maritime and commercial documentation relative to Spain in America is held by the Archivio de Stato in Naples.

England

Most of the documentation found in British repositories concerning Mexico is diplomatic in nature. However, diverse types of records found their way into British archives as a result of pirate depredations on Spanish ships and ports. The largest concentration of this material is housed in the British Museum. Its Hispanic American collection is divided as follows: America in General, North America, the Antilles and the Caribbean, South America, and the Philippines and Oceana. Manuscripts pertinent to New Spain are in the division on North America. Many of these are geographic descriptions and travel accounts. Several, because of their thoroughness, have been copied and deposited in other European and American archives.

The "State Papers" in the Public Record Office provide data on the common frontier shared by Great Britain and Spain in North America. In a similar way papers preserved in the archives of the Foreign Office pertain to Spanish-British relations, particularly in regard to the lower Mississippi River valley. Papers of the Colonial Office frequently treat of similar information.

France, Denmark, Germany

Most of the Mexican material in the Bibliothèque Nationale (Paris) is in the Colección Aubin-Goupil. Included here are the Spanish writings of Garcés, Kino, and Palou. Most of this collection is on microfilm at the Museo Nacional in Mexico City. In the manuscript section of the library, the Colección Margny concerns the French in the Spanish borderlands. Documents relative to New Spain are also found in the Fonds des Manuscrits Espagnols and the Fonds des Manuscrits Mexicains. The section "Cartes et Plans" has cartographic material, as does the Bibliothèque de la Société de Géographie, also housed in the library.

The National Archives with records from the Bureau of Commerce, the Ministry of Colonies, the Ministry of War, and the Foreign Ministry has documentation of diplomatic and maritime character. Papers in the archives of the Foreign Ministry begin in the early years of the sixteenth century and are rich in information concerning Bourbon Spain. The Bibliothèque del Arsenal preserves material relative to the northern Spanish borderlands.

Other than Italy, France, and England, documentation of interest for northern New Spain can be located in limited quantities in the Royal Library of Copenhagen and in the Bayerisches Hauptstaatsarchiv in Munich. Very little research has been done in eastern Europe; future work there should reveal previously unknown documentation.

ARCHIVES IN THE UNITED STATES

Most documentary repositories in the United States fit into one of four categories: private, religious, university, or government. It would be a monumental task to describe each one having collections concerning New Spain. This essay does not attempt to do so. Some thirty archives and libraries are briefly discussed. The holdings of other depositories are listed and described in the guides and aids which follow this discussion.

A recent and most welcome addition to archival guides is *Spanish and Mexican Records of the American Southwest* by Henry P. Beers (Tucson: University of Arizona Press, 1979). The author describes various archives and documentary sources pertinent to the history of the states of New Mexico, Texas, California, and Arizona, providing with each description a brief history of the respective state. No other work of this nature exists, and it fills a large gap in the literature, allowing researchers to better prepare themselves before actual work in the archives begins.

As will become evident in the descriptions of major collections in the United States, a substantial amount of documentation has been transcribed or photocopied from important archives in Mexico, Spain, and the rest of Europe. Thus, it is wise to consult catalogs and guides to U.S. archives and libraries before initiating research in Mexico or Europe. This is especially true for the AGN in Mexico City, the AGI and AHN in Spain, the British Museum and the Public Records Office in London, and the National Library of Paris.

Library of Congress

Three divisions of the United States government maintain collections useful in the study of New Spain. The most important is the Library of Congress. The library itself is arranged by "divisions," with the manuscript division being by far the most consequential. Much of the material in this part of the library is further divided according to "collection." Together, these collections cover all aspects of New Spain with major strengths in the seventeenth, eighteenth, and nineteenth centuries. The Harkness Collection contains a variety of documentation for the colony's early years, most importantly for Cortés and his heirs. Notable, too, are numerous documents pertinent to the Inquisition in Mexico.

The G.R.G. Conway Collection is a duplicate of the collection in the Cambridge University Library (England). Part of this collection is also located in the Gilcrease Institute, Tulsa, Oklahoma. This accumulation of documents is particularly strong concerning the Mexican Inquisition, with special reference to the treatment of foreigners. A substantial amount of this material originated from the AGI in Seville and the AGN in Mexico City.

Spanish Transcripts and Facsimiles, another section of the manuscript division, has documentation from the AGI and the AGN. Information ranges from the early sixteenth century to the second decade of the nineteenth and covers most facets of civil, military, and ecclesiastical activities. A considerable number of records concern Spanish relations with France and the United States. Documents describing Spanish relationships with Indians on the northern frontier are also kept here.

The Woodbury Lowery Collection concentrates on Spanish and Mexican territories which are now part of the United States. These documents cover the period 1538–1800 for New Mexico, 1673–1803 for Texas, and 1588–1800 for California. Additional documentation relative to these areas is located in the Texas Collection and the New Mexico section. In the former, information ranges from the late seventeenth century to the 1830s and is best represented by material on ecclesiastical activities and the Provincias Internas. In the latter, documentation dates from 1621 and continues to the middle of the nineteenth century, covering most aspects of colonial life.

The microfilm collection of the manuscript division is one of the best of its kind in the country, with film from the Real Academia de la Historia, the Biblioteca Nacional, the Biblioteca del Palacio Real, the Archivo Histórico Nacional, the Archivo General de Simancas, the Archivo General de Indias (all in Spain), and the Archivo General de la Nación (Mexico City). Other sections in the manuscript division concern later years, with good coverage of Mexican independence, the Mexican War, and diplomatic relations between the United States and Mexico.

Two additional sections of the manuscript division deserve mention. The Hispanic Law section of the library is the largest single collection of Hispanic American legal material in the world. The Geography and Map Division contains a wide selection of original maps, copies, and special subject maps.

The National Archives and Smithsonian Institution

The National Archives of the United States safeguards records that concern intergovernmental relations between Mexico and the United States. Papers in the archive are arranged by Record Group (RG) in five general divisions: Legislative, Judicial and Diplomatic, Modern Military, Old Military, Social and Economic, and Cartographic and Audiovisual. Approximately one-fourth of the record groups pertain to Latin America. Those of most value concerning Mexico are:

RG 21 Records of the District Courts of the United States

RG 46 Records of the United States Senate (from 1789)

RG 76 Records of Boundary and Claims Commissions and Arbitrations

RG 84 Records of Foreign Service Posts of the Department of State

RG 94 Records of the Adjutant General's Office (1800–1939)

RG 107 Records of the Secretary of War (most of this transferred to RG 94)

RG 123 Records of the United States Court of Claims

RG 233 Records of the United States House of Representatives (from 1789)

RG 360 Records of the Continental Congress and Constitutional Convention (early United States–Spanish relations)

The most important record group in the National Archives is RG 59—General Records of the Department of State. Papers in this group date from the late eighteenth century and continue into the first decade of the twentieth, including, in addition to broad ranging diplomatic documentation, the Territorial Papers of the Secretary of State. This information resulted from the State Department's authority over the territories of Arizona, New Mexico, and California.

Although many government offices store records and have in-house libraries, most Mexican documentation has been deposited in the Library of Congress or the National Archives. The only other government supported agency to preserve material of note is the Smithsonian Institution with important material on North American Indians.

Colleges and Universities

The nation's universities conserve the major portion of available documentation on New Spain. The Bancroft Library at the University of California at Berkeley and the Nettie Lee Benson Latin American Collection at the University of Texas at Austin have the most extensive collections. The Bancroft Library maintains thousands of pages of manuscripts relative to northern Mexico and Jesuit activities there, and its microfilm collection rivals that of the Library of Congress. Some ten million pages of documents have been filmed in:

England The British Museum and the Public Records Office

France   Archives Nationaux and the Bibliothéque Nationale

Mexico   AGN, the Biblioteca Nacional, the Archivo Histórico Militar, the Museo Nacional, the Biblioteca Pública de Jalisco (Guadalajara), and regional archives

	in San Luis Potosí, Ciudad Juárez, and Parral
Spain	AGI, the Real Academia de la Historia, the Biblioteca Nacional, the Archivo Histórico Nacional, the Archivo General de Simancas, and the Museo Naval

Also in California, San Diego State University is now building a microfilm collection of materials copied from the Bancroft Library.

The Nettie Lee Benson Latin American Collection at the University of Texas covers a wide range of time and subject matter. Within the NLBLAC, the W.B. Stephens Collection has documents dating from the late sixteenth century, with a variety of personal papers pertinent to the borderlands. Documentation concerning the independence period of Mexican history is preserved in the Juan E. Hernández y Dávalos Collection. Material specific to Texas and the immediate area is housed in the Texas Collection. The substantial microfilm section maintains records copied from several small Mexican archives, the Public Records Office of Great Britain, and the National Archives of the United States. There is significant documentation from the AGN in Mexico City, with ramos "Historia," "Provincias Internas," and "Correspondencia de los virreys" filmed in their entirety.

The University of Texas Archives supplement the NLBLAC. This material focuses on the Spanish and Mexican periods of the American Southwest. Included here is the Bexar Archive, with documentation beginning in 1717 and continuing to 1836, and the Nacogdoches Archive with material from 1729 to 1836. Also preserved in the UT Archives are transcripts and photocopies from the AGI (Seville) and local archives in Mexico.

Other Texas archives of value include the Archivo Parroquial de San Fernando (San Antonio) and the Archivo de San Agustín de Laredo (St. Mary's University, San Antonio). The first preserves parish registers and documentation on Franciscan activities, and the latter relates to the Laredo area between 1749 and the 1860s.

The DeGolyer Foundation Library of Southern Methodist University (Dallas) has important information, the most notable being documentation concerning land disputes in Durango between 1659 and 1764 and early nineteenth century missionary correspondence. The special collections division of the University of Texas at El Paso Library has on microfilm all or parts of municipal archives from Parral, Durango, Chihuahua, Ciudad Juárez, and Janos, as well as the cathedral archives of Durango and Ciudad Juárez.

The John Carter Brown Library at Brown University (Rhode Island) has a strong collection emphasizing early chroniclers, Franciscan and Jesuit information, and indigenous languages. The Bein-ecke Rare Books Library and the Western Americana Collection at Yale contain early Mexican imprints and information on the Southwest for the first half of the nineteenth century.

St. Louis University (St. Louis, Missouri) has a valuable microfilm collection on Jesuit history in Mexico. At the university's Pius XII Library, the Knights of Columbus Film Collection has over eleven million manuscript pages from the Vatican Library, the Roman archives of the Society of Jesus, the AGI (Pastells Collection), and the Fondo Gesuitico al Gesú di Roma. There is also substantial documentation from various Mexican repositories. Indiana University and the University of Michigan maintain significant collections. The Lilly Library at Indiana has a number of early Mexican publications, as well as records relative to Jesuit and Franciscan activities in New Spain. The William L. Clements Library of the University of Michigan preserves a broad range of material, with emphasis on early chroniclers and historians.

Documentation in the New Mexico State Records Center (Santa Fe) covers the period 1621–1821 and is strongest for the eighteenth and nineteenth centuries. Data on the Pueblo Revolt, local residencias, frontier defenses, and Spanish-Indian relations are available. The papers of the archive division are accessible on microfilm. Material relative to land grants is located in the archives of the Court of Private Land Claims (Santa Fe) and the Department of Interior's Bureau of Land Management (Santa Fe). The Zimmerman Library at the University of New Mexico (Albuquerque) maintains a significant microfilm collection strong in diplomatic history and a several-hundred-volume set of copied manuscripts covering a variety of topics focusing on New Spain from the mid-sixteenth century to 1750.

The microfilm collection of the library of the University of Arizona (Tucson) contains a copy of the Archivo del Hidalgo de Parral, the Spanish Archives of New Mexico, the Bexar Archive, and the records and registers of several northern Mexico parishes. At the Arizona State Museum, also located at the University of Arizona, is the American Division of the Jesuit Historical Institute. The AD-JHI maintains microfilm collections of the Jesuit province of Mexico, the Pablo Pastells documents, extensive selections from the AGN and AGI, and miscellaneous copies from Bancroft, Texas, and various European archives. Associated with the AD-JHI is the Documentary Relations of the Southwest project which has reviewed tens of thousands of documents from all the principal archives of Mexico and the United States and selected those that pertain to the greater Southwest. These have been thoroughly analyzed and computer-indexed in a variety of ways. The computer tapes, printouts, indexes, and microfilm are all available at the DRSW.

Private Institutions

Several private institutions in the United States have collections dealing with the southwestern borderland region. The Henry E. Huntington Library (San Marino, California) contains pertinent documentation for areas previously under Spanish and Mexican sovereignty. Information ranges from the early seventeenth to mid-nineteenth centuries and is notable for records of the Mexican Inquisition (1525–1824), the correspondence of Eusebio Francisco Kino, and documents concerning José de Gálvez (1763–1794).

The Newberry Library (Chicago) has preserved material relative to Spanish colonial legislation and early explorations in the New World, and it maintains a valuable collection of rare books from the sixteenth, seventeenth, and eighteenth centuries. Information concerning the Indians of Mexico is located in the library's Edward E. Ayer Collection.

Exploration and travel accounts for the borderlands are housed in the Thomas Gilcrease Institute of American History and Art (Tulsa, Oklahoma). Material relative to the activities of fathers Kino and Serra is also available, as is part of the Conway Collection (the entire collection resting in the Library of Congress and the Cambridge University Library in Great Britain).

There are three private collections in New York City worthy of mention. The American Museum of Natural History is most noted for its material on North American anthropology, ethnography, and archaeology. The American Geographic Society possesses the single most important collection of geographical data in the United States. In a cultural vein, the Hispanic Society of America has a fine library collection of early imprints concerning the humanities and the arts.

Public Libraries

Two public libraries in the United States have important holdings. The New York Public Library is noted for the Obadiah Rich Collection which contains a variety of material for colonial Mexico, most of it copied from archives in Spain. Over one thousand rare books printed before 1800 are held in the rare book section. The Sutro Branch of the California State Library System has significant information concerning Mexican independence and a unique collection of early nineteenth century periodicals.

Religious Holdings

Few ecclesiastical archives in the United States contain Mexican documentation. The Santa Barbara Mission Archive-Library (Santa Barbara, California) has rare books and records for the Franciscan missions of Alta California (1769–1848). The Santa Barbara holdings are complemented by the archive of the Archdiocese of Santa Fe, New Mexico, which preserves Franciscan mission records from 1680 to 1850, records of the archdiocese from 1678 to the present, and parish registers for the seventeenth, eighteenth, and nineteenth centuries. The Academy of American Franciscan History in Washington, D.C., also has information relative to Franciscan activities in the Southwest.

The Church of Jesus Christ of Latter-day Saints (Mormon) has contributed immeasurably to biographical and genealogical research for New Spain. An aggressive microfilming program has resulted in the preservation of many parish and civil archives in Mexico. This microfilm is available in the genealogical library (Salt Lake City, Utah) and the Academia Mexicana de Genealogía y Heráldica in Mexico City. A published guide to this collection is also available.

GENERAL GUIDES AND AIDS TO DOCUMENTARY COLLECTIONS

MEXICO

General

Alessio Robles, Vito. *Bosquejos Históricos.* México, D.F.: Editorial Polis, 1938.

Barbena, Elsa B., ed. *Directorio de bibliotecas de la ciudad de México. Directory of Mexico City Libraries.* 2d ed. México, D.F.: 1967.

Boletín Interamericano de Archivos. Since 1974.

Bolton, Herbert E. *Guide to the Materials for the History of the United States in the Principal Archives of Mexico.* Washington, D.C.: The Carnegie Institution, 1913.

Somewhat dated in various of his descriptions, but still very useful. In addition to covering the archives of Mexico City, Bolton's labors took him to every Mexican state with archives containing material relevant to the United States.

Carrera Stampa, Manuel. *Archivalia Mexicana.* México, D.F.: Publicaciones del Instituto de Historia, 1952.

Good coverage of Mexican archives.

Colegio de México. Centro de Estudios Históricos. *Bibliografía histórica mexicana.*

Current information.

Gamoneda, Francisco. "Archivos (de México)." Included in *México. Historia de su evolución constructiva.* Tomo IV, 99–119. Edited by Félix Palavicini. México, D.F.: 1945.

García y García, J. Jesús. *Guía de archivos contiene material de interés para el estudio del desarrollo socioeconómico de México.* México, D.F.: UNAM, 1972.

Limited to archives in Mexico City. Excellent descriptions of holdings in most of the important archives of the city.

Genealogical Society, The Church of Jesus Christ of Latter-day Saints. *Genealogical Record Sources in Mexico.* Salt Lake City, Utah: 1970.

Gómez Canedo, Lino, O.F.M. *Los archivos de la historia de América.* 2 vols. México, D.F.: Instituto Panamericano de Geografía e Historia, 1961.

This is the best single source on archives for the study of Mexican history. Treats the United States and Europe as well as Mexico.

Greenleaf, Richard E., and Michael C. Meyer, eds. *Research in Mexican History: Topics, Methodology, Sources and a Practical Guide to Field Research.* Lincoln, Nebraska: University of Nebraska Press, 1973.

Recent and practical. Essays on the more important archives of Mexico City and research in Mexican history.

Gropp, Arthur E., ed. *A Bibliography of Latin American Bibliographies.* Metuchen, New Jersey: 1968. Supplement, 1971.

Hackett, Charles W., ed. *Historical Documents Relating to New Mexico, Nueva Vizcaya and Approaches Thereto, to 1773.* 3 vols. Washington, D.C.: The Carnegie Institution, 1923, 1926, 1937.

Handbook of Latin American Studies.

Hill, Roscoe R. "Ecclesiastical Archives in Latin America," *Archivum,* 4 (1954), 135–144.

———. "Latin American Archivology, 1948–1953," *HAHR,* 30 (February 1950), 115–139; 31 (February 1951), 152–176; 32 (August 1952), 458–482; 34 (May 1954), 256–279.

———. *The National Archives of Latin America.* Cambridge: Harvard University Press, 1945.

Millares Carlo, Agustín. *Los archivos municipales de Latinoamerica, libros de actas y colecciones documentales; apuntes bibliográficos.* Maracaibo, Venezuela: 1961.

———. "Notas bibliográficas acerca de los archivos municipales, ediciones de acuerdos y colecciones de documentos concejiles," *Revista de Historia de América,* 35 & 36 (January-December 1953), 175–208; 44 (December 1957), 393–428.

———. *Repertorio bibliográfico de los archivos mexicanos y de los europeos y norteamericanos de interés para la historia de México.* México, D.F.: UNAM, 1959.

Millares Carlo, Agustín and José Ignacio Mantecón. *Repertorio bibliográfico de los archivos mexicanos y de las colecciones diplomáticos fundamentales para la historia de México.* México, D.F.: Imprenta Aldina, 1948.

Pompa y Pompa, Antonio. "Contribución del Instituto Nacional de Antropología e Historia para la conservación de los archivos mexicanos fuera de la capital," *Memoria del Primer Congreso de Historiadores de México y los Estados Unidos . . . Monterrey, Nuevo León.* México, D.F.: Editorial Cultura, 1950.

Revista de Historia de América. "Bibliografía de Historia de América."

Current information.

Revista Interamericana de Bibliografía.

Zavala, Silvio. *Francisco del Paso y Troncoso. Su misión en Europa, 1892–1916.* México, D.F.: Departamento Autónoma de Prensa y Publicidad, 1939.

MEXICO CITY
El Archivo General de la Nación

Archivo General de la Nación. Departamento de Publicaciones del Archivo. Serie: Guías y Catálogos.

On-going publication series which produces the indexes of the various *ramos* of the AGN.

Boletín del Archivo General de la Nación. Since 1930.

Besides articles of historical character originating from research done in the archive, this periodical carries recent information on the status of the archive, its holdings, acquisitions, publications and new indexes in progress.

Civeira Taboada, Miguel, and María Bribiesca Sumano. *Guía descriptiva de los ramos que constituyen el Archivo General de la Nación.* México, D.F.: AGN, 1977.

Lists the 159 ramos of the AGN with a description of each, providing a general idea of the contents, the time period covered and relationships with other parts of the archive. If an index is available, this too, is noted.

Mariscal, Mario. *Reseña histórica del Archivo General de la Nación, 1550–1946.* México, D.F.: Secretaría de Gobernación, 1946.

Most complete history of the AGN. Study of the beginnings, growth, organization and operation of Mexico's most important archive.

Rubio Mañé, Jorge Ignacio. *El Archivo General de la Nación, México, D.F.* México, D.F.: Editorial Cultura, 1940. Also appears in *Revista de Historia de América,* 9 (August 1940), as "El Archivo General de la Nación, México, Distrito Federal."

Urrutia de Stebelski, Cristina, et al. *Inventario de ramos, guías e indices actualizados al mes de marzo de 1977, Archivo General de la Nación.* México, D.F.: AGN, 1977.

Excellent supplement to *Guía descriptiva*

(Civeira Taboada & Bribiesca Sumano). Lists the sections and ramos, the number of volumes in each and notes the existence of any guide or inventory for all or part of any ramo.

El Archivo Histórico de Hacienda

Hernández, Agustín. *Guía del Archivo Histórico de Hacienda, Siglos XVI al XIX.* México, D. F.: Secretaría de Hacienda y Crédito Público, 1940.

A list of documents in the archive broken down into the archive's sections, with individual documents listed under these section headings. The date and author, the length of the document and the individual legajo (volume) number are supplied.

Rodríguez de Lebrija, Esperanza. *Indice analítico de la guía del Archivo Histórico de Hacienda.* México, D.F.: AGN, 1975.

Used in conjunction with the guide by Hernández, this provides the quickest access to material in the AHH. Its analytical listing includes people, places, things and events in alphabetical order.

La Biblioteca Nacional

Carrasco Puente, Rafael. *Historia de la Biblioteca Nacional de México.* México, D.F.: Imprenta Universitaria, 1949.

Iguiniz, Juan B. "La Biblioteca Nacional de México," *Revista de Historia de América,* #8 (1940), 57–86.

Río, Ignacio del. *Guía del Archivo Franciscano de la Biblioteca Nacional de México.* México, D.F.: UNAM, 1975.

Rios, Enrique E. "Indice geográfico de manuscritos que se conservan en la Biblioteca Nacional," *Investigaciones Históricas,* October, 1938–39.

Instituto Nacional de Antropología e Historia

Juárez A., Bárbara. *Archivos microfilmados por la Biblioteca Nacional de México.* (Inventario). NP. ND.

Morales, Francisco. *Inventario del Fondo Franciscano del Museo de Antropología e Historia de México.* Washington, D.C.: 1978.

Ulloa Ortiz, Berta. "Catálogo de los fondos del Centro de Documentación del Museo Nacional de Historia, Castillo de Chapultepec," *Anales del Instituto Nacional de Antropología e Historia.* IV, #2 (1952).

El Museo Nacional

Caballero, J. Guadalupe Antonio. "La Biblioteca del Museo Nacional de Arqueología, Historia y Etnografía," *Anales del Museo Nacional,* 4th series, 5 (1927), 168–223.

Zavala, Silvio. "Catálogo de los fondos del centro del documentación del Museo Nacional de Historia, en el Castillo de Chapultepec," *Memoria de la Academia Mexicana de la Historia*, 10 (1951), 459–95.

El Archivo Histórico Militar Mexicano (Defensa)

Alessio Robles, Vito, et al. *Guía del Archivo Histórico Militar Mexicana*. Tomo I. México, D.F.: Dirección del Archivo Militar, 1948.

Torre Villar, Ernesto de. "El Archivo Histórico Militar de la Secretaría de la defensa nacional (México, D.F.)," *Revista de Historia de América*, 23 (1947).

Centro de Estudios de Historia de México, CONDUMEX, S.A.

Sierra, Carlos J. "El Centro de Estudios de Historia de México," *Boletín Bibliográfico de la Secretaría de Hacienda y Crédito Público*, #359 (January 15, 1967).

Archivo General de Notarías

Millares Carlo, Agustín, and José Ignacio Mantecón. "El Archivo de Notariás del Departamento del Distrito Federal (México, D.F.)," *Revista de Historia de América*, (June 1944), 69–118.

————. *Indice y extractos de los protocolos del Archivo de Notarías de México*. México, D.F.: El Colegio de México, 1945.

El Archivo del Arzobispado

Costeloe, Michael P. "Guide to the Chapter Archives of the Archbishopric of Mexico," *HAHR*, 45 (February 1965), 53–63.

MEXICAN STATES

In addition to the guides that follow, pertinent information concerning repositories in the various states is found in the following guides listed in the first portion of this bibliography on pages 39–40: Alessio Robles, *Bosquejos Históricos;* Bolton, *Guide to the Materials . . .*; Carrera Stampa, *Archivalia Mexicana;* Gómez Canedo, *Los archivos . . .*; and Pompa y Pompa, "Contribución del Instituto . . ."

Baja California

Aguirre, Amado. *Documentos para la historia de Baja California*. Introduction by Miguel León-Portilla. México, D.F. and Tijuana: Centro de Investigaciones, UNAM-UABC, 1977.

Cota Sandoval, José Andrés. *Archivo Histórico de Baja California Sur Pablo L. Martínez, Catálogo, Ramo I, La Colonia, 1744–1821*. La Paz: Cuadernos de Divulgación del Gobierno de Baja California Sur, #40, 1974.

León-Portilla, Miguel. "El Archivo Histórico de Baja California Sur, sus antecedentes y su reciente creación," *Memorias de la Academia Mexicana de la Historia*, 29:4 (October–December 1970), 300–319.

Mathes, Michael. "Baja California Mission Records," *Southwestern Mission Research Center Newsletter* (Tucson, University of Arizona), 11:35 (May 1977), 7.

Chihuahua

Hackett, Charles W., ed. *Historical Documents Relating to New Mexico, Nueva Vizcaya and Approaches Thereto, to 1773*. 3 vols. Washington, D.C.: The Carnegie Institution, 1923, 1926, 1937.

Hewitt, Harry P. "El Archivo de Hidalgo del Parral, 1631–1821." *Microfilm Review*, January 1972.

Rosaldo, Renato, et al. *El Archivo de Hidalgo del Parral, Index, 1631–1821*. Tucson: Arizona Silhouettes, 1961.

West, Robert C. "The Municipal Archive of Parral, Chihuahua, Mexico," *Handbook of Latin American Studies*, 6 (1940).

Coahuila

Bailey, David C., and William H. Beezley. *A Guide to Historical Sources in Saltillo, Coahuila*. East Lansing, Michigan: Latin American Studies Center, Monograph Series, #13, 1975.

Durango

Gallegos C., José Ignacio. "Durango; la historia y sus instrumentos," *Historia Mexicana*, 11:2 (October–December 1961), 314–20.

Porras, Guillermo. "Los archivos de Durango," *Divulgación Histórica*, 4:3 (July 1943), 164–66.

Saravia, Atanasio G. *Inventario general de los libros y papeles del excelentísimo ayuntamiento de Durango*. México, D.F.: 1948.

Jalisco (Guadalajara)

Castañeda, Carmen. "Los archivos de Guadalajara," *Historia Mexicana*, 97 (1975), 143–62.

Kroeber, Clifton. "La Biblioteca Pública del estado de Jalisco, Guadalajara," *HAHR*, 44 (August 1964), 377–81.

Mora, Miguel L., and Moisés González Navarro. "Jalisco; la historia y sus instrumentos," *Historia Mexicana*, 1:1 (July–September 1951), 143–46.

Van Young, Eric. "Los archivos históricos de Guadalajara." *Historia Mexicana*, January-March 1975.

Páez Brotchie, Luis. *La Nueva Galicia a través de su viejo Archivo Judicial. Indice analítico de los Archivos de la Audiencia de la Nueva Galicia o de Guadalajara y del Supremo Tribunal de Justicia del Estado de Jalisco*. México, D.F.: Porrúa e hijos, 1940.

————. "La importancia de nuestros archivos," *Estudios Históricos*, 1:1 (January 1943) (Guadalajara).

Nuevo León

Cavazos Garza, Israel. "Guía del ramo militar del Archivo General del Estado de Nuevo León, 1797–1850," *Humanitas*, 12. Monterrey: Centro de Estudios Humanísticos, Universidad de Nuevo León.

————. *Catálogo y síntesis de los protocolos del Archivo Municipal de Monterrey, 1599–1700*. Monterrey: Publicaciones del Instituto Tecnológico de Monterrey, Serie: Historia, 4, 1966.

————. "Catálogo y síntesis de los protocolos del Archivo Municipal de Monterrey, 1700–1725," *Humanitas*, 1973. Monterrey: Centro de Estudios Humanísticos, Universidad de Nuevo León.

————. "El Archivo Parroquial de Villaldama," *Vida Universitaria*, 13 (April 1, 1960). Monterrey.

————. "Nuevo León; la historia y sus instrumentos," *Historia Mexicana*, 1:3 (January–March 1952), 494–515.

Hoyo, Eugenio del. *Historia del Nuevo Reino de León, 1577–1723*. 2 vols. (Vol. 2). Monterrey: Publicaciones del Instituto Tecnológico de Monterrey, Serie: Historia, 13, 1972.

————. *Indice del ramo de causas criminales del Archivo Municipal de Monterrey*. Monterrey: Publicaciones del Instituto Tecnológico de Monterrey, Serie: Historia, 2, 1963.

————. *Indice de documentos existentes en el Archivo Municipal de Monterrey para el estudio de las tribus nómadas del Nuevo Reino de León, fines del siglo XVI a principios del siglo XIX*. N.P. N.D.

————. *Indice de documentos del Archivo Municipal de Monterrey para el estudio de la esclavitud y las encomiendas de indios en el Nuevo Reino de León, fines del siglo XVI a principios del siglo XIX*. N.P. N.D.

Mendirichaga y Cueva, Tomás. "Breve reseña del archivo parroquial de la catedral de Monterrey," *Humanitas*, 1962–1966. (#3, 1962, 377–88; #4, 1963, 247; #5, 1964, 413–19; #7, 1966, 341–51).

San Luis Potosí

Meade, Joaquín. "San Luis Potosí; la historia y sus instrumentos," *Estilo, Revista de Cultura*, 39 (July–September 1956), 155–78.

Montejano y Aguiñaga, Rafael. *Catálogo de los manuscritos de la Biblioteca Pública de la Universidad Autónoma de San Luis Potosí*. San Luis Potosí: Universidad Nacional Autónoma, 1958.

Sonora

López, E. Y. *Bibliografía de Sonora*. Hermosillo: Ediciones Fátima, 1960.

Radding de Murrieta, Cynthia. *Catálogo del Archivo de la Parroquia de la Purísima Concepción de los Alamos, 1685–1900*. Hermosillo: Centro Regional del Noroeste, INAH, #22, 1976.

Torres Chávez, María Lourdes, and Cynthia Radding de Murrieta. *Catálogo del Archivo Histórico del Estado de Sonora, Tomos I & II*. Hermosillo: Centro Regional del Noroeste, INAH, #12, 1974, 1975.

SPAIN
General

Biblioteca Nacional. Servicio Nacional de Información Bibliográfico y Documental.

Boletín del Centro de Estudios Americanistas.

Boletín de la Dirección General de Archivos y Bibliotecas.

Born, Lester K. *Unpublished Bibliographic Tools in Certain Archives and Libraries of Europe: A Partial List*. Washington, D.C.: The Library of Congress, 1952.

Burrus, Ernest J., S.J. "An Introduction to Bibliographic Tools in Spanish Archives and Manuscript Collections Relating to Hispanic America," *HAHR*, 35:4 (November 1955), 443–83.

Carrera Stampa, Manuel. *Misiones mexicanas en archivos europeos*. México, D.F.: Instituto Panamericano de Geografía e Historia, #93, 1949.

Dirección General de Archivos y Bibliotecas: Servicio de Publicaciones del Ministerio de Educación Nacional. *Guía de los archivos de Madrid*, and *Guía de las bibliotecas de Madrid*. Madrid: Ministerio de Educación, 1952, 1953. Ongoing publication series.

Dirección General de Archivos y Bibliotecas. *Boletín del Servicio Nacional de Microfilm*. (Madrid).

Dirección General de Archivos y Bibliotecas. *Guía de fuentes para la historia de Ibero-América conservados en España*. 2 vols. Madrid: 1966–1969.

Gómez Canedo, Lino, O.F.M. *Los Archivos de la historia de América*. 2 vols. México, D.F.: Instituto Panamericano de Geografía e Historia, 1961.

Greenleaf, Richard E. "Mexican Inquisition Materials in Spanish Archives," *The Americas*, 20 (April 1964), 416–20.

Hill, Roscoe R. *American Missions in European Archives*. México, D.F.: Instituto Panamericano de Geografía e Historia, 1951.

Lejarza, Fidel de, O.F.M. "Los archivos españoles y la Misionología," *Misionalia Hispánica* (Madrid), 4:12 (1947), 525–85.

Millares Carlo, Agustín. *Repertorio bibliográfico de los archivos mexicanos y de los europeos* y norteamericanos de interés para la historia de México. México, D.F.: UNAM, 1959.

Robertson, James Alexander. *List of Documents in Spanish Archives Relating to the History of the United States, which have been Printed or of which Transcripts are Preserved in American Libraries.* Washington, D.C.: The Carnegie Institution, 1910.

Rodríguez Marín, Francisco. *Guía histórica y descriptiva de los archivos, bibliotecas y museos arqueológicos de España.* Madrid: 1916.

Rodríguez Moñino, A. "Los manuscritos americanos en las bibliotecas madrileñas," *Bulletin Hispanique,* 58 (1956), 51–76.

Sánchez Alonso, Benito. *Fuentes de la historia española e hispanoamericana. Ensayo de bibliografía sistemática de impresos y manuscritos que ilustran la historia política de España y de sus antiguas posesiones de Ultramar.* 3d ed. Madrid: Consejo Superior de Investigaciones Científicas. Instituto "Miguel de Cervantes." Publicaciones de la "Revista de Filología Española," 1952.

Sánchez Belda, Luis. *Bibliografía de archivos españoles y de archivística.* Madrid: 1963.

Santiago Rodríguez, Miguel. *Documentos y manuscritos genealógicos.* Madrid: Ministerio de Educación Pública. Dirección de Archivos y Bibliotecas, 1954.

Schäfer, Ernst. *Indice de la colección de documentos inéditos de Indias editada por Pacheco, Cárdenas, Torres de Mendoza, y otros (1 serie, tomos 1–42) y la Real Academia de la Historia (2 serie, tomos 1–25).* 2 vols. (Consejo Superior de Investigaciones Científicas, Instituto "Gonzalo Fernández de Oviedo"). Madrid: Gráficas Ultra, S.A., 1946–1947.

Serís, Homero. "The Libraries and Archives of Madrid." *Hispanic-American Studies.* Coral Gables, Florida: University of Miami, Hispanic-American Institute, 1939.

Shepherd, William R. *Guide to the Materials for the History of the United States in Spanish Archives.* Washington, D.C.: The Carnegie Institution, 1907.

Torre Revello, José. *Los archivos españoles.* Buenos Aires: Instituto de Investigaciones Históricas, #36, 1927.

Tudela de la Orden, José. *Los manuscritos de América en las bibliotecas de España.* Madrid: Ediciones Cultura Hispánica, 1954.

El Archivo General de Indias

Archivo de Indias. *Indice de documentos de Nueva España existentes en el Archivo de Indias de Sevilla.* 4 vols. México, D.F.: Imprenta de la Secretaría de Relaciones Exteriores, 1928–1931.

Bermúdez Plata, Cristóbal. *El Archivo General de Indias de Sevilla, sede del Americanismo.* Madrid: 1951.

Catálogo de pasajeros a Indias durante los siglos XVI, XVII, XVIII. Vol. I (1509–1534); Vol. II (1535–1538); Vol. III (1539–1559). Sevilla: AGI, 1940, 1942, 1946. An on-going publication series.

Chapman, Charles E. *Catalogue of Materials in the Archivo General de Indias for the History of the Pacific Coast and the American Southwest.* Berkeley: University of California Press, 1919.

Hanke, Lewis, and Celso Rodríguez. *Guía de las fuentes en el Archivo General de Indias para el estudio de la administración virreinal española en México y en el Perú, 1535–1700.* Köln, Germany: Eöhln, 1977.

Indice de documentos de Nueva España existentes en el Archivo General de Indias de Sevilla. 4 vols. México, D.F.: Monografías Bibliográficas Mejicanas, Nos. 1, 12, 14, 22, 23. 1928–1931. (Paso y Troncoso, Francisco del.)

Peña y Cámara, José María de la. *Archivo General de Indias de Sevilla.* Madrid: 1958.

———. *A List of the Spanish Residencias in the Archives of the Indies.* Washington, D.C.: The Library of Congress, 1955.

Rubio y Moreno, Luis. *Pasajeros a Indias. Catálogo metodológico de las informaciones y licencias de los que allí pasaron, existentes en el Archivo General de Indias. Siglo primero de la colonización de América, 1492–1592.* 2 vols. Madrid: Compañía Iberoamericana de Publicaciones, S.A., 1930–1931.

Torre Revello, José. *El Archivo General de Indias de Sevilla: Historia y clasificación de sus fondos.* Buenos Aires: Instituto de Investigaciones Históricas, 1929.

———. *Inventarios del Archivo General de Indias.* Buenos Aires: Instituto de Investigaciones Históricas, #28, 1926.

Torres Lanzas, Pedro. "Catálogo de legajos," *Boletín del Centro de Estudios Americanistas,* 1919. (Sevilla)

———. *Independencia de América. Fuentes para su estudio. Catálogo de documentos conservados en el Archivo General de Indias de Sevilla.* 1st series. 6 vols. Madrid: Tipografía de la Sociedad de Publicaciones Históricas, 1912. 2d series. 2 vols. Sevilla: Tipografía Zarzuela, 1924–1925.

———. *Relación descriptiva de los mapas, planos . . . de México y Floridas, existentes en el Archivo General de Indias.* 5 vols. Sevilla: Imprenta de El Mercantil, 1900–1906.

———, and Germán Latorre. *Catálogo-cuadro general de la documentación.* Sevilla: AGI, 1918.

La Biblioteca Nacional

Castro, Manuel, O.F.M. *Manuscritos franciscanos de la Biblioteca Nacional de Madrid.* Madrid: Ministerio de Educación y Ciencia, 1973.

Cuesta, Luisa. *Catálogo de obras iberoamericanos y filipinas de la Biblioteca Nacional de Madrid.* Madrid: 1953.

Estrada, Genaro. *Manuscritos sobre México en la Biblioteca Nacional de Madrid.* Madrid: Cuadernos Mexicanos de la Embajada de México en España, 1933.

Ministerio de Educación Nacional. *Inventario general de manuscritos de la Biblioteca Nacional.* 9 vols. Madrid: Ministerio de Educación Nacional, 1953.

Museo-Biblioteca de Ultramar. Catálogo de la Biblioteca. Madrid: 1900.

Paz, Julián. *Catálogo de manuscritos de América existentes en la Biblioteca Nacional.* Madrid: Tipografía de Archivos, 1933.

————. *Manuscritos sobre México en la Biblioteca Nacional de Madrid.* Madrid: Cuadernos Mexicanos de la Embajada de México en España. 1933.

Paz Remolar, Ramón, and José López de Toro. *Inventario general de manuscritos de la Biblioteca Nacional.* 9 vols. Madrid: Dirección General de Archivos y Bibliotecas, 1953, 1956, 1957.

Ponce de León Freyre, Eduardo. *Guía del lector en la Biblioteca Nacional: Historia, organización, fondos.* Madrid: 1949.

Real Academia de la Historia

Ballestros y Beretta, Antonio. *Catálogo de la colección de don Juan Bautista Muñoz.* 3 vols. Madrid: Real Academia de la Historia, 1954–1958.

Boletín de la Real Academia de la Historia

Castañeda Alcover, Vicente. *La Real Academia de la Historia, 1735–1930.* Madrid: Tipografía de Archivos, 1930.

Olarra Garmendia, José, and Doña María Luisa Larramendi. *Indices de la correspondencia entre la Nunciatura en España y la Santa Sede, durante el Reinado de Felipe II.* Madrid: Real Academia de la Historia, 1949.

Pezuela, Jacobo de la. "La Colección Muñoz en la Real Academia de la Historia," *Boletín de la Real Academia de la Historia,* 79 (1929), 75–79.

Rodríguez-Moñino, A., ed. *Catálogo de los documentos de América en la colección de jesuitas en la Academia de la Historia.* Bajadoz: Institución de Servicios Culturales de la Diputación de Bajadoz, 1949.

El Archivo General de Simancas

Alcarez Terán, Concepción. *Guerra y Marina. I: Epoca de Carlos I de España y V de Alemania. Catálogo XVIII.* Valladolid: 1949.

Alcocer y Martínez, Mariano. *Archivo General de Simancas. Guía del investigador.* Valladolid: Imprenta de la Casa Social Católica, 1923.

Archivo General de Simancas. *Guía del Archivo General de Simancas.* Madrid: Dirección General de Archivos y Bibliotecas, 1958.

Catálogo de las informaciones genealógicas de los pretendientes a cargas del Santo Oficio. Valladolid: 1928.

Magdalena, Ricardo. *Titulos de Indias.* Valladolid: Patronato Nacional de Archivos Históricos, *Catálogo XX del Archivo General de Simancas.* 1954.

Paz, Julián. "Catálogo de los mapas que se conservan en el Archivo General de Simancas," *Revista de archivos, bibliotecas y museos,* III (1899), 524.

Plaza, Angel de la. *Archivo General de Simancas; Guía del investigador.* Valladolid: 1962.

El Archivo Histórico Nacional

González Palencia, Angel. *Extracto del catálogo de los documentos del Consejo de Indias conservados en la sección de Consejos del Archivo Histórico Nacional.* Madrid: 1920.

Gutiérrez del Arroyo, Consuelo. *La sección Universidades del Archivo Histórico Nacional.* Madrid: 1952.

Javierre Mur, Aurea, and Consuelo Gutiérrez del Arroyo. *Guía de la sección de ordenes militares.* Madrid: Patronato Nacional de Archivos Históricos, 1949.

Pescador del Hoyo, Carmen. *Archivo Histórico Nacional. Documentos de Indias. Siglos XV-XIX. Catálogo de la serie existente en la Sección de Diversos.* Madrid: Dirección General de Archivos y Bibliotecas, 1954.

Sánchez Belda, Luis. *Guía del Archivo Histórico Nacional.* Madrid: 1958.

La Biblioteca del Palacio Real

Domínguez Bordona, Jesús. *Catálogo de la Biblioteca de Palacio. Tomo IX. Manuscritos de América.* Madrid: Tipografía de Archivos, 1933.

Gijón, E. "América en la Biblioteca de Palacio," *Boletín de la Dirección General de Archivos y Bibliotecas,* 1:7 (1952), 42–54.

Torre Revello, José. *Biblioteca de Palacio en Madrid.* Buenos Aires: Publicaciones del Instituto de Investigaciones Históricas, #83, 1942.

Military Archives

Boletín de la Biblioteca Central Militar. Since 1945.

Catálogo del Archivo de Mapas, Planos y Memorias del Depósito de la Guerra. Madrid: Servicio Geográfico del Ejército, 1901.

Guillén Tato, Julio F. *Indice de los expedientes y papeles de la Sección de Indiferente del Archivo Central de la Marina.* Madrid: Instituto Histórico de la Marina, 1951.

————. *Indice de los papeles de la Sección Corso y Presas, 1784–1838.* 2 vols. Madrid: Institutos "Francisco de Vitoria" a "Histórico de la Marina," 1953.

————. *Independencia de América. Indice de los papeles de expediciones de Indias.* 3 vols. Madrid: Instituto Histórico de la Marina, 1953.

————. *Repertorio de los manuscritos, cartas, planos y dibujos relativos a las Californias existentes en este museo (Museo Naval).* Madrid: El Museo Naval, 1932.

Martínez Friera, Joaquín. "La Biblioteca Central Militar. Su museo y archivos," *Revue d'Histoire Internationale Militaire,* #9 (1950), 285–93.

Servicio Histórico Militar y Servicio Geográfico del Ejército. *Cartografía y relaciones históricas de Ultramar.*

Vela, Vicente V. *Indice de la colección de documentos de Fernández de Navarrete que posee el Museo Naval.* Madrid: El Museo Naval y El Instituto de la Marina, 1940.

Other Archives

Catálogo de los fondos americanos del Archivo de Protocolos de Sevilla. 5 vols. Madrid: Publicaciones del Instituto Hispano-Cubano de Historia de América de Sevilla, 1930–1937.

Esteve Barba, Francisco. *Catálogo de la Colección de Manuscritos Borbón-Lorenzana (La Biblioteca Provincial de Toledo).* Madrid: 1942.

Gutiérrez, Mariano, O.S.A. *Noticia de los manuscritos escurialenses a la historia y costumbres de los indios americanos.* Madrid: 1909.

Gutiérrez del Caño, Marcelino. *Catálogo de los manuscritos existentes en la Biblioteca Universitaria de Valencia.* N.P. N.D.

Torre Revello, José. *Archivo General Central en Alcalá de Henares. Reseña histórica y clasificación de sus fondos.* Buenos Aires: Instituto de Investigaciones Históricas, 1926.

Zarcos Cueva, P., S. J. *Catálogo de los manuscritos Castellanos de la Real Biblioteca de El Escorial.* 3 vols. Madrid: Imprenta Helénica, 1924–1929.

EUROPE

General

Born, Lester K. *Unpublished Bibliographic Tools in Certain Archives and Libraries of Europe: A Partial List.* Washington, D.C.: The Library of Congress, 1952.

Carrera Stampa, Manuel. *Misiones mexicanas en archivos europeos.* México, D.F.: Instituto Panamericano de Geografía e Historia, #93, 1949.

Donoso, Ricardo. *Fuentes documentales para la historia de la independencia de América. Misión de investigación en los archivos europeos.* México, D.F.: 1960.

García Ruiz, Alfonso. "La misión del historiador José de Jesús Núñez y Domínguez en archivos de Europa (1937–1939)," *Anales del Instituto Nacional de Antropología e Historia,* 2 (1947), 321–71.

Gómez Canedo, Lino, O.F.M. *Los archivos de la historia de América.* 2 vols. México, D.F.: Instituto Panamericano de Geografía e Historia, 1961.

Hanke, Lewis. "Materials for Research on Texas History in European Archives and Libraries," *Southwestern Historical Quarterly,* 59 (January 1956), 335–43.

Lewanski, Richard C. *Subject Collections in European Libraries: A Directory and Bibliographical Guide.* New York: Bowker, 1965.

Matteson, David M. *List of Manuscripts Concerning American History Preserved in European Libraries and Noted in their Published Catalogues and Similar Printed Lists.* Washington, D.C.: The Carnegie Institution, 1925.

Millares Carlo, Agustín. *Repertorio bibliográfico de los archivos mexicanos y de los europeos y norteamericanos de interés para la historia de México.* México, D.F.: UNAM, 1959.

Thomas, Daniel H., and Lynn M. Case. *Guide to the Diplomatic Archives of Western Europe.* Philadelphia: University of Pennsylvania Press, 1959.

ITALY

Archivio Vaticano. *Bibliografia dell' Archivio Vaticano.* 3 vols. Vatican City: 1962–1965.

Archivum: Revue International de Archives. Paris. Since 1951.

Bannon, John Francis, S.J. "The Saint Louis University Collection of Jesuitica Americana," *HAHR,* 37 (1957), 82–88.

Bignami Odier, Jeanne. *Guide au Departement des Manuscrits de la Bibliotheque du Vatican.* N.P. N.D.

Borges, Pedro. "Documentación americana en el Archivo General O.F.M. de Roma," *Archivo Ibero-Americano,* 19 (January–June 1959), 5–119.

Born, Lester K. *Unpublished Bibliographic Tools in Certain Archives and Libraries of Europe: A Partial List.* Washington, D.C.: The Library of Congress, 1952.

Burrus, Ernest J., S.J. "The Bandelier Collection in the Vatican Library," *Manuscripta,* 10 (July 1966), 67–84.

————. "Research Opportunities in Italian Archives and Manuscript Collections for Students of Hispanic American History," *HAHR,* 39:2 (August 1959), 428–63.

————. "Hispanic Americana in the Manuscripts of Bologna, Italy," *Manuscripta,* (October 1959).

————. "Mexican Historical Documents in the Central Jesuit Archives," *Manuscripta,* 12 (November 1968), 133–61.

Carrera Stampa, Manuel. *Misiones mexicanas en archivos europeos.* México, D.F.: Instituto Panamericano de Geografía e Historia, #93, 1949.

Fish, Carl R. *Guide to the Materials for American History in Roman and other Italian Archives.* Washington, D.C.: The Carnegie Institution, 1911.

Gómez Canedo, Lino, O.F.M. *Los archivos de la historia de América.* 2 vols. México, D.F.: Instituto Panamericano de Geografía e Historia, 1961.

Gómez Pérez, José. *Manuscritos españoles en la Biblioteca Central de Roma.* Madrid: Dirección General de Relaciones Culturales, 1956.

Guzmán, Eulalia. *Manuscritos sobre México en archivos de Italia.* México, D.F.: Sociedad Mexicana de Geografía y Estadística, 1964.

Lewanski, Richard C. *Subject Collections in European Libraries: A Directory and Bibliographical Guide.* New York: 1965.

Millares Carlo, Agustín. *Repertorio bibliográfico de los archivos mexicanos y de los europeos y norteamericanos de interés para la historia de México.* México, D.F.: UNAM, 1959.

Olarra Garmendia, José, and Doña María Luisa Larramendi. *Indices de la correspondencia entre la Nunciatura en España y la Santa Sede, durante el reinado de Felipe II.* Madrid: Real Academia de la Historia, 1948–1949.

Revelli Beaumont, Pedro. *Terre d'America e archivi d'Italia Milano.* Instituto Cristoforo Colombo, 1926.

Teschitel, Joseph. "Archivum Romanum Societatis Iesu," *Archivum,* 4 (1954), 145–52.

Weber, Francis J. "Roman Archives of Propaganda Fide," *American Catholic Historical Society Records,* 76 (December 1965), 245–48.

ENGLAND

Andrews, Charles M. *Guide to the Materials for American History, to 1783, in the Public Record Office of Great Britain.* 2 vols. Washington, D.C.: The Carnegie Institution, 1912–1914.

Andrews, Charles M., and Frances G. Davenport. *Guide to the Manuscript Materials, for the History of the United States to 1783, in the British Museum, in minor London Archives, and in the libraries of Oxford and Cambridge.* Washington, D.C.: The Carnegie Institution, 1908.

Bell, Herbert C., and David W. Parker. *Guide to British West Indian Archive Materials in London and the Islands for the History of the United States.* Washington, D.C.: The Carnegie Institution, 1926.

Born, Lester K. *Unpublished Bibliographic Tools in Certain Archives and Libraries of Europe: A Partial List.* Washington, D.C.: The Library of Congress, 1952.

British Museum. *Catalogue of Additions, 1843–1950.*

Calderón Quijano, José Antonio. *Guía de los documentos, mapas y planas sobre historia de América y España moderna en la Biblioteca Nacional de Paris, Museo Británico y Public Record Office de Londres.* Sevilla: Escuela de Estudios Hispano Americanos, 1962.

Carrera Stampa, Manuel. *Misiones mexicanas en archivos europeos.* México, D.F.: Instituto Panamericano de Geografía e Historia, #93, 1949.

"Documentos relativos a América existentes en el Foreign Office," *Boletín del Instituto de Investigaciones Históricas,* 5:29–32; 6:33–35.

Gayangos y Arce, Pascual de. *Catalogue of the Manuscripts in the Spanish Language in the British Museum.* 4 vols. London: Wm. Clowes and Sons, 1875–1893.

Gómez Canedo, Lino, O.F.M. *Los archivos de la historia de América.* 2 vols. México, D.F.: Instituto Panamericano de Geografía e Historia, 1961.

Grajales Ramos, Gloria. *Guía de documentos para la historia de México en archivos ingleses, siglo XIX.* México, D.F.: UNAM, 1969.

Great Britain. *Catalogue of the Colonial Office Library.* 15 vols. Boston: 1964.

————. *A Guide to Government Libraries.* London: 1958.

————. Public Record Office. *Guide to the Contents of the Public Record Office.* 2 vols. London: 1963.

Griffin, Grace Gardner. *A Guide to Manuscripts*

Relating to American History in British De-positories; Reproduced for the Manuscript Division of the Library of Congress. Washington, D.C.: The Library of Congress, 1946.

Guiseppi, M.S. *A Guide to the Manuscripts Pre-served in the Public Record Office.* London: 1923–1924.

Hepworth, Philip. *Archives and Manuscripts in Libraries.* 2d ed. London: 1964.

Historical Manuscripts Commission. *Record Repositories in Great Britain.* 2d ed. London: 1966.

Irwin, Raymond, and Ronald Staveley, eds. *The Libraries of London.* 2d ed. London: 1961.

Lewanski, Richard C. *Subject Collections in European Libraries: A Directory and Bibliographical Guide.* New York: 1965.

Millares Carlo, Agustín. *Repertorio bibliográfico de los archivos mexicanos y de los europeos y norteamericanos de interés para la historia de México.* México, D.F.: UNAM, 1959.

Paullin, Charles O., and Frederic L. Paxson. *Guide to the Materials in London Archives for the History of the United States since 1783.* Washington, D.C.: The Carnegie Institution, 1914.

Pugh, R.B. *The Records of the Colonial and Dominions Offices.* London: 1964.

Stevens, B.F. *Catalogue Index of Manuscripts in the Archives of England, France, Holland and Spain, relating to America, 1763–1783.* 180 vols. N.P. N.D.

Street, J. "The G.R.C. Conway Collection in the Cambridge University Library," *HAHR,* 27:1 (1957), 60–81.

Thomas, Henry. *Short Title Catalogue of Books Printed in Spain and of Spanish Books Printed Elsewhere in Europe Before 1601, Now in the British Museum.* London: 1921.

————. "Short Title Catalogue of Portuguese Books and of Spanish-American Books Printed before 1601 now in the British Museum," *Revue Hispanique,* 65 (1926), 265–315.

————. *Short Title Catalogue of Spanish-American Books Printed Before 1601 now in the British Museum.* London: 1944.

University of London. Institute of Latin American Studies. *Guide to Latin American Collections in London Libraries.* London: 1967.

Walford, A.J. "Latin America in British Libraries and Archives," *Revista Interamericana de Bibliografía,* 1: 3–4 (1951).

Walne, Peter, ed. *A Guide to the Manuscripts For the History of Latin America and the Caribbean in the British Isles.* London: Oxford University Press and the University of London, 1973.

Webster, B.K. *Britain and the Independence of Latin America, 1812–1830. Select Documents from the Foreign Office Archives.* 2 vols. London: Oxford University Press, 1938.

FRANCE

Bibliothéque Nationale. *Catalogue des manuscrits Americains de la Bibliothéque Nationale.* Paris: 1925.

Boban, Eugene. *Documents pour servir a l' histoire du Mexique. Catalogue raisonné de la collection de M.E. Eugene Goupil (ancienne collection J.M.A. Aubin). . . .* 2 vols., and one volume atlas. Paris: Ernest Leroux, 1891.

Calderón Quijano, José Antonio. *Guía de los documentos, mapas y planas sobre historia de América y España moderna en la Biblioteca Nacional de París, Museo Británico y Public Record Office de Londres.* Sevilla: Escuela de Estudios Hispano Americanos, 1962.

Gómez Canedo, Lino, O.F.M. *Los archivos de la historia de América.* 2 vols. México, D.F.: Instituto Panamericano de Geografía e Historia, 1961.

Leland, Waldo G., et. al. *Guide to Materials for American History in the Libraries and Archives of Paris.* 2 vols. Washington, D.C.: The Carnegie Institution, 1932.

Millares Carlo, Agustín. *Repertorio bibliográfico de los archivos mexicanos y de los europeos y norteamericanos de interés para la historia de México.* México, D.F.: UNAM, 1959.

Morel-Fato, M. Alfred. *Catalogue des manuscrits espagnols et portugais de la Bibliothéque Nationale.* Paris: Imprimerie Nationale, 1881–1892.

Nuñez y Domínguez, José de Jesús. "Documentos existentes en la Biblioteca Nacional de París relativos a Chihuahua y Durango," *Boletín de la Sociedad Chihuahuense de Estudios Históricos,* 2:4 (September 4, 1930), 128–30, 133.

Omont, Henri A. *Catalogue des manuscrits Mexicains.* Paris: 1899.

Paz, Julian. *Documentos relativos a España existentes en los Archivos Nacionales de París. Catálogo y extractos de más de 2,000 documentos de los años 1276–1844.* Madrid: Publicaciones del Instituto de Valencia de don Juan, 1934.

Weskmann, Luis. "Un gran archivo histórico mexicano en París," *Historia Mexicana,* 8:1 (July–September 1958), 81–94.

OTHER EUROPEAN LOCATIONS

Butler, Ruth Lapham. "The Latin American Manuscripts in the Royal Library at Copenhagen," *Handbook of Latin American Studies,* 1936.

Faust, Albert B. *Guide to the Materials for American History in Swiss and Austrian Archives.* Washington, D.C.: The Carnegie Institution, 1916.

Golder, Frank. *Guide to the Materials for American History in Russian Archives.* 2 vols. Washington, D.C.: The Carnegie Institution, 1917, 1937.

Kraft, Walter C. *Codices Vindobonenses Hispanici: A Catalog of the Spanish, Portuguese, and Catalan Manuscripts in the Austrian National Library in Vienna.* Corvallis, Oregon: 1957.

Learned, Marion Dexter. *Guide to the Manuscript Materials Relating to American History in the German State Archives.* Washington, D.C.: The Carnegie Institution, 1912.

Velásquez, María del Carmen. "Documentos mexicanos en Austria," *Historia Mexicana,* 10 (1961), 509–26.

UNITED STATES

General

American Archivist

Ash, Lee, and Denis Lorenz, eds. *Subject Collections: A Guide to Special Book Collections and Subject Emphasis as Reported by University, College, Public, and Special Libraries in the United States and Canada.* 3d. ed. New York: 1967.

Beers, Henry Putney. *Spanish and Mexican Records of the American Southwest: A Bibliographical Guide to Archives and Manuscript Sources.* Tucson: University of Arizona Press, 1979.

Besterman, Theodore. *A World Bibliography of Bibliographies and of Bibliographical Catalogues, Calendars, Abstracts, Digests, Indexes, and the Like.* 4th ed. 5 vols. Lausanne: 1965–1966.

Billington, Ray Allen. "Guides to American History Manuscript Collections in the United States," *The Mississippi Valley Historical Review,* 38 (December 1951), 467–96.

Butler, Ruth Lapham. "Important Acquisitions of Manuscript and Rare Printed Material Relating to Latin America in the Libraries of the United States," *Handbook of Latin American Studies,* 11 (1945), 360–64.

Cottler, Susan M. et. al. *Preliminary Survey of the Mexican Collection.* Finding Aids to the Microfilmed Manuscript Collection of the Genealogical Society of Utah, #1. Salt Lake City: University of Utah Press, 1978.

Critendon, Christopher, and Doris Godard. *Historical Societies in the United States and Canada: A Handbook.* Washington: 1944.

Directory of Archives and Manuscript Repositories. Washington, D.C.: National Historical Publications and Records Commission, 1978.

Ellis, John A. *A Guide to American Catholic History.* Milwaukee: Bruce Publishing Co., 1959.

Evans, G. Edward. "A Guide to Pre-1750 Manuscripts in the United States Relating to Mexico and the Southwestern United States, with Emphasis on Their Value to Anthropologists," *Ethnohistory,* 17 (Winter–Spring 1970), 63–90.

————, and Frank J. Morales. "Fuentes de la historia de México en archivos norteamericanos," *Historia Mexicana,* 18 (January–March 1969), 432–62.

Fernández de Córdoba, Joaquín. "Nuestros tesoros bibliográficos en los Estados Unidos." *Historia Mexicana,* 5:1 (1956), 123–60; and 6:1 (1956), 129–60.

————. *Tesoros bibliográficos de México en los Estados Unidos.* México, D.F.: 1959.

Gómez Canedo, Lino, O.F.M. *Los archivos de la historia de América.* 2 vols. México, D.F.: Instituto Panamericano de Geografía e Historia, 1961.

————. "Some Franciscan Sources in the Archives and Libraries of America," *Americas,* 13 (October 1956), 141–74.

Hale, Richard W. *Guide to Photocopied Historical Materials in the United States and Canada.* Ithaca, New York: Cornell University Press, 1961.

Hamer, Philip M. *A Guide to Archives and Manuscripts in the United States.* New Haven: Yale University Press, 1961.

Handbook of Latin American Studies.

Haro, Robert P. ed. *Latin Americana Research in the United States and Canada: A Guide and Directory.* Chicago: 1971.

Hilton, Ronald, ed. *Handbook of Hispanic Source Materials and Research Organizations in the United States.* 2d ed. Stanford: Stanford University Press, 1956.

————. *Los estudios hispánicos en los Estados Unidos. Archivos-Bibliotecas-Museos-Sociedades científicas.* Translated and revised by Lino Gómez Canedo. Madrid: Instituto de Cultura Hispánica, 1957.

Hispanic American Historical Review (HAHR).

Historical Records Survey. *Guide to the Depositories of Manuscript Collections in the United States.* By state.

Millares Carlo, Agustín. *Repertorio bibliográfico de los archivos mexicanos y de los europeos y norteamericanos de interés para la historia de México.* México, D.F.: UNAM, 1959.

Patterson, Jerry E. *Latin American Manuscripts in United States Libraries: A Guide to Printed Sources.* Washington, D.C.: 1965.

Society of American Archivists. *College and University Archives in the United States and Canada.* Ann Arbor, Michigan: University of Michigan Press, 1966.

Steck, Francis B. *A Tentative Guide to Historical Materials on the Spanish Borderlands.* Philadelphia: The Catholic Historical Society of Philadelphia, 1943.

Vollmar, Edward R., S.J. *The Catholic Church in America; an Historical Bibliography.* New Brunswick, New Jersey: The Scarecrow Press, 1956.

Winter, Oscar O. *A Classified Bibliography of the Periodical Literature of the Trans-Mississippi West (1811–1957). Volume II, Archives and Manuscripts.* Bloomington, Indiana: Indiana University Press, 1961.

Washington, D.C.

Bickel, Richard B., ed. *Manuscripts on Microfilm: A Checklist of the Holdings in the Manuscript Division.* (Library of Congress). Washington, D.C.: Government Printing Office, 1975.

Childs, James B. "Hispanic American Government Documents in the Library of Congress," *HAHR,* 6 (February–August 1926), 134–41.

Cortes, Vincenta. "Manuscripts Concerning Mexico and Central America in the Library of Congress, Washington, D.C.," *The Americas,* 18 (January 1962), 255–96.

Cossío, J.L. "La Biblioteca del Congreso de los Estados Unidos de Norte América," *Boletín de la Sociedad Mexicana de Geografía y Estadística,* 59 (1944).

Fitzgerald, David, ed. *Index of Publications, Articles and Maps Relating to Mexico in the War Department Library.* Washington, D.C.: 1896.

Garrison, Curtis W. "List of Manuscript Collections in the Library of Congress to July 1931," *Annual Report of the American Historical Association for the year 1930.* Washington, D.C.: Vol. I, 123–249.

Handbook of Manuscripts in the Library of Congress. Washington, D.C.: Government Printing Office, 1918.

Harrison, John P. *Materials in the National Archives Relating to the Mexican States of Sonora, Sinaloa and Baja California.* Washington, D.C.: The National Archives, Reference Information Papers, #42, 1952.

————. "The Archives of the United States Diplomatic and Consular Posts in Latin America," *HAHR,* 33 (February 1953), 168–83.

Harrison, John P., ed. *Guide to Materials on Latin America in the National Archives.* 2 vols. Washington, D.C.: 1961 and 1970.

Hufford, Harold E., and Watson Caudill. *Preliminary Inventory of the Records of the U.S. Senate.* Washington, D.C.: Government Printing Office, 1950.

Kahler, Mary Ellis, ed. *The Harkness Collection in the Library of Congress. Manuscripts Concerning Mexico, A Guide.* Washington, D.C.: Library of Congress, 1974.

Lounsbury, Ralph G. "Materials in the National Archives for the History of New Mexico before 1848," *New Mexico Historical Review,* 21 (1946), 247–56.

Martin, Thomas P. "Transcripts, Facsimiles, and Manuscripts in the Spanish Language in the Library of Congress, 1929," *HAHR,* 9 (May 1929), 243–46.

Phillips, Philip Lee. *The Lowery Collection: A Descriptive List of Maps of the Spanish Possessions Within the Present Limits of the United States, 1502–1820.* Washington, D.C.: Government Printing Office, 1912.

Powell, C. Percy. "List of Manuscript Collections Received in the Library of Congress, July 1931, to July 1938," *Annual Report of the American Historical Association for the Year 1937.* Washington, D.C.: Vol. I, 147–83.

Prologue: The Journal of the National Archives. Since 1968.

Rhoads, James B., ed. *Catalog of National Archives Microfilm Publications.* Washington, D.C.: General Services Administration, 1978.

Salado Alvarez, Victoriano. "Breve noticia de algunos manuscritos de interés histórico para México, que se encuentran en los archivos y bibliotecas de Washington, D.C.," *Anales del Museo Nacional de Arqueología, Historia y Etnología,* 3d época, I (1900), 1–24.

Shelley, Fred. "Manuscripts in the Library of Congress: 1800–1900," *The American Archivist,* 11:1 (January 1948), 3–17.

United States Library of Congress. "Hispanica," Library of Congress Quarterly Journal of Current Acquisitions.

————. *Inventory of Documents from Spanish, Mexican and Cuban Archives in the Library of Congress.* Washington: 1940.

————. *The National Union Catalog of Manuscript Collections, 1959–1970.* 10 vols. Published at Ann Arbor, Michigan: J.W. Edwards, Inc., 1959–1961; Hamden, Connecticut: The String Press, Inc., 1962; and Washington, D.C.: The Library of Congress, 1963–1970.

United States National Archives. *Guide to the Records in the National Archives.* Washington, D.C.: Government Printing Office, 1948.

————. *List of National Archive Microfilm Publications, 1953.* Washington, D.C.: The National Archives, 1953.

————. *United States Congress, House of Representatives, House Files. Records of the U.S. House of Representatives.* (RG 233).

————. *United States Congress, Senate, Senate Files. Records of the U.S. Senate.* (RG 46).

————. *United States Department of the Navy. Naval Records and Library Collections.* (RG 45).

————. *United States War Department, Records of the Adjutant General's Office.* (RG 94).

————. *United States Department of State. General Records of the Department of State.* (RG 59).

————. *United States Department of Justice. General Records of the Department of Justice.* (RG 60).

————. *United States Department of Interior. Bureau of Land Management.* (RG 49).

————. *Records of the Office of the Secretary of the Interior.* (RG 48).

————. (Kelsay, Laura E.) *List of Cartographic Records of the General Land Office.* (RG 49). Washington, D.C.: 1964.

United States Library of Congress and Records Service. *Records of the National Archives and Record Service.* (Record Group 64).

STATES

Arizona

Colley, Charles C. *Documents of Southwestern History: a Guide to the Manuscript Collections of the Arizona Historical Society.* Tucson: Arizona Historical Society, 1972.

Mills, Todd. "Western Manuscripts in the University of Arizona Library," *Arizona and the West,* 22 (Spring 1980), 5–66.

United States Survey of Federal Archives, Arizona. *Inventory of Federal Archives in the States, Series VIII, The Department of the Interior, No. 3, Arizona.* Tucson: 1939.

University of Arizona Library, Microforms Section. *Guide to Film 811, Parish Archives of Sonora and Sinaloa.* Tucson: University of Arizona Library, 1976.

Wallace, Andrew, ed. *Sources and Readings in Arizona History; a Checklist of Literature Concerning Arizona's Past.* Tucson: Arizona Historical Society, 1965.

California

Abajian, James. "Preliminary Listing of Manuscript Collections in the Library of the California Historical Society," *California Historical Society Quarterly,* 33 (December 1954), 372–76.

Bancroft Library, University of California. *Index to Printed Maps.* Boston: G.K. Hall, 1964.

Barlow, R.H. "The 18th Century *Relaciones Geográficas:* A Bibliography," *Tlalocan,* I (1943), 54–70, 362–63. (Bancroft Library).

————. "Los manuscritos de la Biblioteca Bancroft que pertenecieron a la antigua colección de don José Fernando Ramírez," *Memorias de la Academia de la Historia* (Mexico), 2:2 (April–June 1943), 189–200.

California, University of, at Los Angeles. *Guide to Special Collections in the Library of the University of California at Los Angeles (UCLA).* Los Angeles: University of California at Los Angeles Library, Occasional Papers, #7, 1958.

Carpenter, Edwin H., Jr. "Checklist of the Official Imprints of the Administration of Revilla Gigedo the Younger, 1789–1794," *Papers of the Bibliographical Society of America,* XLVI (1952), 215–63. (Huntington Library).

Catalogue of Maps of America from the Sixteenth to the Nineteenth Centuries. London: 1924. (Huntington Library).

Catalogue of Mexican Pamphlets in the Sutro Collection. 14 vols. San Francisco: 1939–1940.

Chapin, Edward L. *A Selected Bibliography of Southern California Maps.* Berkeley: University of California Press, 1953.

Chávez, Angélico. "Some Original New Mexico Documents in California Libraries," *New Mexico Historical Review,* 25:3 (July 1950), 244–53.

Curthbert, Norma B. *American Manuscript Collections in the Huntington Library for the History of the Seventeenth and Eighteenth Centuries.* San Marino: The Huntington Library, 1941.

Dillon, Richard H. "The Sutro Library," *News Notes of California Libraries,* 51 (April 1956), 338–52.

————. "Sutro Library's Resources in Latin Americana," *HAHR,* XLV (May 1965), 267–74.

Dunne, Peter M. "Jesuit Annual Letters in the Bancroft Library," *Mid America,* 20 (1938), 263–72.

Ferguson, M.J. "The Sutro Branch of the California State Library," *News and Notes of California Libraries,* 12:2 (1917).

Fisher, Mary Ann. *A Preliminary Guide to the Microfilm Collection in the Bancroft Library.* Berkeley: University of California Press, 1955.

Gars, A.I., ed. *Library Catalogue of Works on the Catholic Church by Spanish, Portuguese and*

Spanish-American Writers Before 1800. San Francisco: The Sutro Library, 1941.

Geiger, Maynard J., O.F.M. *Calendar of Documents in the Santa Barbara Mission Archives.* Washington, D.C.: Academy of American Franciscan History, 1947.

Hammond, George P. "Manuscript Collections in the Berkeley Library," *American Archivist,* 13 (January 1950), 15–26.

Haselden, R.H. "Manuscript Collections in the Huntington Library," *Archives and Libraries: Papers* (American Library Association). Chicago: 1939. Pp. 71–79.

Historical Records Survey. *Guide to Depositories of Manuscript Collections in the United States: California.* Los Angeles: 1941.

Huntington Library. "Huntington Library Collections," *Huntington Library Bulletin,* I (May 1931), 33–106.

Liebman, Seymour B. "The Abecedario and a Check-List of Mexican Inquisition Documents at the Henry E. Huntington Library," *HAHR,* XLIV (November 1964), 554–67.

Louis, Ronald, and Silveira de Braganza, eds. *San Diego, California: A Bicentennial Bibliography, 1769–1969.* San Diego 200th Anniversary, Inc., 1969.

Morgan, Dale L., and George P. Hammond, eds. *A Guide to the Manuscript Collections of the Bancroft Library.* 2 vols. Berkeley: University of California Press, 1963.

Nasatir, A.P. *French Activities in California. An Archival Calendar-Guide.* San Francisco: Stanford University Press, 1945.

Parish, John C. "California Books and Manuscripts in the Huntington Library," *Huntington Library Bulletin,* #7 (April 1935).

Radin, Paul, ed. *Catalogue of the Mexican Pamphlets in the Sutro Collection.* 3 vols. San Francisco: The Sutro Library, 1939–1940.

St. John's Seminary, Camarillo, California. Estelle Doheny Collection. *One Hundred Manuscripts and Books from the Estelle Doheny Collection in the Edward L. Doheny Memorial Library, St. John's Seminary, Camarillo, California.* Los Angeles: Anderson and Ritchie, 1950.

San Diego Historical Society. *A Guide to the Research Collections of the San Diego Historical Society, Located in the Serra Museum, Presidio Hill.* San Diego: The Society, 1964.

Schultz, Herbert C., et al. *Ten Centuries of Manuscripts in the Huntington Library.* San Marino: The Huntington Library, 1962.

Weber, Francis J. "The Los Angeles Chancery Archives," *The Americas,* 21 (April 1965), 410–20.

———. "The San Francisco Chancery Archives," *The Americas* 20 (January 1964), 313–21.

Wright, D.M. *A Guide to the Mariano Guadalupe Vallejo Documents for the History of California, 1780–1875.* Berkeley: University of California Press, 1953.

Connecticut (Yale University)

Goddard, Jeanne, et al. *A Catalogue of the Frederick W. and Carrie S. Beinecke Collection of Western Americana, Volume I, Manuscripts.* New Haven: Yale University Press, 1965.

Patterson, Jerry E. "Spanish and Spanish American Manuscripts in the Yale University Library," *The Yale University Library Gazette,* 31:3 (1957), 110–13.

Withington, Mary C. *A Catalogue of Manuscripts in the Collection of Western Americana Founded by William Robertson Coe, Yale University Library.* New Haven: Yale University Press, 1952.

Illinois (Newberry Library)

Butler, Ruth Lapham. *A Bibliographical Checklist of North and Middle American Indian Linguistics in the "Edward E. Ayer Collection."* 2 vols. Chicago: Newberry Library, 1941.

———. *A Checklist of Manuscripts in the Edward E. Ayer Collection.* Chicago: The Newberry Library, 1937.

Coale, Robert P. "Evaluation of a Research Library Collection: Latin American Colonial History at the Newberry," *Library Quarterly,* 35 (1965), 173–84.

Hussey, Roland Denis. "Manuscript Hispanic Americana in the Ayer Collection of the Newberry Library, Chicago," *HAHR,* 10:1 (February 1930), 113–17.

Pargellis, Stanley. "Manuscript Collections in the Newberry Library," *Illinois Libraries,* 40 (1958), 314–20.

Smith, Clara A. *A List of Manuscript Maps in the Edward E. Ayer Collection.* Chicago: Newberry Library, 1927.

Indiana (Indiana University, Lilly Library)

Lilly Library. *Mexican Manuscripts in the Lilly Library.* Bloomington, Indiana: The Lilly Library, N.D.

Louisiana (Tulane University)

Griffith, Connie G. "Collections in the Manuscript Section of Howard-Tilton Memorial Library, Tulane University," *Louisiana History,* I (1960), 321–27.

Irvine, Marie H. *Administrative Papers: Copies Relating to New Spain.* New Orleans: (Tulane University), 1939.

Middle American Research Institute. *An Inventory of the Collection of the Middle American Research Institute.* New Orleans: 1941.

————. *Maps in the Frederick K. Hoffman Collection.* New Orleans: 1939.

Massachusetts (Harvard University)

Hussey, Roland Denis. "Manuscript Hispanic Americana in the Harvard College Library," *HAHR,* 17:2 (May 1937), 259–77.

Michigan (William L. Clements Library, University of Michigan)

Brun, Christian. *Guide to the Manuscript Maps in the William L. Clements Library.* Ann Arbor, Michigan: 1959.

Clements, William L. *Uncommon, Scarce, and Rare Books Relating to American History During the Discovery and Colonial Periods Together with Other Americana from the Library of William L. Clements.* Bay City, Michigan: 1924.

Erving, William S. *Guide to the Manuscript Collections in the William L. Clements Library.* 2d ed. Ann Arbor, Michigan: The William L. Clements Library, 1953. Supplement, 1959.

Peckham, Howard H. *Guide to the Manuscript Collection in the William L. Clements Library.* Ann Arbor, Michigan: University of Michigan Press, 1944.

University of Michigan. *Americana, 1493–1860 in the William L. Clements Library.* 7 vols. Boston: 1971.

Missouri (St. Louis University)

Bannon, John Francis, S.J. "The Saint Louis University Collection of Jesuitica Americana," *HAHR,* 37:1 (1957), 82–88.

Mateos, P. Francisco. "La colección Pastells de documentos sobre América y Filipinas," *Revista de Indias,* 27 (January–March 1947), 7–52.

New Mexico

Chávez, Angélico, O.F.M. *Archives of the Archdiocese of Santa Fe, 1678–1900.* Washington, D.C.: Academy of American Franciscan History, 1957.

Díaz, Albert J. *A Guide to the Microfilm of Papers Relating to New Mexico Land Grants.* Albuquerque: University of New Mexico Press, 1960.

————. *Manuscripts and Records in the University of New Mexico Library.* University of New Mexico Library, 1957.

————. "University of New Mexico Special Collections," *New Mexico Historical Review,* 33 (July–October 1958), 235–51, 316–21.

Historical Records Survey, Illinois. *Checklist of New Mexico Imprints and Publications, 1784–1876; Imprints, 1834–1876; Publications, 1784–1876.* (Lansing?), Michigan: Michigan Historical Records Survey, 1942.

Jenkins, Myra Ellen. *Calendar of the Mexican Archives of New Mexico, 1821–1846.* Santa Fe: State of New Mexico Records Center, 1970.

————. *Guide to the Microfilm of the Spanish Archives of New Mexico, 1621–1821, in the Archives Division of the State of New Mexico Records Center.* Santa Fe: State of New Mexico Records Center, 1967.

————. *Guide to the Microfilm Edition of the Mexican Archives of New Mexico, 1821–1846, in the Archives Division of the State of New Mexico Records Center.* Santa Fe: State of New Mexico Records Center, 1969.

————. *Calendar of the Spanish Archives of New Mexico, 1621–1821.* Santa Fe: New Mexico State Records Center, 1968.

Porrúa Turanzas, José. *Documentos para servir a la historia del Nuevo México, 1538–1778.* Madrid: 1962.

Scholes, France V. "Manuscripts for the History of New Mexico in the National Library of Mexico City," *The New Mexico Historical Review,* 3 (1928), 301–23.

Swadesh, Frances L. *20,000 Years of History: a New Mexico Bibliography. With an Ethnohistorical Introduction.* Santa Fe: Sunstone Press, 1973.

Twitchell, Ralph E. *The Spanish Archives of New Mexico.* 2 vols. Cedar Rapids, Iowa: The Torch Press, 1914.

New York

American Geographical Society. *Research Catalogue of the American Geographical Society.* 15 vols. Boston: 1962.

American Jewish Historical Society. *Manuscript Collections.* New York: 1967.

Carreño, Alberto María. "Documentos relacionados con la historia de México en la Nueva Biblioteca Pública de Nueva York," *Anales del Museo Nacional de Arqueología, Historia y Etnología* (Mexico), 4 (1912), 489–504.

Hispanic Society of America. *Catalogue of the Library.* 10 vols. Boston: 1962.

————. *A History of the Hispanic Society of America, Museum and Library (1904–1954) with a Survey of Collections.* New York: 1954.

New York Public Library. "List of Works in the New York Public Library relating to Mexico," *Bulletin of the New York Public Library*, 13 (October 1909), 622–62; (November 1909), 675–737; (December 1909), 748–829.

―――――. "Manuscript Collections in the New York Public Library," *Bulletin of the New York Public Library*, 5 (July 1901), 306–36, Supplement, 19 (February 1915), 149–62.

―――――. *Dictionary Catalog of the Manuscript Division of the New York Public Library*. 2 vols. Boston: 1967.

Penney, Clara Louisa. *List of Books Printed Before 1601 in the Library of the Hispanic Society of America*. New York: The Hispanic Society of America, 1929.

―――――. *List of Books Printed 1601–1700 in the Library of the Hispanic Society of America*. New York: The Hispanic Society of America, 1938.

North Carolina (Duke University)

Tilley, Nannie M., and N. Lee Goodwin. *Guide to the Manuscript Collections in the Duke University Library*. Durham, North Carolina: Duke University Press, 1947.

Oklahoma (The Thomas Gilcrease Institute)

Cadenhead, Evie E., Jr. "The G.R.G. Conway Collection in the Gilcrease Institute: A Checklist," *HAHR*, 38 (May 1958), 373–82.

Strout, Clevy L. *A Catalog of Hispanic Documents in the Thomas Gilcrease Institute*. Tulsa: The Thomas Gilcrease Institute of American History and Art, 1962.

―――――. "Literary-Historical Treasures in the Thomas Gilcrease Institute of American History and Art," *HAHR*, 43 (May 1963), 267–70.

Rhode Island (Brown University, The John Carter Brown Library)

Van den Eynde, Damian, O.F.M. "The Franciscan Manuscripts in the John Carter Brown Library, Providence, Rhode Island, U.S.A.," *Archivum Franciscum Historicum*, 21 (1938), 219–22.

―――――. "Calendar of Spanish Documents in the John Carter Brown Library," *HAHR*, 16:4 (November 1936), 564–607.

Wagner, Henry R. "Hispanic Americana in the John Carter Brown Library," in *Essays Honoring Lawrence C. Wroth*. Portland, Maine: 1951. Pp. 423–55.

Wroth, Lawrence C. *The First Century of the John Carter Brown Library: A History with a Guide to the Collection*. Providence: 1946.

Texas

Bolton, Herbert E. "Spanish Mission Records at San Antonio," *Texas State Historical Association Quarterly*, 10 (April 1907), 297–307.

Castañeda, Carlos E. *A Report on the Spanish Archives in San Antonio, Texas*. San Antonio: The Yanaguana Society, 1937.

Castañeda, Carlos E., and Jack A. Dabbs. *Guide to the Latin American Manuscripts in the University of Texas Library*. Cambridge: Harvard University Press, 1939.

―――――. *Independent Mexico in Documents: Independence, Empire, and Republic. A Calendar of the Juan Hernández y Dávalos Manuscript Collection, The University of Texas Library*. México, D.F.: Editorial Jus, 1954.

Connor, Seymour V. *A Preliminary Guide to the Archives of Texas*. Austin: Texas State Library, 1956.

Dabbs, Jack A. *The Mariano Riva Palacio Archives: A Guide*. 2 vols. México, D.F.: 1967–1968.

Day, James M., et al. *Maps of Texas, 1527–1900; the Map Collection of the Texas State Archives*. Austin: The Pemberton Press, 1964.

Day, James M., and Donna Yarbrough. *Handbook of Texas Archival and Manuscript Depositories*. Austin: Texas State Library, Monograph Series #5, 1966.

De Golyer, Everett L., Jr. *The Degolyer Foundation*. Dallas: 1962.

Diekemper, Barnaby, O.F.M. *Guide to the Catholic Archive at San Antonio*. San Antonio: The Catholic Archives and the Béxar County Historical Commission, 1977.

Gómez de Orozco, Federico. *Catálogo de la colección de manuscritos relativos a la historia de América formada por Joaquín García Icazbalceta*. México, D.F.: Secretaría de Relaciones Exteriores, 1927.

González Navarro, Moisés. "Papeles manuscritos en Texas," *Historia Mexicana*, 6 (1958), 466–67.

Haggard, John V. "El Archivo de Béxar," *Historia Mexicana*, #19 (July 1955–June 1956).

Kielman, Chester V. *Guide to the Microfilm Edition of the Béxar Archives 1717–1803; 1804–1821; 1822–1836*. 3 vols. Austin: University of Texas Archives Microfilm Publication, 1967, 1969, 1971.

―――――. *The University of Texas Archives: A Guide to the Historical Manuscripts in the University of Texas Library*. Austin: University of Texas Press, 1967.

Lane, M. Claude (Sister). *Catholic Archives of Texas; History and Preliminary Inventory.* Houston: Sacred Heart Dominican College, 1961.

Pacheco Moreno, Manuel. "Las colecciones mexicanas de la Universidad de Austin, Texas," *Sociedad Chihuahuense de Estudios Históricos, Boletín,* 4 (January 1943), 308–11.

Raines, Cadwell W. *A Bibliography of Texas: Being a Descriptive List of Books, Pamphlets, and Documents Relating to Texas in Print and Manuscript since 1536.* Austin: Gammel, 1896.

Santos, Richard G. "A Preliminary Survey of the San Fernando Archives," *Texas Libraries,* 28 (Winter 1966–1967), 152–72.

————. "An Annotated Survey of the Spanish Archives of Laredo at St. Mary's University of Texas," *Texana,* 4 (Spring 1966), 41–46.

————. "Documentos para la historia de México en los archivos de San Antonio, Texas," *Revista de Historia de América,* 53 and 54 (January–December 1967).

Smither, Harriet. "The Archives of Texas," *The American Archivist,* 3:3 (July 1940), 187–200.

Spell, Lota May. *Research Materials for the Study of Latin America at the University of Texas.* Austin: University of Texas Press, 1954.

————. "The Mier Archives," *HAHR,* 12:3 (August 1932), 359–75.

Streeter, Thomas W. *Bibliography of Texas, 1795–1845.* 5 vols. Cambridge: Harvard University Press, 1955–1960.

Taylor, Virginia H. *The Spanish Archives of the General Land Office of Texas.* Austin: Lone Star Press, 1955.

Torok, Mildred. *Guide to Collections: The University of Texas at El Paso Archives.* El Paso: 1972.

THE STRUCTURE OF COLONIAL GOVERNMENT

A rudimentary understanding of the organization and operation of Spain's overseas empire is useful in assessing the definitive value of a document. This section presents an overview of the structure and function of Spanish colonial government with the obvious proviso that exceptions were almost as prevalent as the rule. The analysis that follows is dictated by modern concepts of the division of powers in government and does not represent a conceptualization common to the colonial mind.

Structure and attention to detail characterized Spanish colonial government in the Western Hemisphere. Responsibilities in the chain of command were clearly defined, but the system admitted many exceptions. As the chart on page 58 shows, the viceroy and audiencia controlled the policy and operation of every branch of government, subject only to the Crown and the Council of the Indies.

In practice, although not in theory, Spanish colonial government operated in a scheme of a separation of powers. Five distinct spheres of colonial government existed, sometimes working in consort, sometimes contesting for power and resources. These five—the political/administrative, judicial, military, financial, and ecclesiastical — can be clearly delineated as to purpose and function.

GOBIERNO

The viceroy was the supreme executive in the colonies. He had certain latitude to initiate his own programs or legislation without having to ask the Council of the Indies or the Crown. If, however, his actions proved to be unpopular, the virreinal audiencia could pressure him for change. As he sat as president ex officio of this body, he had to be receptive to them. Indeed, they could go over his head to the Council of the Indies. The pretorial and subordinate audiencias could also bypass the viceroy, as could the provincial executives, by appealing to Spain. Thus the successful viceroy took care not to anger certain other officials in the colonial government.

The audiencia, primarily a judicial body acting as a court of appeals, did have some legislative power. Generally, legislative deliberations included the viceroy for purposes of smooth and efficient government. However, the audiencia could issue its own directives in some cases.

The structure and character of New World government derived from the Spanish experience during the long reconquest of the Iberian peninsula and from the basic realities of New World geography. The viceroy had responsibility for the whole realm. The realm (kingdom) was divided into smaller units called *provincias*. In charge of each provincia was the *gobernador*. He could be a *gobernador y capitán general* if he also headed the provincial military establishment. If he lived in the capital city of the province, the gobernador sat as ex officio president of the pretorial audiencia. His relationship to his province and the respective audiencia paralleled that of the viceroy and his relationship to the realm and the virreinal audiencia. Within his province the gobernador (and capitán general) had tremendous authority, having to answer only to the viceroy. Geographical distance played an important role. The viceroy's power to do as he saw fit was enhanced by the space and time separating him from Spain. Similarly, the gobernador, especially if he governed a frontier province far from Mexico City, had a certain advantage due to distance and time.

If an audiencia resided in the capital city of the province, the gobernador presided ex officio as its president. In this case, the audiencia was pretorial. The area of each audiencia's jurisdiction was called the *presidencia*. If an audiencia did not reside in the capital and the gobernador did not sit with it, the audiencia was labeled subordinate. However, this title did not mean it had less importance or power than a pretorial audiencia. The decisions it made were final within its own jurisdiction.

An *alcalde mayor* or *corregidor* governed smaller geographical areas. Such an area could consist of a district embracing several small towns or just one community. In New Spain the executive was commonly called the alcalde mayor. When corregidor is mentioned, it usually occurs in the context of an Indian community which he governed. These were communities under crown control and subject to tribute. Like the viceroy, the members of the audiencias, and the provincial governors, the alcaldes mayores and corregidores were crown appointees or, at least, their appointments had to be approved by the crown.

Each town or municipality had a governing body called the *cabildo*. If the community happened to be Mexico City or one of the provincial capitals, the viceroy or gobernador might sit on the cabildo, or at least exercise a substantial amount of influence in its deliberations. The composition of a cabildo depended on the area and population where it operated. As a general rule, the cabildo comprised the following officials: two *alcaldes ordinarios*, who served as local magistrates; several *regidores* or councilors; an *alférez real*, who was a regidor but held higher rank and substituted for the alcalde ordinario; the *alguacil mayor*, the community's law enforcement officer; the *depositario general*, a public trust official; the *fiel ejecutor*, who checked weights and measures, the supply and control of vital foodstuffs, and often set market prices; and the *receptor de penas*, the collector of judicial fines. The last four officials may or may not have been regidores. Other important local officials existed but did not sit on the cabildo. The *procurador general (síndico)* served as the town's attorney. The *mayordomo* acted as the custodian of public property. The *justicia mayor* was the deputy of the alcalde mayor. The *escribano* served as scribe and notary.

Regidores could be elected to the cabildo. However, after the first few years, it became common for the outgoing regidores to nominate their replacements. The gobernador of the province or the respective audiencia needed to approve these nominations. In capital cities, where a seat on the cabildo meant more than in a small community, the crown might appoint *regidores perpetuos* (for life). The regidores elected the alcaldes ordinarios but not from among their own membership. While the regidor watched over town affairs in conjunction with the alcalde mayor, the alcaldes ordinarios handled the litigation which arose in the community. Until the early seventeenth century, *oficiales reales* (treasury officials) might sit on the cabildo with a vote, technically holding rank over the regidores.

This system of government remained unchanged in its basic structure until the introduction of the *intendencias* under the Bourbons. Initiated in 1764 and fully instituted by 1790, this reorganization eliminated all governmental and administrative units below or inferior to the audiencia. An *intendente* assumed the duties of gobernador, corregidor, and alcalde mayor. This new system was designed to centralize the colonial empire in order to govern it more efficiently, to obtain more revenue from it, and to provide a better defense against the aggressive English. Consequently, greater centralization led to larger geographic administrative units.

The intendente became a gobernador and alcalde mayor all in one, being responsible for the intendencia down to the municipal level. *Subdelegados,* officials in charge of smaller units within the inten-

dencia called *partidos,* assisted him in his duties. The chain of command was thus changed with the subdelegado responsible to the intendente and the intendente responsible to the audiencia and the viceroy. To further assure the crown's control in this centralizing reform, the intendente received his appointment from the King. By preference the appointee was a *peninsular* (born in Spain), thus increasing even more the centralization of power in Spain.

JUSTICIA

At the local level of justice, a civil or criminal case came before the alcalde ordinario. In the instance of a minor infraction of the law, the escribano might pass judgment and assess a fine (subject to appeal). However, the alcalde ordinario heard most cases. His decision could be appealed to the audiencia of the province. If the audiencia chose to hear an appeal, its decision in all but the rarest of cases was final. The citizen in question could, if he so desired, petition the King. However, owing to the complexity and time involved in such an appeal, this procedure was not often employed.

The three types of audiencias (virreinal, pretorial, subordinate) had original jurisdiction in certain cases. On such occasions, their decisions might be appealed to the Council of the Indies. However, the audiencia functioned primarily as a court of appeals from the lesser courts, and decisions rendered in such instances were final.

The viceroy had only peripheral influence in judicial matters. He could not overrule the decision of an audiencia, nor could he call a case up from a lower court. He could, however, determine which cases were of a political/administrative character and which were judicial. Thus in some situations, he could work around the audiencia by declaring the nature of a case. The viceroy did have the power of pardon.

Although cases involving large sums of money or high-level corruption did come before the audiencias, the court with primary jurisdiction resolved most cases. In a few instances, cases concerning very large amounts of money or very high-level corruption went to the Council of the Indies.

In addition to routine judicial procedure, the audiencia performed other judicial functions. They heard appeals from special administrative courts. They also took appeals in certain cases rising from the ecclesiastical courts. The *visita* and the *residencia* served as checks on most officials in the structure of colonial government. A *juez de residencia* (judge of residence) directed the residencia which served to review an individual's performance during his term of office. Ideally, the juez would be an *oidor* from the provincial audiencia. However, it became common for the incoming official to act as the judge of the retiring official, thus making the residencia subject to various political pressures. If the official was found wanting, the judge could make his decision and pass sentence. All residencias had to be forwarded to the Council of the Indies. A visita was an inspection of a province (a local visita) carried out by the gobernador of that province. An inspection of the whole kingdom or realm (a general visita) could have been conducted by an oidor of the virreinal audiencia. Ideally, however, such a general inspection would be presided over by a person appointed in Spain who had no ties of any sort with the colony. The findings of a visita or residencia became crucial in the life of a colonial official, and he tended to be mindful of possible consequences.

MILITAR

The viceroy directed the colonial military establishment. In New Spain this meant he was head of very little. No standing army existed until late in the eighteenth century. Officially, the viceroy in his military capacity held the rank and title of *capitán general*.

In the provinces the military command rested with a lieutenant capitán general (often referred to as the capitán general). Frequently, especially in frontier provinces, the gobernador filled this role. If he did not, the lieutenant governor (*teniente de gobernador*) often served as capitán general.

The presidio served as the only regular military establishment in the provinces. A regular army capitán or *teniente* commanded each presidio and was responsible to the provincial capitán general. In times of danger the gobernador called up the militia which consisted of most able-bodied men in the area or the substitutes they paid to stand in for them. Most respected citizens held a brevet rank, usually that of capitán. This accounts for the appearance in documents of vast numbers of military officers. If the capitán general saw fit, he could augment presidial troops and the militia with friendly Indians, who often outnumbered the Spaniards in military campaigns.

HACIENDA

The complexity of colonial government came to a head in the administration of colonial finance. The viceroy and the virreinal audiencia were responsible for the collection of all forms of wealth due the crown and for its shipment to Spain. However, at every level of government below the viceroy, officials of the treasury had coordinate authority with regular government officials in financial matters.

Local officials collected the taxes or contracted the job to private individuals. The money was then passed on to treasury officials. Working together, the gobernadores of the provincias and the treasury officials collected the royal fifth and tribute. The *Junta Superior de la Real Hacienda* (composed of members of the virreinal audiencia, the viceroy and treasury officials) did the final auditing of the books. A similar group existed at the provincial level.

The viceroy and the audiencias had some control over the dispersement of funds. Large annual expenditures for the maintenance of the colony had to be approved in Spain, but for matters of an emergency nature the viceroy did have access to a general fund.

ECLESIASTICO

Nothing may appear as complex and incomprehensible as the structure and function of the colonial church in New Spain. Every basic textbook on Latin America presents some discussion on the church and especially the Patronato Real whereby the King of Spain controlled the appointment of the secular hierarchy in return for accepting the financial obligations of the church throughout the empire. The entire system was an outgrowth of feudal concepts of rights and privileges that are not of primary concern here. A straightforward description of the organization of the hierarchy and the religious orders will suffice.

Below the political levels of ecclesiastical involvement as seen in the roles of the King, Council, and Viceroy, the church reflected the common distinction of regular and secular clergy. The regular clergy were members of recognized and approved religious institutes. This status was granted by the Roman Pontiff. Members of the religious orders were classified as "regulars" because they followed an approved religious "rule" (regula). The clergy who were not members of such approved institutes, and who ordinarily did not take solemn vows, were classified as members of the secular clergy. The idea of the secular clergy was that by not following a religious rule, these clergy "stayed in the world." Normally they did not take vows of poverty and as such were permitted to own property and acquire personal wealth.

The secular clergy were most frequently installed in the positions of hierarchical authority. Archbishops, bishops, and vicars controlled the affairs of the church. Because of the missionary character of the church in New Spain there were many instances in which a member of a religious order was appointed to the hierarchy. This was especially true of Franciscans, Dominicans, and Augustinians. Often the person consecrated as bishop was also an *hidalgo*, which only served to complicate the understanding of the roles they played. The ecclesiastical provinces over which the hierarchy served were known as dioceses. Jurisdiction in each diocese was jealously guarded because this affected both authority and the power to raise funds.

At the lower levels of organization in the secular church were the parishes of the diocese. These units were served by a *párroco* or *cura*. In case these local units were administered by regular clergy, they had obligations to their religious superiors as well as the bishop. Conflict of interest and authority was not uncommon.

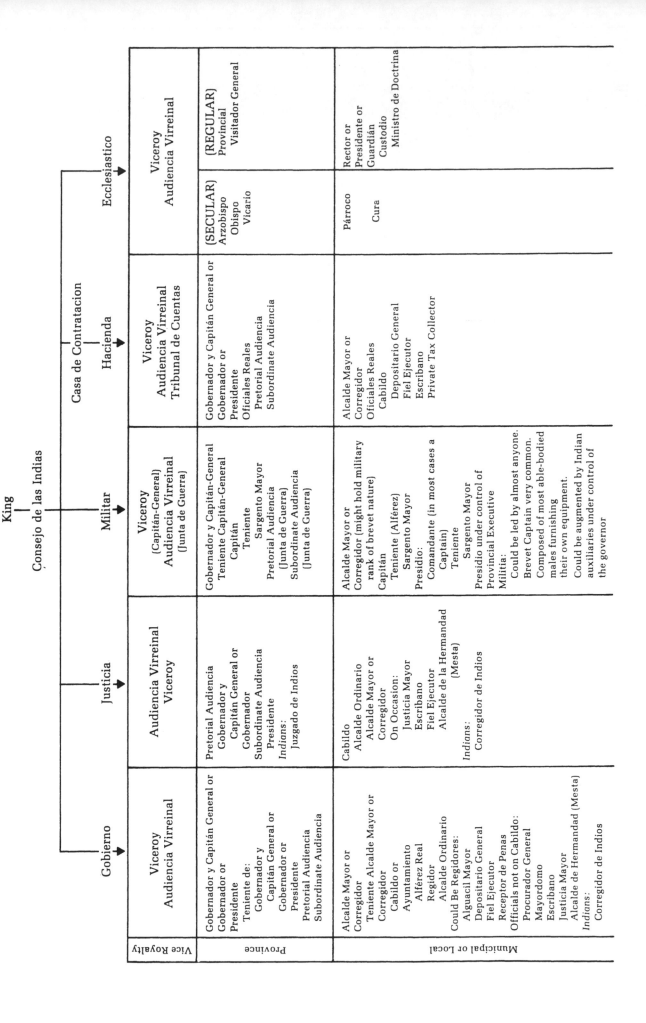

King

Consejo de las Indias

	Gobierno	Justicia	Militar	Hacienda	Ecclesiastico (SECULAR)	Ecclesiastico (REGULAR)
Vice Royalty	Viceroy / Audiencia Virreinal	Audiencia Virreinal / Viceroy	Viceroy (Capitán-General) / Audiencia Virreinal / (Junta de Guerra)	Viceroy / Audiencia Virreinal / Tribunal de Cuentas	Viceroy / Audiencia Virreinal	

Province	Gobernador y Capitán General or Gobernador or Presidente
	Teniente de:
	  Gobernador y
	    Capitán General or
	  Gobernador or
	  Presidente
	Pretorial Audiencia
	Subordinate Audiencia
		Pretorial Audiencia
		Gobernador y
		  Capitán General or
		Gobernador
		Subordinate Audiencia
		  Presidente
		Indians:
		  Juzgado de Indios
			Gobernador y Capitán-General
			Teniente Capitán-General
			Capitán
			  Teniente
			    Sargento Mayor
			Pretorial Audiencia
			  (Junta de Guerra)
			Subordinate Audiencia
			  (Junta de Guerra)
				Gobernador y Capitán General or
				Gobernador or
				Presidente
				Oficiales Reales
				Pretorial Audiencia
				Subordinate Audiencia
					Arzobispo
					Obispo
					  Vicario
						Provincial
						Visitador General

Municipal or Local	Alcalde Mayor or
	Corregidor
	Teniente Alcalde Mayor or
	Corregidor
	Cabildo or
	Ayuntamiento
	  Alférez Real
	  Regidor
	  Alcalde Ordinario
	Could Be Regidores:
	  Alguacil Mayor
	  Depositario General
	  Fiel Ejecutor
	  Receptor de Penas
	Officials not on Cabildo:
	  Procurador General
	  Mayordomo
	  Escribano
	  Justicia Mayor
	  Alcalde de Hermandad (Mesta)
	Indians:
	  Corregidor de Indios
		Cabildo
		Alcalde Ordinario
		Alcalde Mayor or
		Corregidor
		On Occasion:
		  Justicia Mayor
		  Escribano
		  Fiel Ejecutor
		  Alcalde de la Hermandad
		    (Mesta)
		Indians:
		  Corregidor de Indios
			Alcalde Mayor or
			Corregidor (might hold military
			  rank of brevet nature)
			Capitán
			  Teniente (Alférez)
			    Sargento Mayor
			Presidio:
			  Comandante (in most cases a
			    Captain)
			    Teniente
			      Sargento Mayor
			  Presidio under control of
			    Provincial Executive
			Militia:
			  Could be led by almost anyone.
			  Brevet Captain very common.
			  Composed of most able-bodied
			    males furnishing
			    their own equipment.
			  Could be augmented by Indian
			    auxiliaries under control of
			    the governor
				Alcalde Mayor or
				Corregidor
				Oficiales Reales
				Cabildo
				  Depositario General
				  Fiel Ejecutor
				  Escribano
				  Private Tax Collector
					Párroco
					  Cura
						Rector or
						Presidente or
						Guardián
						  Custodio
						  Ministro de Doctrina

Branches from Consejo de las Indias: Gobierno, Justicia, Militar, Casa de Contratacion / Hacienda, Ecclesiastico

The organization of the regular clergy was quite distinct. In general the religious orders were organized around the concepts of various apostolates. Thus, work in missions, colleges, hospitals, and monasteries dominated the scene. The missions were not directly responsible to the bishop, and the regular clergy assigned to various missions received their assignment from the regional superior, called a provincial. While a provincial superior is the next highest to a general superior in the regular clergy, he does not enjoy the power of a bishop. In fact, the superiors general of the religious orders are seldom if ever bishops. The lines of authority and organization are separate and distinct.

Within the apostolates of the colleges and charitable works the religious orders had less independence. These areas were always the gray areas in the exercise of authority and gave rise to most litigation over tithes, benefices, and privileges. The rectors of colleges, universities, and residences were appointed by the provincial superior but had obligations to meet with respect to the secular church as well.

In the structure of the missions there were further divisions of authority and responsibility. The provincial superiors appointed rectors, presidents, or guardians over regional areas, depending on the particular religious order concerned. These regional areas were then further divided into missions and custodias that paralleled the secular organization of parishes; but these local divisions were not legally the same as parishes. The priest at a local church was a *cura* if it were a parish; he was a *ministro de doctrina* if it were a mission.

These are only some of the more gross divisions of structure and function in the colonial church of New Spain. There are many important nuances to know if one's research delves deeply into church affairs. But for general purposes it is sufficient to recognize that the church was not a monolithic system of rigid hierarchical control.

Consejo de las Indias

1492–1524

Juan Rodríguez de Fonseca, member of the Council of Castile was chief councilor to the crown on American affairs.

This group came to include:

> Junta de asunto de Indios
> Procurador
> Relator
> Abogado de los pleitos de las Indias

The group was administrative only. Judicial matters still rested with the Council of Castile.

1524

El Real y Supremo Consejo de las Indias. The Council of the Indies was established and given autonomous rank as a "royal and supreme" council.

Structure of the council:
President (or Grand Chancellor)
The original composition: Consejeros (four or five)
Fiscal
Relator
Secretario
Escribiente de cuentas
Usher

Added later:
Receptor
Contadores (three)
Solicitors (procuradores—two)
Abogado and procurador for poor suitors
Capellán
Notarios
Portero
Alguacil
Historiador
Cosmógrafo
Profesor de matemáticas

As time went on, the number of councilors increased, as did the supporting bureaucracy.

Audiencias

Virrey, gobernador: Presidente (ex officio) of virreinal and pretorial audiencias.

Structure (idealized):

	Regent	
Oidores (8)	Alcaldes de Crimen (4)	Fiscales (2, civil criminal)

Minor officials

Alguacil	Relatores	Abogado
Capellán	Notarios	(for the poor)

Subordinate audiencias followed the same structure, but with fewer major officials and sometimes without some minor officials.

Special Administrative Courts: With primary jurisdiction in their respective areas.

Mesta	Aduanas
Consulado	Protomedicato
Casa de moneda	Real cuerpo de minería
Tribunal de cuentas	Acordada

Cases heard and decided here could be appealed to an audiencia.
Certain decisions of ecclesiastical courts could be appealed to an audiencia.
No case could be appealed from one audiencia to another.
Oidores of audiencias had outside duties: Jueces de verificación
Visitadores
Jueces de residencia
Pesquisas

Audiencias contained several important committees or subcommittees:

Junta de guerra
Junta superior de la real hacienda
Tribunal de cuentas
Asuntos de Indios
Ad hoc

POLITICAL EVOLUTION
OF
NORTHERN NEW SPAIN

Political and administrative units in northern New Spain during the Spanish colonial period changed names and description so often that they defy precise definition. Indeed, changes in administrative philosophy during the seventeenth and eighteenth centuries introduced new nomenclature and revised jurisdictional boundaries. The arrangement of units prior to the creation of the Provincias Internas in 1776 was one thing, and the eventual shift to the system of intendencias in 1786 was another. Each new arrangement reflected a combination of complex factors as the Spanish crown attempted to produce more effective government.

In the earliest years of administrative expansion Spanish royal officials often accepted indigenous political divisions. These units were simply incorporated into the Spanish plan of organization, or in other cases were slightly modified in response to need or convenience. In other words, there was no wholesale obliteration of native organization. Adaptation was the byword. When the continent was still largely unknown, titles to land granted to *conquistadores* and *adelantados* were general in nature, leaving administrative boundaries in newly conquered and settled areas vague and imprecise. But as the frontier expanded northward with the concomitant opening of missions, mines, and haciendas, need arose for more closely defined jurisdictions and boundaries. In the later years of northern political organization more attention was given by the crown to conformity to abstract design than to political and administrative realities.

REINOS AND PROVINCIAS, 1540–1776

The inconsistent delineation of geographical areas belonging to various administrative authorities was itself compounded by the problems of nomenclature. In the earlier years large areas were included under the title "reino." Simultaneously all or parts of these areas were called "provincias," which finally became the dominant name for a major political subdivision. One must be cautious in evaluating the meaning of an administrative label such as "reino" or "provincia" because it may imply a true change in administrative character, it may denote the persistence of an older administrative division, or it may be only a traditional reference to a now-changed political reality.

As the Spanish advance continued northward, new political divisions were more exactly defined. By the 1770s most of the areas of northern New Spain had designated boundaries and jurisdictions. Some changes were introduced with the creation of the Provincias Internas and the Intendencias. The following chronological table gives the dates of the most significant administrative establishments and changes through the eighteenth century.

1527	Audiencia y Chanchillería Real de México
1530	Culiacán (villa)
1548	Audiencia y Chanchillería Real de Guadalajara de la Galicia en la Nueva España (Nueva Galicia)
1561	Reino de Nueva Vizcaya (1562; Francisco Ibarra, governor)
1563	Guadiana (Durango)
1582	Provincia de Nuevo León
1587	Sinaloa (first successful alcaldía mayor)
1598	Provincia de Nuevo México
1631	San Joseph del Parral (Real de Minas)
1637	Provincia de Sonora (Nueva Andalucía)
1643	Sonora returns to dependence on Sinaloa as an alcaldía mayor
1648	Sonora as an alcaldía mayor dependent on Nueva Vizcaya
1673	Provincia de Ostímuri
1674	Provincia de Coahuila (Nueva Estremadura) (separated from Nueva Vizcaya)
1676	Ostímuri under a justicia mayor, independent of Sonora and Sinaloa
1680	Provincia de Nuevo México abandoned
1691	Ostímuri as an alcaldía mayor
1692	Provincia de Nuevo México (reconquered by Diego de Vargas)
1697	California (Real Presidio de Loreto)
1708	Chihuahua as an alcaldía mayor
1716	Provincia de Texas (separated from Coahuila)
1732	Sonora, Sinaloa, and Ostímuri (leave jurisdiction of Nueva Vizcaya to become Provincia de Sonora y Sinaloa, including Culiacán and Rosario)
1746	Nuevo Santander settled
1764	Provincia de Nuevo Santander (independent of Nueva Vizcaya)

1767 Provincia de California
1776 Provincias Internas
1786 System of Intendencias
      Distritos de Saltillo and Parras attached
      to Coahuila (Nueva Estremadura) leaving
      jurisdiction of Nueva Vizcaya
1804 Provincias de Baja and Alta California

Provincia de Sinaloa
Provincia de Sonora (when first combined,
    Sonora and Sinaloa were
    called Nueva Navarra)
Provincia de Nayarit (Nuevo Reino de Toledo)
Provincia de Californias
Provincia de Nuevo México de Santa Fe

The information below provides a classification of the political divisions in northern New Spain in existence prior to 1776 and 1786. Along with the chronological listing this provides a description of the general political evolution of the area, keeping in mind that some areas underwent changes of jurisdiction throughout.

Major Political Administrative Divisions Prior to 1776

Reino de México (Nueva España)—
with five major provincias
    Provincia de México
    Provincia de Tlaxcala
    Provincia de la Puebla de los Angeles
    Provincia de Antequera (Oaxaca)
    Provincia (Reino) de Michoacán (Valladolid)
Reino de Nueva Galicia—
with three major provincias
    Provincia de Jalisco
    Provincia de Zacatecas
    Provincia de Colima
Gobernación de la Nueva Vizcaya—
with two major provincias
    Provincia de Guadiana (Durango)
    Provincia de Chihuahua
Gobernación de Yucatán—
with three major provincias
Nuevo Reino de León
Colonia de Nuevo Santander
Provincia de Coahuila (Nueva Estremadura)

This geographical organization admitted many exceptions. Smaller, peripheral areas often shifted from the jurisdiction of one audiencia or provincia to another.

With the establishment of the Provincias Internas (1776) and the further modification into the Intendencias (1786) the organizational scheme changed markedly, although previous territorial classifications retained important influences. Definitively proposed as early as 1752, the Provincias Internas finally became a reality in 1776. Essentially the northernmost territories of New Spain required more compelling authority from local administrators because of the distance from viceregal control in Mexico City. The Spanish crown was keenly aware of the lack of administrative control in the northern provinces which resulted partially from failure to pacify native groups and partially from pressures exerted by other European powers encroaching on the poorly defined perimeters of New Spain. Consequently, the Spaniards relied on the creation of the Provincias Internas which had a distinctly military character. The commander of the region had direct access to Spain, thus bypassing the viceroy in Mexico. In the beginning the Provincias Internas comprised Nueva Vizcaya, Sinaloa, Sonora, the Californias, Coahuila, Texas, and Nuevo México. These areas came under the strongly independent command of a single appointee. The information that follows outlines the major aspects of the administrative structure and many of the changes it experienced prior to the wars of independence.

PROVINCIAS INTERNAS, 1776–1824

Teodoro Francisco de Croix, independent of viceroy
    August 1776, named
    October 1777, assumed
    August 1783, left

Sonora, Sinaloa, Texas
Coahuila, the Californias,
Nueva Vizcaya, Nuevo México

Felipe de Neve (interim), independent of viceroy
    February 1783, named
    August 1783, assumed
    August 1784, died

Same

José Antonio Rengel, independent of viceroy
    August 1784, assumed
    April 1786, left

Same

————In January 1785, the Provincias Internas became dependent to the viceroy————

Jacobo Ugarte y Loyola, dependent on viceroy
    October 1785, named
    April 1786, assumed
    January 1791, left

Same, until October 1786

————In October 1786, the Provincias Internas was divided into three commands. Ugarte y Loyola remained as commander-in-chief with the two commanders of the newly created divisions subordinate to him————

Jacobo Ugarte y Loyola, dependent on viceroy
    October 1786

Sonora, Sinaloa, the Californias

José Antonio Rengel, under Ugarte y Loyola
    April 1786, assumed
    October 1787, left

Nueva Vizcaya, Nuevo México

Juan de Ugalde, under Ugarte y Loyola
    October 1786, assumed
    January 1788, change of position

Texas, Coahuila, Nuevo León, Nuevo Santander, los distritos de Saltillo and Parras

————In March 1788, two separate and equal commands were created, with both commanders dependent on the viceroy—

Jacobo Ugarte y Loyola, dependent on viceroy
    March 1788
    April 1791, left

Provincias Internas de Poniente (Nueva Vizcaya, Nuevo México, Sonora, Sinaloa, the Californias)

Juan de Ugalde, dependent on viceroy
    March 1788
    April 1791, left

Provincias Internas de Oriente (Nuevo León Nuevo Santander, Coahuila, Texas, los distritos de Saltillo and Parras)

————In March 1790, Ugarte y Loyola named supreme commander over both east and west, dependent on the viceroy, with Ugalde as second in command—

Pedro de Nava, replaces Ugarte y Loyola, dependent on viceroy
    March 1790, named
    April 1791, assumed

    Ramón de Castro, replaces Ugalde, dependent on Nava
        June 1790, named
        April 1971, assumed
        1793, left

————By royal order of November 1792 and viceregal directive of February 1793, the Provincias Internas were reunited as one unit, independent of the viceroy—

Pedro de Nava, independent of viceroy
    1792, named
    February 1793, assumed
    1802, left

Sonora y Sinaloa, Nuevo México, Nueva Vizcaya, Texas, Coahuila, los distritos de Saltillo and Parras. Nuevo León, Nuevo Santander, and the Californias are separated and become dependent on the viceroy.

Nemesio Salcedo y Salcedo, independent of viceroy
    1802, assumed
    July 1813, left

Same

————In May 1804, the Provincias Internas was again ordered divided. However, this order never went into effect. Consequently, Salcedo y Salcedo remained as commander of a singular unit until 1813.

————A royal order of May 1811 directed the Provincias Internas be divided into two units. This was communicated to Mexico twice, once in December of 1811 and again in July of 1812. The order was effected in October 1813, with each commander being equal and dependent on the viceroy.

Bernardo Bonavia y Zapata, dependent on viceroy
    February 1813, named
    July 1813, assumed
    November 1817, left

Provincias Internas de Occidente (Nueva Vizcaya, Nuevo México, Sonora y Sinaloa)

Joaquín de Arredondo, dependent on viceroy

Provincias Internas de Oriente (Coahuila, Texas, Nuevo Santander, Nuevo León, los distritos de Saltillo and Parras)

Alejo García Conde, dependent on viceroy, replaces Bonavia y Zapata, November 1817

————In October 1818, the two commands of the Provincias Internas lose what power they had maintained to this point to the viceroy.

Mariano de Urrea as sole commander, dependent on the new government of Mexico
    July 1822, assumed

Antonio Cordero, as sole commander, under the Mexican government
    July 1822, assumed
    March 1823, left

Gaspar de Ochoa, as sole commander, dependent on the Mexican government
    March 1823, assumed
    1824, left

After 1824 this area was no longer called the Provincias Internas and evolved into a military district under the government of Mexico.

INTENDENCIAS
1770–1824

The second major revision in colonial government originated with the introduction of the intendency system in New Spain in 1786. The intendencias had been implemented in Spain in 1718 as part of the Bourbon reforms. They first began to appear in New Spain in 1770 when Pedro Corbalán was named governor and intendent of Sonora. The rest of New Spain came under this reorganization in 1786. Territorial revisions which resulted from this change had as a base the previous colonial divisions of the area. With the exception of Nuevo México, the Californias, and the gobernacíon of Tlaxcala, which remained under viceregal jurisdiction, all of New Spain was divided into intendencias. Twelve such administrative units were established: México, Puebla de los Angeles, Nueva Veracruz, Mérida de Yucatán, Antequera de Oaxaca, Valladolid de Michoacán, Santa Fe de Guanajuato, San Luis Potosí, Guadalajara, Zacatecas, Durango, and Arizpe. This was to be the general political-administrative structure of colonial government until Mexican independence.

The intendent and the lesser officials, the subdelegados, replaced the gobernador and the alcalde mayor. In the northern areas of New Spain which had comprised the Provincias Internas, the intendent generally exercised complete authority except in military affairs, which remained in the hands of the commanders of the Provincias Internas. However, in the case of the intendencies of Durango and Arizpe (Nueva Vizcaya and Sonora y Sinaloa), the commander of the Provincias Internas often found himself as acting intendent with fiscal and military authority. Judicial and administrative matters not inclusively local in nature were still in the hands of the respective audiencias. The information on pages 109–10 and 112–13 indicates the intendents and their dates of tenure in the two intendencies which covered northern New Spain.

MONEY AND CURRENCY

The purpose of this discussion is to make the interpretation of financial information in the documents somewhat easier and more exact. Colonial monies are not compared here to any modern standard such as the U.S. dollar because such a comparison is difficult to validate. The common gold or silver peso was important only for what it would buy then, not for what it might buy now by conjecture.

Two important factors should be borne in mind when dealing with colonial currency. Distance is the first; in matters of money as in all other facets of colonial life, values were affected by distance from authority. Regulations that were set in Spain did not always find ready acceptance or compliance in the colonies. What the Viceroy demanded in Mexico City might or might not be effective in the far northern frontier of New Spain. Second, when money is exchanged for goods, the quantity of the commodity should be determined. The variety of weights and measures for different items was plethoric, often leading to confusion regarding the quantity in question; a *carga* (load), for example, differed in volume and weight for different products.

When Ferdinand and Isabella came to power, the monetary system of the Spains was still dominated by regional confusion. Henry IV (1454-1474) had attempted to revalue gold and silver based on the value of the old *maravedí*; he accomplished very little. In 1497 under the Catholic Kings, the existing system was replaced by the *Ordenanza de Medina del Campo*, which made the *excelente de la Granada* the standard denomination for gold; the base for silver was the *real de plata*. Thus, at the beginning of colonization in the New World the excelente was valued at 375 maravedís, or 11 silver reales plus one maravedí. The real de plata was valued at 34 maravedís. Hence the ratio of value between gold and silver currencies was established at approximately 11 to 1.

For the first two or three decades of the sixteenth century few coins were circulated in New Spain. Most commerce relied on credit or barter until the gold and silver from the Aztec treasury and the new mines came into currency. Colonists complained to Spain about the lack of coinage. In response the Crown authorized the shipment of silver and copper coins to Mexico in the form of *vellón*. Until the Mexican mint began production in 1537, Spain enjoyed a lucrative trade in currency. The real de plata, valued at 34 maravedís in Spain, sold in Mexico for 44; the disparity was explained by the risk of shipping and the cost of accounting.

The circulation of gold in Mexico was specifically prohibited, but the law was ineffectively enforced. Because the mints were not yet in existence, gold changed hands in the form of fine dust, bars, or other odd shapes. In any given transaction the value of the gold was suspect because of the difference in scales, the impurities in the gold, and the simple unreliability of a man's word. Beginning in 1526 individuals could take their gold to the Royal Smelter and Assay office where it was cast into slugs of 1, 2, or 4 *tomines* (a measure of weight equal to 12 grains or ⅛ of a gold peso). If the person preferred, the gold could be cast into pieces each weighing 1, 2, or 4 pesos *(de oro)*, 1 peso being equal to 96 grains. The most common form of gold coinage came to be called the *castellano*, which was the ordinary gold coin on the Peninsula. For silver the common standard became the piece of eight reales. In Spain the castellano was valued at 450 maravedís; the piece of eight (silver) was valued at 275 maravedís. Eventually each coin came to be called a "peso" in the colonies. thus referring to a "weight" of gold or silver *(peso de oro and peso de plata).*

As silver was scarce in the early days of the New World, gold became the most common medium of exchange and value. Several types of gold pesos (weights) were accepted in the economy, the difference among them being in their purity. These pesos de oro can be divided into two types—high and low quality—which were determined by the fineness of the metal. Although there was some variance in value, each group became settled by the mid-sixteenth century. Pesos of high quality had an accepted value of 450 maravedís; they were the:

peso de oro	peso
"mejor común"	de oro ensayado
castellano de oro	peso de oro
peso de oro de minas	peso de oro
peso de oro	de minas
de ley perfecta	de ley perfecta

The pesos of low quality equaled 272 maravedís:
  peso de oro común
    (sometimes valued at 300 maravedís)
  peso de oro de tepuzque
  peso corriente
  peso de lo que corre

Lower quality pesos were the most common. The peso de oro de tepuzque, whose purity was diluted by its copper content, was fashioned into crude pieces for daily commerce. The gold *tomín* (⅛ of a peso) became the equivalent of one silver real after 1538. In 1536, the value of the silver real in Mexico was reduced from 44 to 34 maravedís as the mint in Mexico City began production. From then on throughout the colonial period, the *tomín de peso de oro de tepuzque* (or any low grade peso) equaled one real de plata. Thus the common low grade gold peso equaled the silver peso. Large-scale transactions often took place in pesos of high quality; be-cause this is the case, the reading of documents can be confusing if the title of the peso in question is not given.

After the opening of the mint in Mexico City, silver coinage began to replace that of gold. Until 1728 this system remained intact, although a devaluation occurred in Spain in 1686. In 1728 Philip V devalued the silver and gold coins on both sides of the Atlantic by lowering the content of pure metal.

As previously mentioned, gold was not a legal medium of exchange in the colonies. In 1676, owing to growing pressure from New Spain, the Crown allowed the minting of gold coins. Despite the new availability of gold coinage, silver remained the most common currency.

Copper was minted in Mexico City in the 1540s, 1550s, and 1560s. It was considered necessary for small transactions, but the Indian populace held the copper coins in such low esteem they often threw them away or melted them down for other uses. Hence copper coinage was discontinued.

Gold

Marco (½ lb or 8–8.5 onzas)	Onza	Doblón	Escudo	Peso	Tomín	Grano	Maravedí
1 =	8.5	17	68	136	1,088	13,056	36,992
	1 =	2	8	16	128	1,536	4,352
		1 =	4	8	64	768	2,176
			1 =	2	16	192	544
				1 =	8	96	272
					1 =	12	34
						1 =	2.83
							1

Silver

Marco	Ducado	Peso	Peseta	Real	Vellón	Grano	Maravedí
1 =	6	8.5	17	68	170	816	2,312
	1 =	1.417	2.83	11.30	28.60	136	385
		1 =	4	8	20	96	272
			1 =	4	10	48	136
				1 =	2.5	12	34
					1 =	4.8	13.6
						1 =	2.83
							1

WEIGHTS AND MEASURES

Documents resulting from the three hundred years of Spanish control in northern Mexico and the southwestern portion of the United States frequently contain references to various weights and measures. This section of the *Guide* is designed to simplify the confusion attached to the Spanish system of measurement and thereby aid in the reading and interpretation of colonial documents.

Much of the confusion in the interpretation of these weights and measures results from their lack of specificity. There is little that can be done about this problem, except to clarify and make consistent what is already known. This lack of exactness was not solely a Spanish problem—a lack of scientific knowledge prevented any society's attempts at precision. Not until the introduction of the metric system in Spain and Mexico did a semblance of accuracy and standardization appear. Furthermore, only recently with the use of atomic clocks and satellites have we been able to attain reliable precision.

The complexity and lack of order in the standards of colonial Mexico arise from the fact that measurements used in Spain had been received and adapted over the centuries from the Phoenicians, the Greeks, Moslims from Africa, and especially the Romans. Furthermore, many of these units had as an historical base the length of an arm *(braza)* or a leg, or the distance a man could walk in a determined amount of time. Spanish regionalism complicated this situation even more. At the time of the conquest of Mexico, nearly every province in Spain had a system of measurement that in many cases only faintly resembled the official standards of Castile. This regional confusion accompanied the Spanish to the Western Hemisphere and remained. In the late sixteenth century some order was introduced with the royal decree that the *vara* of Burgos would henceforth be the standard length. While this helped to no small degree, the value of the Burgos vara remained in question, as it does today. This confusion has carried over into the historical literature. While much of it is unavoidable, many of the discrepancies might have been prevented had authors not tried to make exact a system grounded in imprecision and regional variation.

Even though the following charts and explanations define various of the weights and measures common to New Spain with some precision and relate them to the more exact metric and SAE standards, care should be taken. In many instances one term was used to denote a variety of measurements. Some units changed values in relation to the commodity they were used to reckon. And, as is the case with the league, a certain unit might change in value over a period of time.

The chart for linear measures is based on the vara of Burgos. Although there is no consensus as such, the value of this vara is generally accepted as .8359 meter or 32.909 inches. Other values for this particular unit found in historical literature are .836 and .838 meter. Outside of Mexico, this relative value differs even more. However, using the vara as the basic unit of measure, extrapolation from any value attached to it will lead to a fairly consistent system. The league *(legua)* used in the chart is that which contains 5,000 varas and is equivalent to 4,179.5 meters or 2.59699 miles. The league changed in value perhaps more than any other unit, being based as it was on the value of a degree which was directly related to the known circumference of the earth. The length of the *braza* depended on whether it was being used to measure length or height. The *codo real (de ribera)* was used primarily in shipbuilding. For purposes of conversion from metric to SAE, one millimeter = .03937 inch; one meter = 39.3696 inches or 3.2808 feet. For the sake of convenience, the table of ratios is included. Use of this table will produce relatively close equivalencies but will not be as accurate as the chart or individual computation.

RATIOS FOR COMMON SPANISH LINEAR MEASUREMENTS

Legua : milla	1 : 3
Milla : estadio	1 : 8
Estadio : cordel (69 varas)	1 : 3.0188
Cordel (69 varas) : cordel (50 varas)	1 : 1.38
Cordel (50 varas) : cordel (10 varas)	1 : 5
Cordel (10 varas) : estadal	1 : 2.5
Estadal : marca	1 : 1.391
Marca : toesa	1 : 1.236
Toesa : braza	1 : 1.1628
Braza: paso geométrico	1 : 1.2
Paso geométrico : vara	1 : 1.666
Vara : paso ordinario	1 : 1.2

Paso ordinario : codo real	1 : 1.249
Codo real : codo (geométrico)	1 : 1.333
Codo (geométrico) : pie	1 : 1.5
Pie : palmo mayor	1 : 1.333
Palmo mayor : sesma	1 : 1.5
Sesma : palmo menor	1 : 2
Palmo menor : pulgada	1 : 3
Pulgada : dedo	1 : 1.333
Dedo : línea	**1 : 9**
Línea : punto	1 : 12

AREA MEASUREMENTS

Units of measure utilized to ascertain the size of or to construct a specific area are directly related to the linear measures chart. The basic unit employed was the square *vara*. A square vara contained 1,296 square *pulgadas*. Other squared units common in delineating areas were the square *pie*, square *palmo*, square *pulgada*, and square *línea*. Conversion of these measurements to a higher or lower unit of value can be accomplished with the use of the linear measures chart.

DRY MEASUREMENTS

In a like manner, the basic unit for dry measures was the cubic *vara*. Computations of this sort can also be made from the linear measurements chart. In addition to the cubic vara, other common dry or cubic units were the cubic *brazada* (eight cubic varas), cubic *palmo*, and the cubic *pulgada*.

Precise measurement was especially important in the distribution of land. Confusion as to unit equivalencies and imprecision on the part of colonial officials is still evident and important today. Grants of land made in the early years of New Spain are particularly difficult to estimate until the standard and base measure introduced by royal order, the *vara* of Burgos, became official late in the sixteenth century. Up to that time, grants and claims were based on estimates and the quality of land in question.

However, with the use of the vara and a certain

ARID MEASUREMENTS

Two common units of arid measure have been the cause of a certain amount of controversy. The *carga* and the *fanega* (also units of weight) will probably never be assigned a definitive value. However, regardless of the confusion, extrapolation is possible from known quantities. In the chart below, the fanega has been designated as 55.5 liters or 1.575 bushels—the value most often cited in historical literature. Here, the carga is equal to 2 fanegas. This ratio was subject to change depending on the commodity and the value of the carga. The *almud* is the same as a *celemine*.

	Cahiz	Carga	Fanega	Almud	Cuartillo	Cuchara	Liters	Bushels
Cahiz	1	6	12	144	576	1728	666	18.8977
Carga		1	2	24	96	288	111	3.1496
Fanega			1	12	48	144	55.5	1.575
Almud				1	4	12	4.625	4.1995 quarts
Cuartillo					1	3	1.156	1.0496 quarts
Cuchara						1	.0385	.03495 quarts

AGRARIAN LAND MEASUREMENTS

Type	Dimensions in varas	Hectares	Acres
Hacienda	5,000 x 25,000	8,734.11	21,581.6
Sitio de ganado mayor	5,000 x 5,000	1,746.82	4,316.32
Sitio de ganado menor	3,333.3 x 3,333.3	776.36	1,918.33
Criadero de ganado mayor	2,500 x 2,500	436.71	1,079.08
Criadero de ganado menor	1,666.65 x 1,666.65	194.09	479.58
Fundo legal	1,200 x 1,200	100.62	248.62
Solar	1,000 x 1,000	69.87	172.65
Caballería	1,104 x 552	42.58	105.22
Suerte	552 x 276	10.65	26.3
Aranzada (marco real)	80 x 80	.45	1.105
Solar para molino, casa, o venta	50 x 50	.18	.432

CHART OF LINEAR MEASURES

	CODO DE RIBERA	PASO ORDINARIO	VARA	PASO GEOMETRICO	BRAZA (ESTADO)	TOESA	MARCA	ESTADAL	CORDEL (10 VARAS)	CORDEL (50 VARAS)	CORDEL (69 VARAS)	ESTADIO	MILLA	LEGUA
LEGUA	7,500	6,000	5,000	3,000	2,500	2,149.983	1,739.13	1,250	500	100	72.464	24	3	1
MILLA	2,500	2,000	1,666.666	1,000	833.333	716.660	579.71	416.666	166.666	33.333	24.154	8	1	.333
ESTADIO	312.45	250	208.3	125	104.15	89.568	72.452	52.083	20.83	4.166	3.019	1	.125	.0417
CORDEL (69 VARAS)	103.5	82.8	69	41.4	34.5	29.67	24	17.25	6.9	1.38	1	.3312	.0414	.0138
CORDEL (50 VARAS)	75	60	50	30	25	21.499	17.391	12.5	5	1	.7246	.24	.03	.01
CORDEL (10 VARAS)	15	12	10	6	5	4.299	3.478	2.5	1	.20	.1449	.048	.006	.002
ESTADAL	6	4.8	4	2.4	2	1.72	1.391	1	.4	.08	.058	.0192	.0024	.0008
MARCA	4.313	3.45	2.875	1.915	1.438	1.236	1	.7188	.2875	.0575	.0417	.0138	.0017	.00057
TOESA	3.488	2.791	2.326	1.549	1.1632	1	.8089	.5814	.2326	.0465	.0337	.0112	.0014	.00046
BRAZA (ESTADO)	3	2.4	2	1.2	1	.8599	.6956	.5	.2	.04	.029	.0096	.0012	.0004
PASO GEOMETRICO	2.499	2	1.666	1	.833	.7164	.5795	.4165	.1665	.0333	.0241	.0080	.0010	.00033
VARA	1.5	1.2	1	.66	.5	.4299	.3478	.250	.1	.02	.0145	.0048	.0006	.0002
PASO ORDINARIO	1.249	1	.833	.5	.4165	.3581	.2897	.2083	.0832	.0167	.0121	.004	.0005	.00016
CODO DE RIBERA	1	.7992	.666	.3996	.333	.2864	.2317	.1665	.0666	.0133	.0097	.0032	.0004	.00013
CODO	.75	.6	.5	.3	.25	.215	.1739	.125	.05	.01	.0073	.0024	.0003	.0001
PIE	.4995	.3996	.333	.1998	.1665	.1432	.1158	.0833	.0333	.0067	.0048	.0016	.0002	
PALMO MAYOR	.375	.30	.25	.15	.125	.1075	.0869	.0625	.025	.005	.0036	.0012		
SESMA (JEME)	.249	.1992	.166	.0996	.083	.0714	.0577	.0415	.0166	.0033	.0024	.0008		
PALMO MENOR	.1249	.0999	.0833	.0499	.0417	.0358	.0289	.0208	.0083	.0017	.0012	.0004		
PULGADA	.0416	.0333	.0278	.0167	.0139	.0119	.0097	.0069	.0028	.0005	.0004	.00013		
DEDO	.0312	.0250	.0209	.0125	.0104	.0089	.0073	.0052	.0021	.00041	.0003	.0001		
LINEA	.0035	.0028	.0023	.0014	.0012	.00098	.0008	.00058	.0002					
PUNTO	.00028	.00023	.00019	.00012										

CHART OF LINEAR MEASURES
(continued)

	CODO	PIE	PALMO MAYOR	SESMA (JEME)	PALMO MENOR	PULGADA	DEDO	LINEA	PUNTO	METRIC	SAE
LEGUA	10,000	15,000	20,000	30,000	60,000	180,000	240,000	2,160,000	25,920,000	4179.5	2.59699 Miles
MILLA	3,333.33	5,000	6,666.66	10,000	20,000	60,000	80,000	720,000	8,640,000	1393.166	.86566
ESTADIO	416.6	625	833.125	1,250	2,500	7,500	10,000	90,000	1,080,000	174.118	571.246 Feet
CORDEL (69 VARAS)	138	207	276	414	828	2,484	3,312	29,808	357,420	57.677	189.227
CORDEL (50 VARAS)	100	150	200	300	600	1,800	2,400	21,600	259,000	41.795	137.121
CORDEL (10 VARAS)	20	30	40	60	120	360	480	4,320	51,800	8.359	27.4242
ESTADAL	8	12	16	24	48	144	192	1,728	20,736	3.3436	10.96968
MARCA	5.75	8.625	11.5	17.25	34.5	103.5	138	1,242	14,904	2.4025	7.8821
TOESA	4.651	6.977	9.302	13.954	27.907	83.722	111.629	1,004.66	12,055.9	1.94396	6.3777
BRAZA (ESTADO)	4	6	8	12	24	72	96	864	10,368	1.6718	5.4848
PASO GEOMETRICO	3.322	5	6.665	10	20	60	80	720	8,640	1.3926	4.5688
VARA	2	3	4	6	12	36	48	432	5,184	.8359	2.7424
PASO ORDINARIO	1.666	2.5	3.333	5	10	30	40	360	4,320	.6966	2.2854
CODO DE RIBERA	1.333	2	2.666	4	8	24	33	288	3,456	.5568	1.8283
CODO	1	1.5	2	3	6	18	24	216	2,592	.41795	1.3712
PIE	.666	1	1.333	2	4	12	16	144	1,728	.2786	10.969 Inches
PALMO MAYOR	.50	.75	1	1.5	3	9	12	108	1,296	.20897	8.227
SESMA (JEME)	.332	.5	.666	1	2	6	8	72	864	.1393	5.484
PALMO MENOR	.1666	.25	.333	.5	1	3	4	36	432	.06966	2.7425
PULGADA	.0555	.0833	.111	.1666	.333	1	1.333	12	144	.0232	.914
DEDO	.0416	.0624	.0835	.1250	.2505	.7520	1	9	108	.0174	.6856
LINEA	.0046	.0069	.0093	.0139	.0278	.0832	.1111	1	12	.0019	.076
PUNTO	.00038	.00057	.00077	.00115	.0023	.0069	.0093	.0833	1	.0001583	.00623

standardization of measurements derived therefrom, the dimensions of various types of land holdings are easier to ascertain. Although the vara served as the basic unit of measure, several other standards found frequent use. While not employed to measure as such, the league *(legua)* was often a reference in description. In a more specific sense, the vara, *paso geométrico, cordel* (of 10, 50, and 69 varas) and the *estadal* (4 varas) were the units commonly used.

A *solar* might be anything smaller than a *suerte. Fanegas de sembradura* differed in size according to the crop grown on them. The cabaliería was commonly divided into such fanegas, 12 for the raising of corn and 69 for wheat. A fanega might be further divided into 12 *celemines.* The *fundo legal,* originally 1,440,000 square varas, suffered several reductions in size throughout the colonial period.

MEASURES OF PAPER

	Balón	Resma	Mano	Cuaderno	Sheets
Balón	1	20	400	2,000	10,000
Resma		1	20	100	500
Mano			1	5	25
Cuaderno				1	5

APOTHECARY MEASURES

	Libra	Onza	Dracma	Escrúpulo	Grano	Grams	Troy oz.
Libra	1	12	96	288	5,760	345.180	11.097
Onza		1	8	24	480	28.765	.925
Dracma			1	3	60	3.595	.116
Escrúpulo				1	20	1.198	.039
Grano					1	.059	.0019

LIQUID MEASUREMENTS

Liquids measured by volume present the same problem as units of weight—the greater in value the unit, the less exact the measurement. The only outstanding examples of this are the *pipa* and the *barril.* Both these units have been assigned several values. However, they are included in the chart below with what appear to be their most common equivalencies. Another problem peculiar to liquids is that the base unit of measurement, the *cuartillo,* was defined in terms of water, wine, and olive oil. The equivalent employed here is the most common of the two most frequently cited values for water.

	Pipa	Moyo	Barril	Cántara	Cántara (oil)	Azumbre	Cuartillo	Liters	Gallons
Pipa	1	1.767	6	28.279	36.269	226.235	904.941	456.09	120.5
Moyo		1	3.395	16	20.52	128	512	258.048	68.125
Barril			1	4.743	6.045	37.706	150.823	76.015	20.083
Cántara				1	1.283	8	32	16.128	4.258
Cántara (oil)					1	6.238	24.95	12.576	3.319
Azumbre						1	4	2.016	.532
Cuartillo							1	.504	.133

Olive oil was often measured in the following manner:

1 panilla = 4 onzas
4 panillas = 1 libra
25 libras = 1 arroba (cántara)
1 arroba (cántara) = 12.575 liters
3.319 U.S. gallons

HYDRAULIC MEASURES

	Buey	Surco	Naranja	Limón	Paja	Square Pulgadas	Square Inches	Square Millimeters
Buey	1	48	144	1,152	20,736	1,296	1,082.678	698.5
Surco		1	3	24	432	27	22,556	145.5
Naranja			1	8	144	9	7.519	4.85
Limón (real)				1	18	1.125	.9404	.6067
Paja					1	.625	.5221	.3368

The standard measure for the flow of water was the *buey*, derived from the size of an ox. It was a rectangular opening 1,296 *pulgadas* square. The three largest measures were used primarily for agricultural purposes, while the *limón* and the *paja* were used for urban and culinary flow. The flow or volume of water was measured by taking into account the altitude of the source, the distance the water had to run, and the time taken to fill a receptacle of a known size.

WEIGHTS

Units of weight revolve around the Spanish pound *(libra)* and the *arroba* (25 libras). There is little question as to the value of these two or of the *quintal* (100 libras or 25 arrobas). However, units of measure for weights greater than the quintal are rendered inexact by a variety of factors. Part of this imprecision is due to the regional character of Spanish measures as well as the regional variations of colonial Mexico. Furthermore, larger units such as the *carga, tonel, tonelada,* and the *carretada* were often estimated rather than measured. The carga has suffered most in this respect. Confusion is magnified by the fact that these larger units also served as indicators of volume. Thus the meaning or value of a carga can not be assigned an equivalent on a general colonial level. It must first be determined whether the carga is being used to determine weight or volume. Next, the commodity being measured has to be identified. Most important, the carga itself must be tied to a general local area. A carga of corn in Durango probably differed in weight or volume from a carga of corn in Baja California.

Nevertheless, there are a few guidelines which mitigate some of this complexity. In the sixteenth century, a carga was often defined in terms of what an Indian could carry, as the Indian served as the major beast of burden. This carga, or *carga común,* equaled approximately 50 libras (23 kilograms or 50-7/10 U.S. pounds). This definition apparently evolved from the weight of a specific volume of corn—one-half *fanega* of corn being nearly the same in weight. By the eighteenth century, the mule had become the common beast of burden and the carga changed in meaning. Thus, the value of this unit increased from the approximate 50 pounds to about 306 libras or 140 kgs (308.64 lb). As an example of the complexity and at the same time in an effort to clarify, the following two tables are presented. Notice the relationship of one unit of measure to another for corn and wheat.

Units of weight for corn:

Carga	Fanegas	Quintales	Arrobas	Libras	Kilograms	U.S. pounds
1	3	3	12	300	138.072	304.394
	1	1	4	100	46.025	101.468
		1	4	100	46.025	101.468
			1	25	11.506	25.366

Units of weight for wheat and flour:

Carga	Fanegas	Arrobas	Libras	Kilograms	U.S. pounds
1	4	13	325	149.58	329.764
	1	3.25	81.25	37.395	82.441
	.5	1.625	40.625	18.697	41.219

These tables provide an idea of the relationship of the carga and fanega to lesser weights. However, local variation in the determination of the carga and the fanega prohibit using these or any other calculations as a general rule.

Therefore, the carga of these two commodities, corn and wheat, had differing values. This is true also for other goods: a carga of tobacco or cotton has been measured at 92 kg or 202.82 pounds; of cacao, 37.25 kg or 82.12 pounds. The number of arrobas in a carga varied with the commodity in question. A carga of grain was sometimes measured as 16 arrobas (184.1 kg/405.867 pounds); a carga of honey as 18 arrobas (207.1 kg/456.573 pounds); of sand as 14 arrobas (161.1 kg/355.161 pounds); and of lime or gravel at 12 arrobas (138.1 kg/304.455 pounds).

The *tonel, tonelada,* and *carretada* were other common units of weight in excess of the quintal.

The tonel was equal to 5/6 of a tonelada. The tonelada was often defined as being equivalent to 20 quintales. In this case, the tonelada equaled 920.5 kg or 2, 029.33 lb, and the tonel 767.08 kg or 1,691.11 lb. However, the tonelada was also defined as being equal to 2 *pipas*. A pipa was a container of liquid equal to approximately 120 U.S. gallons or 454.2 liters. With this in mind, and one gallon of water weighing 8.337 lb, a tonelada weighed 2,000.88 lb or 907.59 kg. However, the weight and density of liquids vary, making the tonelada measured in this manner somewhat unreliable. The tonelada was furthermore defined in maritime commerce, where it was more frequently used, as the amount of space occupied by 2 pipas.

However confusing the values of units of weight greater than the quintal may be, values for lesser units are reasonably clear:

	Quintal	Arrobas	Libras	Onza	Adarme	Tomín	Grano	Metric	Pounds/ounces
Quintal	1	4	100	1,600	25,600	76,800	921,600	46.025 kg	101.467 lb
Arroba		1	25	400	6,400	19,200	230,400	11.506	25.367
Libra			1	16	256	768	9,216	460.25 g	16.226 oz
Onza				1	16	48	576	28.77	1.014
Adarme					1	3	36	1.798	.0634
Tomín						1	12	.599	.0211
Grano							1	.0499	.0018

MARITIME MEASUREMENTS

Maritime measures of longitude or distance used by the Spanish between the fourteenth and nineteenth centuries did not remain constant. The lack of consistency was caused by the debate over the length of the *legua* (league). As man's knowledge of science increased, especially in astronomy, measurements used in navigation changed. The length of the league depended ultimately on the circumference of the earth, or what man perceived it to be. By the fifteenth century the Spanish had definite answers, although inaccurate, to the astronomical and mathematical questions posed by long-distance marine travel. Although Spanish mariners were incorrect in their judgment of distance, it is necessary to understand the measurements they did use and the values attached to them.

The most important factor to be borne in mind when working with nautical measurements of the Spanish colonial period is the varying length of the league. Between the fourteenth and nineteenth centuries the Spanish employed leagues ranging from 14 to 22 to the degree of longitude. Columbus based his calculations on a degree of approximately 14 leagues. Early colonial navigators settled, for the most part, on a degree of 17½ leagues. By the middle of the eighteenth century most experts had come to accept 20 leagues to the degree. The league used to determine distance on land measured 5,000 *varas* or 15,000 *pies*. This corresponds roughly to a marine league of 17½ to the degree used during the early years of Spanish colonial growth.

In the sixteenth century, Diego García de Palacio, in his *Instrución Naúthica para el buen uso y regimiento de las Naos (Instrución para navegar),* (1587) outlined marine measurements as follows:

4 grains of barley = 1 dedo
4 dedos = 1 palmo (menor)
4 palmos (menores) = 1 pie
5 pies = 1 paso geométrico (paso de Salomón)
125 pasos geométricos = 1 estadio
8 estadios = 1 milla
3 millas = 1 legua (3,000 pasos geométricos)
1 legua = 15,000 pies

García de Palacio used the degree of 17½ leagues. This structure parallels the measurements commonly employed for measuring distance on land. Until this time sailors had been using different leagues, varying from 14 to 16⅔ to the degree. Generally, they divided the league into 4 *millas* rather

MONETARY MEASUREMENTS

	Marco	Onza	Ochavo	Adarme	Tomín	Grano	Grams	Troy oz.
Marco	1	8	64	128	384	4,608	230.20	7.401
Onza		1	8	16	48	576	28.775	.9251
Ochavo			1	2	6	72	3.597	.1156
Adarme				1	3	36	1.798	.05780
Tomín					1	12	.5995	.01927
Grano						1	.04996	.00160

STANDARD WEIGHTS AND MEASURES IN USE IN MEXICO CITY IN 1620

The *cuartillo* and fractions thereof.
The *arroba* and multiples (usually 2) and fractions thereof.
The *fanega* and fractions thereof.
The *cordel* and fractions thereof.
The *almud* and fractions thereof.
The bronze *cántara*, measured in *arrobas* for wine and honey.
The *vara* and fractions thereof.

Divisions of the *vara*:

Vara	Media	Tercio, o pie	Cuarto, o palmo	Sesma	Pulgada	Línea	Punto
1	2	3	4	6	36	432	5,184
	1	1.5	2	3	18	216	2,592
		1	1⅓	2	12	144	1,728
			1	1½	9	108	1,296
				1	6	72	864
					1	12	144
						1	12
							1

than 3. The *milla marina* is the nautical mile (as opposed to the *nuda* or "knot") and was always accounted to be one-third of a nautical league, with its true value based on the nautical league.

By the eighteenth century, according to Salvador García Franco in *Historia del arte y ciencia de navegar* (1947) and in *La legua náutica en la edad media* (1957), the league had grown. It was accepted as 20 to the degree, and instead of 5,000 varas or 15,000 pies, it contained 6,646 varas or 19,938 pies. In the nineteenth century the league changed once again, growing to 6,666.66 varas or 20,000 pies. The metric equivalent for these three variations began at 4,179.5 meters, went to 5,555.5 meters, and finally to 5,572.7 meters. It should be noted that even though the length of the league grew over the years, subdivisions such as the *vara*, *braza*, and *estadio* did not: more of them were necessary to make up a league of greater length.

Other significant longitudinal measurements used in sailing were the *codo de ribera*, the *braza*, and the *cable*. The codo de ribera and the braza remained constant (see chart on pages 70–71) while the cable fluctuated. García Franco indicates that 1 cable in the eighteenth century contained 110.8 brazas. However, while the cable was a measurement, it was invariably used in estimations, as was the length of a shot fired from a cannon. The length of the cable depended on the length of the rope-walks ashore, which was determined by law. However, application of the law was inconsistent and the length of the cable remains in doubt. The codo de ribera was used primarily in ship building and contained 33 *dedos* as contrasted to the ordinary codo of 24 *dedos*.

Four measures of volume and capacity were frequently employed in the shipping of liquids and in determining a ship's capacity—the *pipa, pipote, tonel,* and *tonelada*. The pipa was the standard measure of liquid capacity and was equal to 136.395 U.S. gallons. The pipote contained 6 pipas. The tonel had a capacity of 272.79 U.S. gallons or 2 pipas. In reference to carrying capacity and volume, the tonelada was referred to as being equal to the tonel, of greater capacity than the tonel and as a designation of space in cubic terms. This last reference amounted to approximately 53.65 cubic feet. The pipa and the tonel should be used when referring to a ship's capacity as they were the most common units employed.

NOMENCLATURE OF NATIVE GROUPS

This alphabetical listing of Indian band and tribal names includes all group designations that have been noted in documents or print pertaining to the area north of the twenty-second parallel and bounded by Louisiana and the Pacific. To date, DRSW archival research has focused on the area of the north Mexican plateau and northwestern New Spain. Consequently, ethnic entries from those areas are more numerous than from any other region. For northeastern Mexico, Texas, and the Californias, greater reliance was placed on secondary sources.

North-central Mexico, especially the region of the greater Bolsón de Mapimí, is extremely confusing and complex with regard to ethnic names. They make up a large percentage of this list. The bewildering number of names is contrasted by an almost complete lack of information about most of them. The reasons for this multitude of band names in the documents are several. Spaniards designated Indian groups in different ways at different times. Some they referred to by an actual name for the band. In some cases a chief's name was used. At other times they were designated by some physical characteristic or description and, not uncommonly, called by the name of their campsite, village, or an associated geographical point.

Spanish knowledge of the native languages was often totally lacking and the recorders of the names no doubt had trouble with transcription. Syllables were sometimes dropped from the longer indigenous names although there was no pattern or consistency to this practice. An apparent Spanish name may actually be only a Spanish word suggested by the sound or form of an Indian one. Nahuatl was widely used in the North through the seventeenth century (its decline seems to actually parallel the demographic demise of these groups) and some bands were probably designated in as many as three languages—the indigenous one, Spanish, and/or Nahuatl. An example may be *Coyotes* (Spanish form of the Nahuatl *coyotl*) and *Cocoyomes* (Nahuatl plural, *cocoyemeh*). The actual group probably called itself by another term in its own language.

Some names occur consistently over a span of time and therefore appear to be stable designations. Many others are seen only a few times and in all likelihood are simply variants of the more stable term. Because chroniclers often translated names into a more familiar language, some names occurring in the list may appear to be distinct when in fact they refer to the same ethnic group. Some names apply only to a single band while others refer to aggregates of bands. At times specific names seem to have acquired generic meaning as the groups themselves became increasingly composite. It is evident that the Spaniards tended to employ generic names for natives located some distance away and specific names for those living nearby.

In the list that follows names are presented alphabetically. Syllabic and orthographic variants are indented under the most commonly occurring and/or accepted form. Beyond the obvious variations given, no attempt is made here to relate groups to each other or to time or place; that would involve a monumental project in itself. Since people were sometimes called by the village or town in which or near which they lived, inclusion of names of Spanish period towns has been held to a minimum. Doubtless the list contains similar names entered as separate designations which refer to the same group, but, where documentary context fails to supply conclusive evidence that they should be grouped, they are treated as distinct.

Aa
A
Aaa
Abayo
Abe
Aba
Abo
Abriache
Acaca
Acafe
Acaf
Acanis
Acansa
Acanza
Acaxee
Acage
Acagee
Acaje
Acajee
Acaxe
Achacome
Achague
Achoj
Achogtatal
Ochayal
Achome
Acohme
Achubale
Acinay
Acinai
Acmueraboida
Acoclame
Acoclama
Acoclane
Acodame
Coclame
Adáes
Adáis
Adáys
Adáyz
Adose
Aes
Afumes
Agdoca
Aguacane
Aguachacha
Aguage
Aavage
Aoiage
Aovage
Aovaje
Avaje
Ovae
Aguaiame
Aguano
Aguastaya
Aguasalla
Aguastalla
Aguatayo
Aguatinejo

Aguatineso
Aguaxani
Aguayan
Aguayam
Aguayo
Aguaxo
Aguidas
Aguilacai
Aguisaca
Ahijado
Ahijito
Ahoge
Ahome
Ahomama
Aiaguia
Aibino
Albino
Aybine
Aybino
Ayuino
Ayvino
Ibine
Aielis
Aiguine
Aijao
Ainais
Aes
Ainay
Ais
Aix
Aynais
Aynays
Ays
Ayses
Aipiel
Aixaos
Ajame
Ajocame
Alalaca
Alasaca
Lalaca
Alamama
Alancos
Alaquines
Alasapa
Alazapa
Alauza
Alayuyo
Alaiuio
Alayuio
Alilluyo
Alcachagua
Alegocha
Alegoche
Alijae
Aliquis
Alliklik
Alobaja
Alobja
Alona

Aloqueño
Alzado
Alsado
Amacava
Amanquex
Amapoala
Amazabare
Amiguara
Amiyaya
Amojave
Amotomanco
Anabudamo
Anacanás
Aname
Anatagua
Ancha
Anchimos
Anchose
Andacamino
Anna
Añimama
Aomania
Aovage
Aobage
Apache
Apaches Cruzados
Apaches de la Lomería
Apaches Enisados
Apaches Escalchufines
Apaches Isleños
Apaches Penxayes
Apagado
Apaixam
Apalachino
Apapax
Apasgame
Apaypatsaus
Ape
Api
Apu
Hape
Heape
Iape
Iapie
Japie
Jeape
Apian
Apillón
Apion
Apompia
Apostatas
Aguitadotdacam
Aquita Doidacam
Aquitadoydacam
Do Aquí Hoidacm
Arácates
Araguays
Aranama
Araname
Arcahome

Arcajoma
Arcanzas
Arco Bueno
Arco Podrido
Arco Tirado
Aretines
Aricado
Aricada
Aripe
Arricara
Asa Toaa
Asay
Osay
Ascahoma
Azcahoma
Ashaque
Asinais
Asinaiz
Asinayes
Assinais
Azinais
Azinays
Asinguatisa
Assares
Atacales
Atacapa
Atacapaze
Atalapa
Attacapa
Attakapa
Atajala
Atalaya
Atangepina
Atapabonda
Atapo
Atasacneu
Atastagones
Atayo
Atemaxaque
Atsina
Aucham Cacalo
Aupuiap
Aujuiap
Ujuiap
Ujuijap
Auxigual
Avavares
Avichita
Avidamoydan
Ayagua
Ayaiula
Ayancuaras
Ayelis
Ayenis
Ayes
Ayjao
Ayona
Ayoves
Ayx

Baba
Babani
Babane
Babia
Babijomama
Babimamar
Babiamamare
Babinamama
Babol
Babola
Babole
Babora
Baborimama
Baborimara
Baburimama
Bamoribama
Bamorimama
Baboroco
Babosarigame
Baboragame
Baboramigame
Baborerigame
Baborigame
Baborisagame
Baboroigame
Babosarica
Babosorigame
Babozaligamen
Babozariga
Babozarigame
Babucaligama
Babusarigame
Babuzarigame
Bauosaregame
Bausaridame
Bauzarigame
Bavaserigame
Bobonizarigame
Bobozaligame
Bobozarigame
Babun
Babury
Babury Dedepo
Bacabichis
Bacacuyo
Bacaranan
Bacarane
Baciroa
Vacinoa
Vaciroa
Baconibito
Bacopo
Bacorame
Baccorame
Bacora
Barocame
Bacoregue
Bacoregui
Bacua
Bacubirito

Bagiopa	Bayecito	Cabellos Blancos	Cahita	Contuna
Bahacehas	Bayocora	Cabellos Colorados	Cahuage	Canube
Bahanero	Bayomane	Cabeza	Cahuameto	Caoco
Baganero	Bazapa	Cabeja	Cahuemeto	Caocozie
Bajanero	Betonijure	Cabesa	Cahuilla	Caocosi
Bahari	Beyocho	Cavesa	Cajalate	Cascosie
Vahare	Biamomama	Caveza	Cajuala	Caucozis
Bahupe	Biamoma	Cabezas Blancas	Cajuencha	Capellone
Daiamamar	Bimama	Cabezas de Huacal	Cafuencha	Capiquamara
Bainos	Biay	Cabia	Cahuenche	Carajo
Bamoa	Bioy	Cabocacis	Cajuenche	Caramiguay
Baimoa	Bibit	Cabri	Calancheños	Carancahua
Baiomanes	Bibis	Cacachaus	Calancha	Carancagua
Baja	Bichuia	Cacafe	Calaraque	Carancaguase
Bajo	Bichoio	Cacae	Calchufine	Carancahuare
Bajamare	Bichoya	Gacaphe	Caliani	Carancahuase
Bajare	Bichuyegua	Cacalote	Californio	Carancahuaye
Baxare	Bidai	Calcalote	Calimona	Carancahuaze
Bajiopa	Bidamamara	Chajalote	Callegué	Carancohuace
Bajopapay	Blanco	Cacaste	Callejué	Karankawa
Bajunero	Blanquillo	Cacastle	Camacraco	Caray
Balerae	Boayo	Cacaxte	Camalucano	Carrai
Bamarimamare	Bohayo	Cacaxtle	Camana	Carray
Bamorimamare	Bobamari	Cascatle	Camanegua	Saray
Bamichicoame	Bobida	Cacateca	Camaneo	Carchiqui
Banamichis	Boboac	Cachopostal	Camiopaja Mara	Carlane
Bapacolani	Babole	Cacahapostal	Camisagua	Carbame
Bapacorapinanaca	Bobore	Cachopostale	Camiseta	Carlana
Bapocare	Bobori	Cachopostate	Camispajamara	Carrizo
Bapacore	Bocaro	Cachuende	Camotero	Casas Chiquitas
Bapusare	Bocas Prietas	Cacoin	Campacua	Casastles
Barbipian	Bocoma	Cacquite	Campagua	Casdudacho
Baroyo	Bocora	Cacuares	Canpacua	Caselobe
Barreteado	Bogisopa	Cacucoat	Canpagua	Casquesa
Barrieno	Bohain	Cacucocit	Canamara	Castizo
Baruano	Boayn	Cacuitataome	Canapuces	Casupugtale
Batayoligla	Bohaym	Cacuitaome	Canaq	Catanacasa
Batayogligla	Vaoyn	Cacuitatahumet	Canatinno	Catqueza
Batayolicla	Vohain	Cacuotaome	Canabatinu	Caquiza
Batayolicua	Bohris	Cavitaome	Canohatino	Catquesa
Batayulica	Bonole	Cacuraco	Canaynas	Catujano
Batlaboyla	Boome	Cacusa	Cancahuas	Catajane
Batlacoyla	Boquillurimamara	Cadajo	Cánceres	Catajuane
Vatayocua	Borrado	Caddo	Canica	Catjuano
Batopila	Barrado	Cadima	Cannecis	Catujane
Guahtopila	Borruca	Cadodacho	Cancis	Catujano
Guatopila	Bozales	Caddudacho	Cannecys	Catujuano
Batopililla	Bozeregamui	Cadodache	Cannesis	Catuxane
Batuca	Brieiatiolyagua	Cadodacho	Cansis	Catuxano
Batucari	Buardava	Cadogdacho	Canzes	Catuxzan
Bauane	Buasdabe	Cadudacho	Cano	Cotujano
Bauiamamare	Buasadaua	Caodache	Cana	Caudacho
Babiamare	Buasdaba	Caodacho	Cane	Caudodocho
Baviamamare	Buasdava	Cododacho	Canna	Caueca
Baviamare	Buchite	Cadima	Canoa	Caugueca
Bavane	Busos	Cagual	Canua	Cauirama
Bayacato		Caguate	Cantiles	Cauisera
Bayaguaniguara	Caba	Caguax	Cantona	Caguicera
Bazaguaniguara	Cabacbitac	Caguas	Cantouahona	Cauicera
Bayamamara	Cabacbitae	Cahigua	Cantuna	Cavisera

Caula
Cauncanayiguara
Cauruama
Causa
Causalo
Causca
Cauta
Cava
  Cavera
  Cavita
Caynaya
  Caynigua
Caynio
Cazcane
Cazosopa
Cenizo
  Cenis
  Cenisa
  Ceniso
  Ceniza
  Censoc
  Censoo
  Chenis
  Senicso
  Seniczo
  Seniso
  Senixso
  Senixzo
  Senizo
  Sinico
  Sinicu
  Siniczo
  Sinixzo
  Zeniza
  Zenizo
Censoc
Cerocahui
  Cerocague
  Cerocagui
  Cerocahue
Cetguane
Chaboya
Chacahuale
  Chacaguale
Chacaiatajo
Chachatiolyagua
Chacuiyacua
Chaguacane
  Chaguacana
Chaguagua
Chaguan
Chaguantapan
Chaiopi
Chajuanahan
Chalame
Chamanca
Chamope
Chane
  Chana
Chapamaco

Chapama
Chapamo
Chapuline
Chaqual
Chaquantapa
Charana
Charayes
Charro
Chatapache
Chauare
Chauchila
Chaulaame
Chavare
Chayopina
  Chayopín
  Chayopine
Chemaya
Chemehuevi
  Chemeguab
  Chemegueb
Chemequi
Chenttis
Cheoca
Cheva
Chibicano
  Chivicano
Chica
  Chicaes
  Chico
Chicanimama
  Chicanima
Chichicuita
Chichilticale
Chichimeca
  Chichimec
  Chichimeco
Chichitame
  Chichitamen
  Chuchitamen
Chicorato
Chicura
Chigame
Chiguagua
  Chigagua
Chilchihuiscan
Chiles
Chilome
  Chilma
  Chilmo
  Chiloma
Chimamale
Chinanche
Chinarra
  Chimarra
  Chinara
  Chinasa
  Chinaso
  Chinaza
  Chinazo
  Chinnara

Chivarra
Chincharra
Chínipas
Chipaine
  Chilpaine
  Chipaindo
  Chipayne
Chiquillo
Chiquita
Chiricahuis
  Chiricaguis
  Chiricahua
Chirno
Chiruma
Chiso
  Chisco
  Chisso
  Chiza
  Chizo
  Chozo
Chivipane
Choctaw
  Chacta
Chol
  Cholz
Chola
Cholome
  Chilome
  Chocolome
  Chokone
  Cholame
  Choloine
  Choloma
  Cholomo
  Cholone
  Coclame
Choma
  Chome
Chomene
Chorrera
Chota
Choumane
Chozo
Chuanimama
Chuchuntica
Chupadero
Churi
Ciaesier
  Ciaefier
Cíbola
  Cébolo
  Cíbolo
  Cívolo
  Síbola
  Síbolo
  Sívolo
  Yíbolo
Cien Orejas
Cimarrón
Cinapécuaro

Cipalda
Cipia
Clamcoet
Cluetau
Coahuilteco
  Coaguileño
  Coaguilleño
  Coahuila
  Coahuileño
  Coavileño
Coama
  Coana
Coapaliguane
  Coapa
Coapite
Coara
  Coaxa
Coauvite
Cobagi
Cobarde
Cochimí
Cochinue
Coclamartube
Coco
  Coxo
Cocobipta
  Cohabita
  Cococomesno
Cocohua
Cocoime
  Cocoiame
  Cocoiome
Cocojita
Cocoma
  Cocom
Cocomaque
  Cocomacaque
Cocomaricopa
  Cocomaripopa
  Cocomarizopa
  Comariapa
  Comaricopa
Cocomeioje
Cocomoguacale
Cocomuliam
Cócopa
  Cócapa
  Cócope
  Cósopa
  Cúcapa
Cocoraboroquiaya
  Coroboroquiaya
Cocosut
  Cocosict
Cocotiolyagua
Cocoxibo
Cocoxima
Cocoxiua
Cocoyome
  Cocoiome

Cocojome
Cocollome
Cocotome
Cocoyame
Cocoye
Cocoyeme
Cocoyolme
Coyume
Coyome
Cuyime
Cocuisam
Cocuytzam
Codam
Coe
Cohumero
Coinama
  Coinam
  Cuinama
  Cuiname
Coioapa
  Coioapae
Cojane
  Cujana
  Cujane
  Cuxane
Cojar
Colabrote
Colas Largas
Colazaque
Colimote
Colina
Colorado
Coltechis
Coma
Comahane
Comales
Comanche
  Comanchi
  Cumanche
  Cumanchi
Comaniopa
Comanito
Comaroya
Comeagame
Comeajeme
Come Caballos
Comecabras
Comecamote
Comecrudos
Come Nariz
Come Nopales
Comesacate
Comesíbolo
Cometuna
Comeviejo
Comeya
Comibopo
Comoporis
Comucha
Comupa

Conapomama
Concho
  Concha
Concumaha
  Conchumaha
Conejo
  Coneco
Conexero
  Conejero
Congrado
Coniani
  Conani
  Coniane
Conicari
  Concuari
  Conicare
Conina
  Cononina
Conquebaco
  Cunquebaco
Contina
Contotore
  Contotole
  Cuntotore
Contraguia
Convaya
Coopabo
Copan
Cora
  Chora
Corcobado
Corica
Coripa
Corizna
Cosari
Cosau
Cosnina
  Cosmina
Coso
Costaños
Cotoaragua
  Cotoayagua
Cotomamar
  Cotohomamar
Cotoname
  Cotonamu
Cototoholome
  Cototoolome
  Totoholome
Cotzales
Coupa
Couylas
Coyote
  Cocoyote
  Coyotero
Cozosopa
Cruiamo
Cruzado
Cuabapae
  Cuabaae

Cuacuytatome
Cuaguila
  Cauila
  Cauguilla
  Quahuila
Cuahuijo
Cuajín
Cuampis
Cuaramaro
Cuartelejo
Cuautomana
Cuayapa
Cuayo
  Coayo
Cuazapayogligla
Cubipane
Cubis
Cubsubi
Cuchanec
Cuchantica
  Cuchuntica
Cuchuta
Cucubipi
Cucusa
Cucuyama
  Cocuytzam
Cudeflecha
Cudobe
Cuecuapay
Cuerco
Cuero
Cueros Quemados
Cueyne
Cufane
  Cufave
Cuguiara
Cui
Cuicuigua
Cuitoa
Cujan
  Coxan
  Cuja
  Cujaco
  Cujart
Cumbres
Cumejero
Cumuripa
  Comoripa
Cunupa
Cupeño
Curia
Cusaco
Cusame
Cutgane
  Cutujane
Cuurbipica
Cuyama
Cuyime

Dacacmuri

Daparabopo
Deadoso
  Dadose
  Deadoce
Decafez
  Decafes
Dedepo
Desorejado
Despesuan
Didui
Diegueño
Dientes Alazanes
Dientes Negros
Diju
  Dija
Ditehagopob
Ditsakana
Doaquioydacam
  Doaquiodacam
  Doaquihoidaun
Doema
Dohobopo
  Dotobopo
Domaxame
Dopobahopob
Duro

Echancote
  Echascote
Ecores Baroyos
Edu
  Edue
Egope
Eguapit
Egue
Emet
Emat
  Emate
  Emete
  Iman
  Yman
  Ymate
  Ymete
Emetjlaba
Emetycara
  Emietycava
Emigdian
Emomama
  Emoma
Enabopo
Enanos
Endere
Enemigos del Cerro
Enojito
Epimama
Epiquamara
Epiquiomar
Esauqui
Escabaca
  Escaba

Escanjaque
  Escanxaque
Escaone
Escapulame
Escomiagamo
Espopolame
Esselen
  Excelen
Estoyto
  Estoytto
Etapai
Etiepen
Euacan
Eudeve
  Eudebe
  Eudobe
  Eudove

Faliquamai
Fancue
Faraone
  Faraon
  Pharaone
  Pharone
  Taraone
Feimama
Fernandeño
Fianque
Filijay
  Filpayay
  Foligais
Flecha Chiquita
Flecha de Palo
Flechazo
Fuerte
Fuerteño
Fusas
Futaaname

Gaapalor
  Gaapa
Gabilacho
Gabrielino
Gamplam
Gandule
Garafe
Garza
Gauchan
Gavilán
  Gabilán
  Gauilán
Gediondo
Genízaro
Gentile
  Jentile
Gerez
Gezene
Gicocoge
Gigora
Gijime

Gila
Gileño
  Giceño
  Jileño
Gincapé
Giorna
Girigaia
Gonzas
Gordos
Gorica
  Giorica
  Goxica
Gorreta
Gozopas
Guacaja
Guacale
  Guacali
Guachichil
  Cuachichila
  Guacacile
  Guacasil
  Guachichile
  Guachiclule
  Huacacil
  Huachichil
Guachita
Guadiamanar
Guaicura
  Guaicuro
  Guaicuru
  Guaycura
  Waicuri
Guaimas
  Gayamas
  Guayamas
  Guaymas
  Guaymis
  Llayemas
  Yaiamas
Guajaguane
Guajolote
  Guejolote
Gualaxise
Gualequa
Gualta
Guamar
  Guamarejo
  Guamaroa
  Guamore
Guampasale
Guamuchicata
  Guamuchicat
  Guamuchiquat
Guanbrauta
Guapica
Guapite
Guapo
Guaquale
Guaquimamara
Guaraba

Guaracata	Guichita	Ervipiame	Horames	Imuris
Guarmare	Guigolote	Gueripiamo	Hores	Xímeris
Guasave	Guiguigoa	Heirvipame	Htucamo	Hynna
Guasabe	Guiguimas	Herbipiamo	Hualapai	
Guascadome	Guijacale	Heruipiane	Gualapai	Iachime
Guastaya	Guilime	Hierbipame	Gualiba	Iacovane
Guasttaya	Guimutiquimamara	Hierbipane	Huallapai	Iatasis
Guaxe	Guineo	Hierbipian	Jaguallapai	Idedepo
Guaxicora	Guiniguio	Hiperbipian	Jualapai	Dedepo
Guayaboa	Guiplote	Hyerbipian	Walapai	Iedododame
Guaypile	Guirate	Irripian	Huamuchigual	Ietan
Guaza	Guiripi	Jerbipiam	Huascaris	Igodosa
Guázabas	Guisacale	Yerbiapame	Huasteco	Igoguib
Guásabes	Guitama	Yerbipiame	Hascalteca	Iguana
Guázavas	Guita	Yerbipian	Hascalteco	Iguanolaxtac
Guázaves	Guitola	Yerbipiane	Huaslec	Ileepo
Guazahuayo	Guilola	Yerebipiamo	Huatamama	Iman
Guasaayo	Guitolo	Yeripiame	Húchiti	Imarina
Guasahaio	Gusiquesale	Yeruijuame	Hueso	Imudaga
Guasahayo	Guyime	Yrbipia	Gueso	Inabopo
Guazaayo	Guzalane	Yurbipian	Hueyquetzal	Enabopo
Gusayo		Hijos de la Pared	Geuiquesal	Inibopo
Huazahaio	Hacho	Hijos de la Sierra	Guericochal	Ynabopo
Huazayo	Haico	Hijos de la Tierra	Guyquechal	Inapaname
Uazahayo	Halchidhoma	Hijos de las Piedras	Huequetzal	Injame
Vazahayo	Halliguamaya	Hijos de Lodo	Huiguechale	Inquero
Guazapare	Hanasina	Hijos de los Palos	Huiquicale	Iopuan
Guacapane	Hanasine	Himen	Queiquechal	Ipandi
Guacapare	Hanimama	Hina	Huhui	Iracancatecuamama
Guarapare	Hapiquamara	Hinechis	Huhuygam	Iritila
Guasapare	Hapore	Hinehis	Huican	Irritila
Guasapari	Hapora	Hinsa	Huicasique	Yritila
Guaspare	Japore	Hiorica	Huichol	Isale
Guazapari	Hasanai	Hio	Huichole	Iscanis
Gucapari	Acinais	Hyo	Huitaaco	Isconis
Gucara	Asinai	Yhio	Huitaro	Izcaniz
Gucoquita	Assinay	Hipalabo	Huitala	Jscanies
Gueimama	Azinais	Hipimamal	Huitalo	Yascanes
Guerisipiamo	Azinays	Hipomamal	Huitero	Yscanes
Guerjuatida	Hainais	Hypimama	Guitalo	Yscanis
Guergaida	Hasinais	Hypimamal	Huite	Iseamis
Guerjoatdo	Hatafee	Hypomama	Uite	Isucho
Guersudan	Havasupai	Ipimama	Humis	Italaca
Guerjudan	Habesupai	Ypimam	Humes	Itoca
Guesecpayolicla	Jabesua	Ypimama	Jume	Ytoca
Guarapaioligla	Hazpipina	Ypomama	Jumi	Itotorame
Guasapagoligla	Hedor Fiero	Hipoco	June	Ituma
Guasapayoligla	Heguaic	Hipólito	Lume	
Guasipayole	Heguan	Hires	Xomi	Jacafes
Guazapayogligla	Hegue	Hisca	Xume	Jacaquinte
Guazapayoligla	Hegui	Hoabonama	Yume	Jacao
Guesapame	Heque	Hoabonoma	Hurabama	Jacajo
Guesecpamot	Hequi	Hobe	Horabam	Jaco
Guesecpayoliglao	Jeque	Hoera	Urabamo	Xacaje
Guesipayole	Hempempalo	Hogue	Huuidacho	Xacajo
Quasapaioligla	Heve	Hoguera	Huvagures	Jacaques
Gueyapaes	Hierbipiame	Hoisuave	Hyamara	Jachime
Guicale	Berttipane	Hoisuaue	Hýmeris	Jaimamar
Guicane	Bervipiane	Hopi	Hímeris	Jajame
Guichaes	Erbipiamo	Hopome	Imeris	Jalame

Xalam	Joba	Kutenai	Mairana	Manos Sordas
Jalane	Joua		Mayrano	Manqui
Xalane	Jove	Lacopsele	Majcagua	Mansiu
Jaloma	Joviale	Lagunero	Malagueco	Manso
Jamajova	Juamaca	Laguna	Malahueco	Manco
Jamajaba	Juama	Laitane	Malaquita	Mansa
Janambre	Juamca	Lamparica	Malaguite	Manzo
Ganambre	Juancana	Lano	Malaguito	Mapaco
Janambría	Jancaz	Laomama	Malas flechas	Mapeana
Xanambre	Juacana	Largo	Malechore	Mapeane
Jano	Juanca	Laymon	Maliabe	Mapoch
Hano	Juaneño	Laymona	Malincheño	Maqualistaca
Yano	Juchipila	Legua	Malinchero	Maqualitaca
Jantajo	Julime	Leguaquin	Malinero	Maquine
Jantapuis	Julimeño	Lemita	Mamacorra	Maraguito
Jaquue	Jutime	Letarive	Mamacera	Maraguita
Jaqueie	Shulime	Letariue	Mamacora	Marahuiayo
Jarame	Tulima	Leujaco	Mamazorra	Marahuito
Harame	Tulime	Lipan	Maman	Maraquita
Jarane	Jumano	Lipillane	Mamen	Maraquite
Xarame	Humano	Lipiyane	Mamarimamari	Marhita
Jaraname	Juman	Liyú	Mamaura	Marhuite
Araname	Jumana	Llanero	Mamaya	Mariquita
Taraname	Jumane	Lobo	Mamiga	Marahuiayo
Taraname Apostata	Jumaneo	Lobsa	Manyga	Mariguanes
Xaraname	Jumzan	Loera	Mamisa	Mariposa
Jaucar	Shumano	Lomisaagua	Mamite	Marneda
Jauca	Jumee	Lorica	Mamete	Marodega
Jaujo	Jumi	Losceana	Mamita	Martaja Mesquite
Jediondo	Sumi	Luiseño	Mamoquana	Masabra
Jegete	Juncata	Lumamar	Mamoquan	Masame
Jémez	Junia	Lumano	Mamorimama	Mascone
Emmes	Honia	Lumbres	Mamorima	Masiabe
Hemes	Hunia		Mamorimamara	Masitabe
Jeueco	Juniana	Mabibit	Mamuasen	Mastajamesquite
Jícaragrande	Jupe	Macacaite	Mamuqui	Masatajamesquite
Hícaragrande	Yupe	Macaname	Mamuya	Matapa
Jicarilla	Jupulame	Macapa	Mana	Matapane
Gicarilla	Juribe	Macapao	Manam	Mataraje
Xicarrilla	Jurive	Macapaqui	Maname	Matarate
Jigualli	Jusile	Macbe	Manahue	Mataraxe
Jigualis	Jusguiopoion	Macheyo	Managua	Mataxcucos
Jijame	Juszalane	Machi	Manague	Matiquica
Hihame		Machiquo	Managui	Matlava
Jigime	Kamia	Macho	Manahua	Matoabra
Jijime	Kanecio	Machomine	Manaue	Matuime
Xijame	Kansa	Macobenamama	Manave	Matuimi
Jimarrones	Kapota	Macoco	Mandone	Maubedan
Jocome	Keliwa	Macoibra	Manguara	Mauitoui
Jacome	Keres	Macoyahui	Manico	Mauyga
Jocoma	Cheres	Macoyaqui	Manicu	Manyga
Jocove	Queres	Macsuam	Minicau	Mauiga
Ocane	Kichais	Macuapaine	Minicu	Mavivit
Ocome	Quichays	Madmeda	Manioja	Maxiconera
Xocome	Quieseys	Maguage	Manyoja	Mayapomi
Jogoso	Quisseis	Maguaos	Manoaca	Mayaye
Jojocome	Quitseis	Magua	Manos	Mayece
Jova	Quitseys	Maha	Manos Colorados	Mayeyes
Hoba	Kiowa	Mahoho	Manos de Perro	Maheyes
Hova	Kunkaak	Maieis	Manos Prietas	Maheyz

Maiey	Michiaba	Musaume	Naquize	Nejora
Malleve	Michis	Mutsun	Naquise	Nifora
Malleye	Miembros Largos		Naras	Nixora
Mayei	Milijai	Nabedache	Naredodacho	Vijora
Mayie	Miligae	Nabadakiou	Narices	Nijote
Maymamamara	Milihae	Nabedacho	Narones	Nios
Mayo	Milijae	Nabedakio	Nasite	Niquité
Maio	Milijay	Nabedakiou	Nasore	Nit-ajende
Maya	Milixay	Nabeidacho	Natajés	Nochi
Mayey	Mimbreños	Nabidacho	Natagées	Necha
Moyo	Mimbres	Nevadizoe	Natagés	Neche
Mayoco	Mimioles	Naborio	Natajée	Nichi
Mayorica	Miopacoa	Nacaachao	Natajís	Noche
Mayrana	Miopacoba	Nacababal	Notage	Nochia
Mazaltipilgua	Miquiaquines	Nacababa	Nata	Nogal
Mazalypilgua	Mischales	Nacabaja	Natal	Nohorache
Mazape	Misuris	Nacabatla	Natcau	Nonoje
Mazarabopo	Mitote	Nacacavora	Natchitoche	Noñojet
Mazayabopo	Moache	Nacacha	Nachetoo	Noñoque
Mazatichigua	Mochiras	Nacameris	Nachitoce	Nonore
Mazume	Mogollón	Nacatzatza	Nachitoche	Nonose
Mazame	Mohave	Nacavura	Nachitoze	Nonotie
Meco	Mojave	Nachito	Nateau	Nonox
Mecocama	Moiote	Nachitoo	Naticoya	Nonoxe
Macocoma	Molia	Nacitos	Natsoo	Novoje
Mecocoma	Molinero	Nacocoma	Naturales	Ynonoje
Médanos	Momon	Ntacocoma	Nava	Norteño
Meguira	Mona	Nacogdoche	Navajo	Nostliguequei
Hehuera	Monqui	Nachadoche	Nabajoe	Nostiguequei
Mehuira	Monquino	Nacodoce	Navaho	Notoni
Meuira	Monso	Nacodog	Navichame	Notrache
Mevira	Mopututur	Nacodogoce	Navidacho	
Menanquen	Moqui	Nacomera	Navedacho	Oba
Menanque	Machi	Nacona	Navonio	Ova
Menequen	Maqui	Nacono	Nayarita	Obaides
Meresalinero	Mochi	Naconi	Naytane	Obaya
Merhuan	Moquinos	Naconome	Nazas	Obaye
Merhuam	Moquis	Nacosura	Nasas	Ovalle
Meriano	Morbana	Nacpache	Nazonis	Ovaya
Mesa	Morcilique	Nadacaos	Nasones	Obebopo
Mescal	Morisco	Nacacahoz	Nasonis	Obebo
Mefcal	Moroamo	Nadacogs	Nasonit	Obesita
Mescata	Movas	Nadacos	Nazones	Ovedsita
Messcal	Mobas	Nagadoche	Nazonio	Ocano
Mexcal	Mowatsis	Nadadora	Nozone	Acani
Mezcal	Moxi	Nadadore	Necha	Cane
Miscal	Mozanamara	Nadesa	Neicha	Ocam
Mixcal	Mruseden	Nadeco	Necpacha	Ocame
Mizcale	Muaches	Nadote	Nacpacia	Ocan
Mescalero	Muca	Nadzoo	Nemantina	Ocana
Mezcalero	Muhuachis	Nagua	Neojodotzi	Ocane
Mesquite	Muladrilla	Naguera	Netafeses	Ochiniguata
Mezquillo	Muliam	Naicha	Nevadizoes	Ocho
Mezquite	Muruame	Nakipa	Névome	Oche
Misquit	Mariame	Namar	Nábome	Ooche
Misquiti	Marueana	Namborica	Nébome	Oclotani
Metontonta	Moroame	Name	Nébone	Ococlame
Mexiquillo	Moroamo	Nanisue	Nicoleño	Ocodame
Mexues	Moruane	Napaname	Nigco	Ococdame
Miaqui	Muruane	Napeste	Nijora	Ocola

Ocora	Osatapa	Pacgal	Pacuasiane	Pamache
Cocore	Osatame	Pachan	Pacuasin	Pamaia
Ocoroni	Osatayolicla	Pachat	Paguasine	Pamajo
Octata	Osatayogligla	Pachol	Pacuchale	Pamajum
Odame	Osatayolic	Pacuchal	Paduca	Pamaque
Hodahame	Osatayolida	Paischal	Padoca	Pamaquepapil
Odaame	Osotayogligla	Paschal	Padouca	Pamasu
Oodame	Osotayoglegla	Pasteal	Padouka	Pamafeo
Odoesmade	Osotdyligla	Patcal	Pagampachic	Pamaseo
Oduesita	Osaugue	Patchal	Pagayame	Pamaujo
Ohoe	Osera	Patehal	Paguana	Pamaus
Hoa	Oquera	Patzal	Pahuana	Pamaya
Oha	Ozara	Patzhal	Pahuanan	Pamaia
Ohe	Osicame	Pauchal	Paguiame	Pamalla
Oho	Ostoyto	Paxchal	Pahaco	Pame
Ojahue	Ostujane	Pachalaque	Paiaia Cuchite	Pamie
Ojo Hondo	Otabua	Pachamal	Paiabuna	Pamorame
Olive	Otaquitatone	Pachana	Pai-Pai	Pamorano
Olibe	Otaquitatome	Pachaque	Paisano	Pampopa
Olobaya	Otauay	Pachaqui	Paizane	Campoa
Omatomanco	Otecameque	Pachasuen	Paysan	Pampo
Amotomanco	Oto	Pachate	Paysano	Pampoa
Omomone	Otocame	Pachaug	Paischale	Pampoca
Omooma	Otucamo	Pachina	Paiuguan	Pampoja
Onat	Otoe	Pacho	Paiupan	Pamposa
Onoje	Otolcoclome	Pacha	Paiute	Panpoc
Ooche	Otolcoclame	Pucha	Pajaca	Pompoc
Oche	Otomí	Pachoche	Pahaque	Pompoja
Odre	Otomoaco	Pacholoco	Paxac	Pompopa
Oodre	Otovage	Pacitalac	Paxaquis	Pampope
Oodam	Otuc	Pacoa	Pajalarne	Pumpoa
Opa	Otuiay	Paca	Pajalatame	Pamuliam
Opacta	Ouichito	Pacco	Pajalache	Pamoliam
Opaguico	Ouigaima	Pacua	Pajalat	Pamuliam
Ópata	Oveibo	Paqua	Pajalate	Pamulam
Opeluza	Ovichria	Patca	Paxalache	Pamulian
Apeluza	Oxao	Patcax	Paxalame	Pamuliem
Opoli	Oyaa	Pacoatal	Paxalate	Pamulies
Oposme	Oydican	Pacoche	Paxalote	Pamulis
Opoxme	Oxdica	Pacpole	Paxalto	Pamulum
Opula	Oymama	Pacpule	Pajam	Panulam
Orame	Oimama	Pacpulo	Pajanto	Pomuluma
Orancho	Oymamare	Pacque	Pajarito	Ypamuliam
Orcoquisac	Oymana	Pactaluc	Paxarito	Pamuti
Orcoguisa		Pacuache	Pajosalam	Pana
Orcogüiza	Paabuna	Pacahuche	Paxasalaun	Panana
Orcoquisa	Paac	Pachuache	Pajuai	Panaque
Orcoquiza	Paace	Pacuachiam	Palahueque	Panchaque
Orcosiza	Pacco	Pacuafin	Palajue	Pancho Cojo
Ore	Pacuaz	Pacuasian	Palague	Pandis
Orejón	Pacuq	Pacuazin	Palenqueque	Panequaimas
Oriental	Paburi	Pacuche	Pallugan	Panipique
Oronirato	Pabori	Pagnache	Palmeto	Pani Pique
Orrorroso	Pacaiopue	Paguache	Palmita	Panis Piques
Ororoso	Pacao	Paguachi	Palo	Panis
Osage	Pachaique	Paguacia	Palo Blanco	Pannis
Osale	Pachacolani	Paquachi	Paloma	Panismaha
Osataba	Pachagua	Paquasian	Pama	Panimacha
Osata	Pachal	Paquatche	Paman	Panimaha
Osatabay	Pacal	Pascuache	Pamaca	Panoga

Pahoga
Pahogua
Paoga
Panpopa
Panquaye
Papabota
Papabrota
Papacolani
Papago
Pápagi
Papahota
Papalote
Papanac
Panac
Papan
Papana
Papanaca
Papanacam
Papanaque
Papanax
Papanoque
Paponaca
Paponal
Popan
Papane
Papani
Papanico
Papayame
Papayo
Papotan
Paquache
Paquachiamo
Paqueye
Paquioba
Paraguane
Paragus
Paran
Parchaque
Parchac
Parchale
Parchena
Parcheque
Parchina
Pardo
Pariguara
Parugan
Pariagan
Parucan
Parusis
Pasajo
Pazajo
Pasita
Passaguate
Pastalbe
Pastaloca
Passtacalo
Passtaculo
Passtalaco
Passtalca
Passtaloca

Passtaloco
Pastalacto
Pastaloco
Pastoloca
Pataloco
Pastancoya
Pastancoiam
Pastancoian
Pastanquia
Pestanquia
Pastate
Pastio
Pastia
Pastilla
Pastis
Paxtis
Pasxa
Patabo
Patacal
Patacalh
Patcal
Pattacat
Patacama
Pataguac
Patagahu
Patagu
Patagua
Pataguaque
Patague
Pataguo
Patahua
Patao
Patau
Patavo
Pato
Patou
Pataguilla
Pataguiya
Patalca
Patarabuey
Patchal
Patilnacal
Patón
Patos de Perro
Patzau
Paceo
Pachao
Pachaug
Paisau
Patsau
Pattsou
Patzar
Pauchau
Pazagual
Psaupsau
Pauchan
Pauit
Pausane
Paufane
Pausana

Pausano
Pauxane
Pauzán
Pauzano
Pausaqui
Paviane
Paxaqual
Paxcaz
Paxnacan
Payaboa
Payaba
Payaguale
Payaguame
Payaguane
Payatammumis
Payaya
Paiaya
Pallaia
Pallaya
Payaia
Payaie
Payate
Payay
Payaye
Peyaye
Payayalaque
Payoan
Pay
Payauan
Payoguan
Payuche
Payuchis
Payugan
Paiugan
Paiuguan
Pajuguan
Pallugan
Payuga
Payuguan
Payuhan
Payuhuan
Paza
Pazac
Pazagual
Pazaguante
Pazaguan
Pazaguate
Pazajo
Pazaju
Pazan
Paysan
Pazary
Pazau
Pazao
Pazchal
Pazolatame
Peana
Pecos
Pecuries
Pedexorcale

Pellejo Blanco
Pelones
Peñol
Penxaje
Penxaye
Pepita
Perico
Pericú
Pericua
Pericue
Periue
Perral
Perros
Pescados
Pessca
Petinique
Pezatillo
Pezatille
Piana
Piane
Piato
Piatto
Picacho
Picuano
Picurís
Picuries
Piedras Blancas
Piedras Chicas
Piegan
Pies de Venado
Piguique
Pilguane
Pima
Pimotologa
Pimotocologa
Pinanaca
Pimanaca
Pinanacame
Pinanacam
Pinanua
Piniquu
Pino
Pinot
Pinto
Pintostejones
Piojo
Piquamara
Piquano
Piquegue
Piguique
Pihuique
Piquigue
Piro
Pisasequi
Pisones
Pita
Pitahay
Pitalac
Pitalague
Pitalaque

Pitali
Pitarday
Piticagan
Pitiqueño
Pitisfiafuile
Plato
Playano
Poarame
Poba
Pojosay
Pausay
Porsay
Pojue
Polacine
Polacme
Pulacman
Polame
Poloora
Pomo
Pomuzeno
Pootajpo
Popora
Popoyehua
Popaega
Popoiegua
Popoiehua
Popoigua
Poponiua
Popoyeua
Popoyihua
Populeño
Poralme
Porras
Poras
Posalme
Poxalma
Poxalme
Posni
Posoama
Postito
Posuama
Potutu
Pozoay
Pozoaie
Praguilis
Prejo
Preso
Prieto
Puapo
Pucha
Puchac
Puchame
Pueblo
Puehaine
Puguahiane
Puguhiane
Puguaque
Pujan
Pulica
Púlique

Púliqui
Puncataguo
Pupilispiaguilis
Puspilis
Putay
  Putaay
  Putahay
  Putai
Putumaca
Puxcane
Puyua
Puzane
Pyhiya

Quaaguapaia
  Coaguapai
  Cuaguapai
  Quaapaya
  Quaaguapaya
  Quaguapaes
  Quaguapaia
  Quaguapaya
Quabasaye
  Quabasay
Quaguimama
Quailo
Quairama
Quamoquane
Quaquithatome
Quartelejo
  Quartelexo
Quautic
  Quactic
Queasenareo
Quechale
  Guechale
Quedejeno
Quem
  Quema
Quemado
Quenicapame
Quenxame
Quepano
  Quepana
Querecho
  Cherecho
  Querės
Queroama
Quesal
Quezy
Quiaquixcaquis
Quicha
Quichau
Quidehais
Quiguaguan
Quiguaguare
Quigyuma
Quimamara
Quimichi
Quimicoa

Quiminipayo
Quimutiquimamara
Quincuano
  Quinicuame
  Quiniquano
Quiniguio
Quiniquiguis
Quiniguyopichico
Quinso
  Quinzo
Quiquehabe
Quiquima
Quiripiamo
Quisabe
Quisachi
Quisis
Quitaca
Quitachim
Quitaea
Quitseis
  Queitseis
  Quitceis
Quituchis
Qunze

Rana
Raton
  Ratonero
Rau
Rayado

Saaquel
Sabaibo
Sabuaguana
Sacaroneño
Saczo
Sadammo
  Sadamo
Sadujane
Saesse
Saguach
Saguaiame
Salapaqueme
Salapeme
Salchomi
Salcocolome
Salina
Salinero
  Salinera
Salineros de Don Cebrián
Salla
Salvaje
  Salbaje
Samampac
Samay
Samenchane
Samioj
Sampanale
Sana
  Chana

Sama
Sanac
Xanna
Zana
Sanague
  Sanaque
Sanaian
  Sanaius
Sanayau
  Sanyau
Sandis
Sanipao
Sanpanale
  Sanpanal
  Sanpanaley
Sanpanasu
Santiago
Saquita
Saraguam
  Saracuame
Sarame
Sarinacanaza
Sarnoso
Satapayogligla
  Satagolila
  Satayolila
Satatie
Satatu
Satzpanal
Sauto
Sayopine
  Chaiopín
  Chayopine
  Saiopine
Sciquipile
Secmoco
Sehyarame
Sejines
Selaia
Semoma
Sendes
Seoporami
Seri
  Ceri
  Here
  Zeri
  Zery
Seromet
Serranía
Serrano
Seuliyolicla
Siabanane
  Chiaguan
  Ciaban
  Ciaguan
  Siaban
  Siabian
  Siaguan
  Tziaban
  Xhiahuan

Xiabane
Xiguan
Ziaban
Ziaguan
Siacueha
Siaexer
  Haeser
  Saeser
  Siaesier
  Xaeser
Siause
  Saesse
  Siaexe
  Siansi
  Siausi
Siboporame
  Sibapolame
  Sibapora
  Sibaporame
  Sibopola
  Sibopolame
  Sibopolo
  Sibopora
  Sipopola
  Sipopolame
  Sivoporame
  Sopolame
  Soporame
Sibubapais
  Sebubapa
  Sibubapa
  Sibubapou
  Suvibapa
Sibuitutilca
Sicpam
Sicribulo
Sicuraba
Sierra Blanca
Siguare
Siguase
Siguiyone
Sijame
  Ciajame
  Cijame
  Hihame
  Jijame
  Scijame
  Scipxame
Sicame
Sicxacama
Siguame
Sijane
Sixame
Syame
Tziame
Xijame
Xixame
Zijame
Zixami
Silangaya

Sillanguaya
Simapa
Simariguanes
Simomo
Sinaloa
  Cinaloa
  Zinaloa
Sin Oreja
Siouan
Sipuan
Siquipil
Siquique
Siquis
Sisibotari
  Cicibotare
  Cicibotari
  Sisibutari
  Sisivotari
  Xixbotare
  Xixibotare
Sisimble
  Asisimbre
  Cicimble
  Cicinble
  Cizimble
  Simble
  Simbli
  Sinible
  Siniple
  Sinple
  Sinsimble
  Sisimbre
  Sisinble
  Xiximble
  Zicimbre
  Zizembre
  Zizimble
Sisimlole
Sisituemeto
Sitana
Sitiminich
Siupán
Soacatino
Soba
  Sobabo
  Sobaybo
Sobaipuri
  Sebaispuri
  Soais
  Sobahipuri
  Sobai
  Sobaighpuro
  Sobaipori
  Sobais
  Sobaisipurio
  Sobajipuri
  Sobajiquris
  Sobaypure
  Sobaypuri
  Sobaxipuri

Sovahipuri
Subaibapa
Sobal
Socatile
Socuina
Sodomamara
Solajame
Sombrero Prieto
Soromet
  Sozomet
Sorones
Sotu
Soxa
  Soxae
Suame
  Suama
Suaqui
  Juaque
  Suaque
  Zuaque
Suatae
Sucuyames
Sue
Sulcha
Sulijame
  Chulajame
  Chulajan
  Chulujan
  Sulajami
  Suliajame
  Suliejame
  Sulujame
  Zolajami
  Zolajan
  Zulajan
Suma
  Cuma
  Juma
  Jumo
  Suama
  Sumar
  Sume
  Sumee
  Summa
  Sumo
  Zuma
Suniglugligla
  Senayoligla
  Simplolila
  Sinayoligla
  Sinilolila
  Siniyoligla
  Solinolicua
  Sonololila
  Sumiguligla
  Suniloligla
  Sunilolila
  Suninoligla
  Suninolila
  Suñiluligla

Sutrebe
Suzaze
Synoqueda

Taamnan
Tabacano
Tabaqueto
Tabehuachis
Tabesua
Tablado
Tacabuy
Tacaguia
  Tacaguiste
Tacame
  Tacane
  Tacome
  Thacame
Tacuitataome
  Tacuitatome
  Taquitatome
Taensa
Tahuacan
  Taguacan
  Taguacane
  Tahuacana
  Tahuancane
Tahuache
  Taguache
Tahuaya
  Taguaya
  Taguayace
  Tahuayace
  Tahuaye
Tahue
  Tahuec
Taimamares
Talamanca
Talapais
Talaquiape
  Tajaguiche
  Talaguic
Talche
Talchedune
  Talchedume
  Talchedun
Talcoyotes
  Talcoyome
  Tatalcoyome
Tallicumais
  Tallicuamay
  Tallicuma
Talopsa
Tamajaba
  Tamafabe
  Tamajab
  Tamalab
Tamara
Tamiguamay
Tamique
Tampacuase

Tampila
Tancabo
Tancahue
  Tancague
  Tancaquie
  Tancaque
Tancame
Tanche
Tanchipa
Tanguaya
Tano
  Tanico
Tanpacayan
Tanpachoa
Taos
  Thaos
Taovacane
  Taovagace
Taovaya
  Tabaya
  Taboayase
  Tahuaya
  Taobaiane
  Taobayace
  Taobaya
  Taobayais
  Taovay
  Taovayace
  Taovayase
  Taovayaze
  Taovayese
  Taquaya
  Tavaya
  Tavayaze
  Tavoiage
  Tavoyachés
  Toaya
Tapacolme
  Tapalcane
  Tapalcolme
Taparabopo
Tapayogligla
Tapia
Tapiel
Tapohoamama
Tapusque
  Tapisque
Taquarabopo
Taquefica
  Taquefil
  Taquefila
Tarahumara
  Tarahumare
  Tarahumari
  Taramane
  Taramara
  Taraumara
  Taraumare
  Taraumaro
  Tarhumara

Tarhumare
Taromara
Tarumare
  Tauromara
  Tharaumara
  Tharaumare
Taraname
Tareguane
  Tareguano
  Tarequaro
Taro
Tastazagonis
Tatalcoyome
Tatamulis
Tatche
Tauanbo
Tawakonis
  Taguacana
  Tahuacana
  Touacana
  Tovacana
  Toyacane
  Tuacana
Tayado
Tayev
Teaname
Teanda
Tebananca
  Tebancana
Tecamo
Techuchapa
Tecinda
Tecla
Tecolame
Tecolote
  Tecolotu
Tecomacaque
  Tecomacaqu
  Tecomaque
Tecuchiapa
  Tecuchiap
Tecuexe
Tegua
  Tegoa
  Tehua
  Teoa
  Tequa
  Tewa
  Teya
Tegüima
Tehata
Tehuacana
Tehueco
  Chegueco
  Tegueco
  Teguiso
  Tepegueco
  Tequeco
  Thegueco
Tejas

Tegas
Texa
Texas
Tejón
  Tetexón
  Texón
Temecula
Temimamar
  Teimamar
  Teneinamar
Temita
Témoris
  Témores
  Tómores
Temoroso
Tena
Tenepajal
Teneymama
Teniania
Tensasame
Tenuco
Teonnarome
Teopa
Teopare
Tepa
Tepahui
  Tepague
  Tepagui
  Tepaguie
  Tepahue
  Tepaque
  Tepaqui
Tepehuan
  Sepequana
  Teguan
  Tegueguan
  Tejuan
  Tepaguane
  Tepecano
  Tepeguana
  Tepeguane
  Tepeguano
  Tepehuane
  Tepehuano
  Tepehuene
  Tepejuane
  Tepeoan
  Tepequan
  Tepeshuana
  Tephuane
  Thepeguane
  Thepehuan
  Thepehuana
Tepeque
  Tepequeco
  Tepetucane
Tepoca
  Tepica
  Tepoque
  Tepoza

Tepoze	Tilijae	Tobaca	Toca	Tucumamara
Tipoca	Tilijaya	Tobaso	Toque	Tucumama
Topoca	Tilixai	Tobasso	Tuca	Tucumuraga
Zepoca	Tilixe	Toboca	Topacolme	Tucurame
Tepolgueguei	Titijaia	Tobosco	Zopacolme	Tuglón
Teponera	Titijay	Tobosso	Topi	Tugue
Tequima	Tilofa	Toboza	Topichis	Tuhacage
Tequisco	Tilojaya	Tobozo	Toremez	Tuicuiguan
Tereodan	Tilpacopal	Tobsos	Toremes	Tuidamoydan
Teodoran	Tilpapay	Tovoso	Torica	Tuigare
Terrodan	Timamar	Tovosso	Torloso	Tuigar
Terocodame	Ticmamar	Yoboso	Toro	Tuigore
Hierquodame	Timama		Toroaca	Tuimamar
Hyroquodame	Timamare	Toca	Torquimamara	Taimamar
Perocodame	Timamore	Tocamomon	Tortuga	Tuimamare
Teocodame	Timpanogo	Tocaymamare	Tosag	Tumama
Teodocodamo	Tintis	Tocaimama	Tosimora	Tumamar
Terocodom	Tiopane	Tocaymamasaesse	Totamomon	Tunmamar
Teroeocodame	Tirangapui	Tocho	Totoclame	Tumanac
Texocodame	Tishim	Toche	Totohame	Tuma
Therocodame	Titioyo	Tococome	Totoholome	Tuman
Thezocodame	Teteoyo	Tocome	Totoolome	Tumana
Toxocodame	Tiupane	Tocone	Totolome	Tumane
Terraba	Tixilxo	Todococdane	Totomono	Tumapacanes
Tetaribe	Tizonazo	Tohaha	Totomoro	Tuncataguo
Teteco	Ticonaco	Tohobapojo	Totolcoyome	Tunsi
Tetecora	Ticonazo	Tohobopo	Totonoca	Tumzi
Tetecore	Tizonaco	Toobopo	Tototorame	Tuque
Tetenagua	Tizonoco	Toida	Itotorame	Tusan
Tetenauorca	Tlacopsele	Tojo	Touacara	Tusane
Tetenobapar	Tlajahuiche	Toho	Tovs	Tuzan
Teterxame	Tlajaguich	Toxa	Tops	Tusares
Tetonbopoca	Tlalcoyome	Toxo	Tova	Tusolivi
Tettecumeno	Tlaxcalteco	Tojuma	Tups	Tuteneiboica
Tetzino	Tlascalteca	Tolocoe	Toyalo	Tzayeos
Teuima	Tlascalteco	Tomahuac	Traname	Tzayeus
Teusasame	Tlempenienniguo	Tomajaba	Trasmama	Tzuname
Texuyame	Tlenamama	Tomascabe	Tratante	
Teymamar	Tloaoorrama	Tomaxpuecpe	Trementina	Uachita
Thao	Toa	Tomayxpucpe	Tresdocodamo	Ubates
Thealis	Toaa	Tomite	Trimomomo	Uchacare
Theloja	Toamare	Tompiro	Ttrimomomo	Uchití
Teloja	Toapa	Tonicas	Tripas	Huchití
Teloxa	Toaja	Tonkawa	Tripas Blancas	Uchitie
Theoloja	Toata	Tancagua	Trueno	Udachita
Theoloxa	Toarame	Tancague	Tuacana	Ujambores
Thiloja	Toaraque	Tancahua	Tuacane	Ujuiap
Thios	Toarma	Tancahue	Tuamca	Upanguaymas
Tibocabopo	Tobacana	Tancaoue	Tuanca	Upanguaimas
Tiburón	Toben	Tancaue	Tuapa	Upanguaymis
Tigua	Toba	Tancauey	Tubar	Jupangueimas
Chigua	Tobe	Tancaque	Tubara	Upiquamara
Téoa	Tova	Tancoye	Tubare	Uquiqualuo
Tigue	Tobitis	Tonmamal	Tubari	Urache
Tiguex	Toboso	Tonmamar	Tubaymamar	Uracha
Tihua	Boboso	Tonojita	Tucara	Ures
Tiwa	Govosso	Tonto	Turcaxa	Hures
Tileja	Teboso	Tonzanmacagua	Tuchano	Huris
Tilijai	Tepoza	Too	Tucano	Uves
Filixaye	Tepoze	Tou	Tuchian	Utaca
Tilihay	Thoboso	Tuu	Tucubante	Ute
		Tooca		

Uta
Utah
Yuta
Yuta Anacapagari
Yuta Muhuachis
Yuta Sabuaganas
Yuta Tabehuachis
Yute
Utiaquies

Vacinoa
Vahane
Vahanero
  Baanero
  Bahanero
  Vaanero
  Vaganero
  Vajanero
  Vanero
Vaiaja
  Vaiatsa
Vaquero
Vasapalles
Vayema
Venado
  Benado
Vende Flechas
Ventureño
Veslaco
Vichilgua
Vidais
  Bibais
  Bidais
  Bidays
  Vidaes
  Vidays
  Vydais
Viddaguimamar
  Biddaguimamar
  Vitdemamar
Viololais
Vívoras
  Víboras
Vocayoes
Vuamariani

Warihio
  Barogio
  Barohio
  Baroquio
  Uarojio
  Varohio
  Vorihio
  Vorohio
Wemintuc
Xaamnacane
Xabatoa
Xacactic
Xacate
  Xacaje
Xalazapa

Jalazapa
Xalepa
Xanamacam
Xanaque
Xanimama
Xantaguis
Xapoz
  Apex
  Xapes
  Xapez
  Xapoz
  Xeapes
  Xiapez
  Xiapoz
  Xoapez
Xaqueban
Xaquibama
Xaquimies
Xaraname
  Arame
  Aranama
  Araname
  Charame
  Charrome
  Harane
  Jarame
  Jaraname
  Jurame
  Sarame
  Saraname
  Schiarame
  Xarame
  Xaranme
  Xarome
  Xharame
  Zarame
Xaunae
Xexet
  Jeget
  Xexte
Xiabus
Xiancocadan
  Xianeocadam
  Xianeocadame
Xiape
  Hiape
Xapi
Xicho
Xicocale
Xicocoxe
  Sicoje
  Xicocoje
  Xicocosse
  Xicocoxe
  Xicose
Xicocuage
Xicona
Xijame
  Zijame
Xilitla
Ximiapas

Xinicare
Xipocale
Xivano
Xixame
Xixime
  Gijime
  Jijime
  Xijime
  Xixeme
Xoabane
  Xoame
Xoman
Xomi
Xonaqui
Xoxame
Xuipulame
  Xupulame
Xuman
  Xuma
Xumee
  Xume

Yabuincariris
Yacealis
Yadoces
Yaiama
Yamomama
  Emoma
  Emomama
  Iamomama
  Imomama
  Yamomaroa
  Ymomama
Yamparica
Yanabopo
Yaoymama
  Oymama
Yaquabuzmama
Yaquat
Yaqui
  Gayqui
  Hiaqui
  Hyaq
  Hyaqui
  Jaqui
  Yaque
  Yegui
  Yiaqui
Yaquimis
Yataioio
Yatasí
  Yatacé
  Yataci
  Yatassé
  Yatassí
  Yatazi
Yavapai
  Yabipai
Yazanac
Ychuimama
Ycruypia

Ydabiri
Yegual
  Iegual
  Yogual
Yerbipia
Yerbuiba
Yergiba
Yeripi
Yeyeraura
Ygoguibas
  Yboquiba
  Igoquib
  Igoquibo
Yguabo
Yguamira
  Guamira
  Iguamira
  Yhuamira
  Yyguamira
Ylame
Ylasaio
Ylaura
Ylauraquasivaha
Ymane
Ymic
Ymitte
Ynojo
  Hinojo
  Ynojuane
  Ynonoje
Yochie
Yoe
  Zoe
Yoera
Yoguocome
Yojuane
  Yocouane
  Yocuane
  Yoguane
  Yojuan
  Yoquan
  Yoquare
  Yujuan
Yome
Yorica
  Horica
  Jorica
  Orica
  Yorca
Yoyehis
Yoytis
Yoxica
Ypanis
  Ypandes
  Ypandis
  Ysandis
Yquineo
Yquitoro
Yrbipias
Ysburpe
Yscanis

Hyscanis
Iscanis
Yscan
Yscanes
Ysconis
Yscohis
Ysiaguan
Ysucho
Ysuguaio
Ysuna
Ytampabichis
Ytocame
Yujan
Yugana
Yuma
  Chuman
  Xuma
  Xuman
Yumyume
Yupimane
Yurbipame
Yuyap
  Muyap
Yxdaroc
Yyuguimi
  Yuyguime

Zacateco
  Cacateco
Zacatile
Zacpoco
  Zacpo
Zacuestacán
Zaguagua
Zaiopine
Zalajan
Zamoi
Zaraguay
Zarra
Zaygs
Zeguaces
Zerquan
  Zorquan
Ziabari
Ziapuan
Zilame
Zipia
  Cipia
Ziquipina
Zoloja
Zoxquan
Zulapan
Zuñi
  Juñi
  Zuni
  Zunie

RACIAL TERMINOLOGY

RACIAL TERMINOLOGY

The following list of racial terms is illustrative of Spanish colonial usage, but is by no means definitive. Spaniards in striving for bureaucratic exactness and perfection were in disagreement. Terminology varied greatly between New Spain and South America; it varied even within New Spain itself. This list, then, represents only the Spanish inclination for a detailed classification of different racial mixtures in New Spain. It should prove helpful in reading colonial documents or secondary sources by giving an approximation of racial definitions.

In many instances in the following list a term is defined by more than one racial combination. While this may be disconcerting to those looking for precision, it is unavoidable because the Spaniards themselves compiled these multiple, racial derivations in their own pursuit of exactness.

peninsular	
gauchupín	
chapetón	European-born Spanish
creole/criollo	American-born Spanish
gente blanca	Spanish and requinterón de mulato
cuasi limpios de origen	Child of Spanish and gente blanca
limpios de origen	Spanish and child of cuasi limpios
mestizo	Spanish and Indian
mestizo blanco	Spanish and Indian (also called coyote)
mestizo castizo	Spanish and mestizo blanco (also called castizo)
cuarterón de mestizo	Spanish and castiza
quinterón de mestizo	
puchuela	Spanish and cuarterón de mestizo
requinterón de mestizo	Spanish and quinterón de mestizo or puchuela
mestizo prieto	mestizo blanco and negro (also called mestizo amestizado)
mestizo pardo	mestizo blanco and mulato pardo (also called mestizo amulatado and coyote)
mestindio	mestizo blanco and Indian
castizo	Spanish and mestizo
torna a Español	Spanish and castizo
mulato	Spanish and negro
mulato blanco	Spanish and negro (also called mulato claro)
mulato morisco	Spanish and mulato blanco
cuarterón de mulato	
tercerón cuatralbo	Spanish and mulato
quinterón de mulato	
octavón	Spanish and cuarterón de mulato
requinterón de mulato	
puchuela de negro	Spanish and quinterón de mulato
mulato prieto	negro and mulato pardo
galfarro	negro and mulato
mulato pardo	negro and Indian (also called: color pardo, color de rapadura, color champurrado, color

	amarillito, color de membrillo, color quebrado, color cocho, color zambaigo, color loro) (geographically labeled: *cochos* in Michoacán, *cambujos* in Oaxaca, *chinos* in Puebla, *jarochos* in Veracruz, *loros* in Chiapas, *zambos* in Guerrero)
mulato obscuro	Indian and mulato
mulato lobo	mulato pardo and Indian
indio alobado	mulato alobado and Indian (alobado being a mulato lobo with few negro characteristics)
tercerón	Spanish and mulato, with Spanish dominant
cuarterón	Spanish and tercerón
	Spanish and mulato
	Spanish and mestizo
	mulato and mestizo
quinterón	Spanish and quarterón (passed for white in some areas)
morisco	Spanish and mulato
bozal	non-Christian, non-Spanish speaking negro from Africa
negro criollo	negro born in New World
zambo	negro or mulato and Indian
	negro and cuarterón
zambo de negro	negro and quinterón
zambo de mulato	mulato and quinterón
zambo de tercerón	tercerón and quinterón
zambo cabra	mulato and negro
zambo grifo	mulato and negro
zambo retorno	mulato and negro
zambaigo (zambahaigo)	negro and Indian
	Indian and chino (oriental)
	lobo and Indian
	barnocino and Indian
	cambujo and Indian
zambo prieto	negro and zambo
tente en el aire	lobo and Indian
	Spanish and torna atrás
	calpo mulato and cambujo
	cuarterón and mulato
	jíbaro and albarazado
	cambujo and Indian
	Spanish and requinterón
	albarazado and salta atrás
salta atrás	quarterón or quinterón and mulato or tercerón
	chino and Indian
	used interchangeably with torna atrás
torna atrás	Spanish and albino
	no te entiende and Indian
lobo	Indian and torna atrás
	cambujo and Indian
	salta atrás and mulato
	Indian and negro
	chino and mulato
lobo torna atrás	lobo and Indian
cambujo (ja)	zambaigo and Indian
	albarazado and negro
	zambaigo and chino

	lobo and Indian
	mulato and zambaigo
	negro and Indian
	Indian and chino
	albarazado and Indian
albarazado	cambujo and mulato
	cambujo and Spanish
	lobo and Indian
	tente en el aire and mulato
	jíbaro and mulato
	cambujo and Indian
	chino and jenízaro
	coyote and morisco
	jíbaro and Indian
barcino	albarazado and mulato
	albarazado and Indian
	albarazado and Spanish
	jíbaro and lobo
coyote	barcino and mulato
	mestizo and Indian
	mulato and Indian
	cuarterón and mestizo
albino	Spanish and morisco
chamiso	coyote and Indian
	mestizo and castizo
	Indian and salta atrás
	Indian and mulato
coyote mestizo	chamiso and mestizo
	Indian and coyote
ahí de estás	coyote mestizo and mulato
	coyote and mestizo
	Indian and no te entiende
	Indian and coyote
barnocino	albarazado and mestizo
chino	oriental
	Spanish and morisco
	Indian and lobo
quarterón de chino	Spanish and chino
jíbaro (gíbaro)	lobo and chino
	albarazado and calpamulato
	calpamulato and Indian
	lobo and mulato
	campomulato and Indian
calpamulato	zambaigo and lobo
	albarazado and negro
	barcino and Indian
	mulato and mestizo
	Indian and mulato
calpamuto	negro and albarazado
campomulato	Indian and barcino
	mestizo and mulato
	lobo and zambaigo
no te entiende	tente en el aire and mulato
cholo	applied to mestizos
jenízaro	cambujo and chino
pardo	Spanish and negro
harnizo	coyote and Spanish
	cambujo and chino
tresalbo	Indian and mestizo

| cuatralbo | Spanish and mestizo |
| tercerón cuatralbo | Spanish and mulato |

Racial terms with literal definitions

amarillito	little yellow one
barcina	large load of straw
barcino	animal with black and white skin
bozal	simple, ignorant, stupid, wild, untamed, a muzzle
cabra	a goat
cafre	barbaric, cruel
camgujo (a)	person of dark color who is strong—animals with dark skin, notably chickens and mules
casta	derogatory term for persons of mixed blood
chapetón	recently arrived European—to have a bad or dangerous time—greenhorn
champurrar/champurrado	to mix one liquor with another
cocho	vulgar name for a parrot
galfarro	hateful, spiteful individual
gachupín	spur
gibar	molest
grifo	spigot, drugged or intoxicated person
jarocho	gruff, insolent—peasant of Veracruz
jenízaro	spider
loro	dark
membrillo	quince
mulato	derivative of *mulo*, meaning the hybrid offspring of a horse and mule
mulecón	male slave between ages seven and twelve
mulecona	female slave between ages seven and twelve
muleque	male slave between ages twelve and sixteen
muleca	female slave between ages twelve and sixteen
negro amembrillado/ amulatado	light-colored negroes
negro atezado/retinto	dark negroes
pardo	brown, applied to various classes of mulatos in a derogatory manner
prieto	dark color, nearly black—dangerous, miserable
quebrado	broken or interrupted
rapadura	action of cutting beard or hair
salta atrás/torna atrás	retrograde in a moral or physical sense
tresalbo	a horse with three white feet
zambo	American monkey. Ferocious, lascivious. Person with bad configuration, knock-kneed with splayed feet.

Miscellaneous terms found either in the names of various groups, in a description of them, or as labels which are too tentative to identify.

cuarterón de salta atrás
quinterón de salta atrás
quinterón de negro
castizo cuatralbo
españolo
lunarejo
meqimistos
merino

LISTS OF COLONIAL OFFICIALS

The following lists of colonial officials are provided as an aid in locating information about events in time and place. Names of viceroys, governors, alcalde mayores and missionaries can frequently be used to identify time or place, serving as an aid in discovering other information.

These lists are by no means definitive. They were compiled from published sources and documentary information. In many cases, for a variety of reasons, published sources disagreed over who held what position at a given time. When such disagreements were encountered, a comparison was made of the data. From such comparison, weighing the sources, these lists were compiled. Known dates appearing in the following lists are either inclusive or dates of appointment.

SPAIN: REYES

Isabel	Queen of Castile, 1474–1504	Carlos II	1665–1700
	(Felipe I as regent, 1504–1506)	Felipe V	1700–1724
Fernando II	King of Aragón, 1479–1516	Luis I	1724
Carlos I	1516–1556	Felipe V	1724–1746
	(Cardinal Francisco Jiménez	Fernando VI	1746–1759
	de Cisneros as regent,	Carlos III	1759–1788
	1516–1517)	Carlos IV	1788–1808
Felipe II	1556–1598	José I (Bonaparte)	1808–1812
Felipe III	1598–1621	Cortés of Cádiz	1812–1814
Felipe IV	1621–1665	Fernando VII	1814–1833

NEW SPAIN: VIRREYES

During the reign of King Carlos I:
October 15, 1535–November 25, 1550   Antonio de Mendoza
November 26, 1550–July 31, 1564   Luis de Velasco

During the reign of King Felipe II:
August 1564–October 1566   Audiencia of México as executive
October 19, 1566–October 18, 1568   Gastón de Peralta
November 5, 1568–October 3, 1580   Martín Enríquez de Almanza
October 4, 1580–June 19, 1583   Lorenzo Suárez de Mendoza
September 25, 1584–October 18, 1585   Pedro Moya y Contreras
October 18, 1585–January 25, 1590   Alvaro Manrique de Zúñiga
January 25, 1590–November 5, 1595   Luis de Velasco (son of 2nd viceroy)
November 5, 1595–October 27, 1603   Gaspár de Zúñiga y Acevedo

During the reign of King Felipe III:
November 27, 1603–August 4, 1607   Juan de Mendoza y Luna
August 1607–June 19, 1611   Luis de Velasco (2nd time)
June 19, 1611–February 22, 1612   Fray García Guerra
October 28, 1612–March 13, 1621   Diego Fernández de Córdoba

During the reign of King Felipe IV:

September 12, 1621–November 1, 1624	Diego Carrillo de Mendoza y Pimentel
November 3, 1624–Sepetmber 16, 1635	Rodrigo Pacheco y Osorio
September 16, 1635–August 27, 1640	Lope Díaz de Armendáriz
August 28, 1640–June 9, 1642	Diego López Pacheco Cabrera y Bobadilla
June 9, 1642–November 23, 1642	Juan de Palafox y Mendoza
November 23, 1642–May 13, 1648	García Sarmiento de Sotomayor
May 13, 1648–April 21, 1649	Marcos de Torres y Rueda
June 28, 1650–August 24, 1653	Luis Enríquez de Guzmán
August 15,1653–September 15, 1660	Francisco Fernández de la Cueva
September 16, 1660–June 29, 1664	Juan de Leyva y de la Cerda
June 29, 1664–October 15, 1664	Diego Osorio de Escobar y Llamas
October 15, 1664–December 8, 1673	Antonio Sebastián de Toledo

During the reign of King Carlos II:

December 8, 1673–December 13, 1673	Pedro Nuño Colón de Portugal y Castro
December 13, 1673–November 30, 1680	Fray Payo Enríquez Afán de Rivera
November 27, 1680–November 16, 1686	Tomás Antonio de la Cerda y Aragón
November 16, 1686–November 20, 1688	Melchor Portocarrero Lazo de la Vega
November 29, 1688–January 21, 1696	Gaspár de la Cerda Sandoval Silva y Mendoza
February 27, 1696–February 2, 1697	Juan de Ortega y Montañez
February 2, 1697–November 4, 1701	José Sarmiento Valladares

During the reign of King Felipe V:

November 4, 1701–December 28, 1702	Juan de Ortega y Montañez
December 28, 1702–January 15, 1711	Francisco Fernández de la Cueva Enríquez
January 15, 1711–August 16, 1716	Fernando de Alencastre Noroña y Silva
August 16, 1716–October 15, 1722	Baltasar de Zúñiga, Guzmán Sotomayor y Mendoza
October 15, 1722–March 16, 1734	Juan de Acuña
March 19, 1734–August 17, 1740	Juan Antonio de Vizarrón y Eguiarreta
August 17, 1740–August 22, 1741	Pedro de Castro Figueroa y Salazar
November 3, 1742–July 8, 1746	Pedro Cebrián y Agustín

During the reign of King Fernando VI:

July 9, 1746–November 9, 1755	Juan Francisco de Güemes y Horcasitas
November 10, 1755–February 5, 1758	Agustín de Ahumada y Villalón

During the reign of King Carlos III:

April 28, 1758–October 5, 1760	Francisco Cajigal de la Vega
October 6, 1760–August 25, 1766	Joaquín de Monserrat
August 25, 1766–September 22, 1771	Carlos Francisco de Croix
September 22, 1771–April 9, 1779	Fray Antonio María de Bucareli y Ursúa
August 23, 1779–April 8, 1783	Martín de Mayorga
April 8, 1783–November 3, 1784	Matías de Gálvez
November 4, 1784–June 16, 1785	President of the audiencia of México as executive
June 17, 1785–November 30, 1786	Bernardo de Gálvez
December, 1786–May 7, 1787	Eusebio Ventura Beleña (regent)
May 8, 1787–August 16, 1787	Alonso Núñez de Haro y Peralta

During the reign of King Carlos IV:

August 17, 1787–October 16, 1789	Manuel Antonio Flores
October 17, 1789–July 12, 1794	Juan Vicente de Güemes Pacheco y de Padilla
July 12, 1794–March 31, 1798	Miguel de la Grúa Talamanca y Branciforte
March 31, 1798–April 30, 1800	Miguel José de Azanza
April 30, 1800–January 4, 1803	Félix Berenguer de Marquina
January 4, 1803–September 15, 1808	José de Iturrigaray

During the reign of King Fernando VII:

September 16, 1808–July 18, 1809	Pedro Garibay
July 19, 1809–May 8, 1810	Francisco Javier de Lizana y Beaumont
May 9, 1810–September 12, 1810	President of audiencia of México as executive
September 13, 1810–February 13, 1813	Francisco Javier Venegas
February 13, 1813–September 19, 1816	Félix María Calleja del Rey
September 19, 1816–July 5, 1821	Juan Ruíz de Apodaca
July 5, 1821–September 14, 1821	Francisco Novella
September 23, 1821–September 26, 1821	Juan O'Donojú

GUADALAJARA: AUDIENCIA

Founded February 13, 1548

Presidentes

July 30, 1580	Gerónimo de Orozco
December 15, 1580	Hernando de Robles
April 22, 1587	Diego García de Valverde
July 24, 1591	Diego de Alfaro
January 11, 1593	Santiago de Vera
January 28, 1607	Juan de Villela
February 11, 1611	Alonso Pérez Merchán
June 22, 1618	Pedro de Otalora
February 10, 1625	Alberto de Acuña
1627	Gerónimo de Paz y Cuéllar
Januaary 14, 1628	Diego Nuñez Morquecho
August 26, 1633	Alonso Pérez de Salazar
January 11, 1636	Juan de Canesco
December 13, 1641	Pedro Fernández de Baeza
August 28, 1654	Antonio de Ulloa y Chaves
April 3, 1662	Antonio Alvarez de Castro
March 2, 1670	Francisco Calderón Romero
June 11, 1673	Juan Miguel de Agurto
March 28, 1677	Diego Nicolás del Puerto
June 15, 1678	Alonso de Ceballos
November 16, 1700	Antonio Vidal Abarca

Oidores

May 21, 1547	Gerónimo Lebrón de Quiñones
May 21, 1547	Miguel de Contreras y Ladrón de Guevara
May 21, 1547	Juan Meléndez de Sepúlveda
May 21, 1547	Hernán Martínez de la Marcha
November 27, 1548	Alonso de Oseguera
September 2, 1553	Gregorio de Villagarcía
February 26, 1556	Pedro Morones
August 1, 1559	Juan Cavallón
December 23, 1560	Francisco de Alarcón
July 9, 1564	Francisco de Mendiola
August 18, 1565	Juan Bautista de Orozco
November 5, 1570	Diego de Bobadilla
April 30, 1572	Santiago de Vera
November 25, 1574	Diego de Santiago del Riego
April 28, 1578	Antonio Maldonado

June 1, 1578	Juan de Pareja
July 5, 1578	Luis Cortés de Mesa
May 20, 1580	Francisco Tello
January 27, 1581	Altamirano
June 1, 1585	Nuño Núñez de Villavicencio
June 1, 1585	Francisco de Pareja
March 13, 1596	Francisco Guillén Chaparro
September 5, 1596	Juan Páez de Vallecillo
February 18, 1596	Palma de Mesa
August 7, 1601	Gaspar de la Fuente
1605–1617	Pedro Arévale Sedeño
March 7, 1608	Diego Muñóz de Cuellar
April 29, 1608	Juan de Avalos y Toledo
March 19, 1609	Bartolomé de la Canal
July 10, 1611	Diego de Medrano
May 26, 1618	Gaspar de Chaves y Sotomayor
May 12, 1620	Pedro Antonio de Villacreces
August 17, 1627	Damián Gentil de Párraga
March 24, 1631	Francisco de Medrano
March 24, 1631	Antonio de Salazar
May 14, 1631	Pedro Noguerol y Córdoba
1631	Antonio Coello de Portugal
December 30, 1632	Andrés Pardo de Lago
March 23, 1637	Juan González Cid
March 23, 1637	Juan Manjarrés
March 9, 1638	Cristobál de Torres
October 23, 1645	Juan Cano
November 26, 1645	Francisco de la Barreda
March 3, 1647	Gerónimo de Aldas y Hernández
July 2, 1651	Juan de Contreras Torres Garnica
September 6, 1652	Fernando de Aguilar
September 30, 1659	Juan de Bolívar y Cruz
November 8, 1663	Cesati del Castelo
June 18, 1664	José Tello de Meneses
July 2, 1669	Gerónimo de Luna
October 10, 1669	Tomás Pizarro Cortés
November 19, 1672	Fernando de Haro y Monterroso
March 29, 1676	Agustín Félix Maldonado de Salazar
June 18, 1677	Gerónimo Chacón Abarca
October 3, 1678	Diego de Acosta Cabrera
April 6, 1680	Pedro de la Bastida
April 8, 1680	Juan de Padilla Guardiola
November 28, 1680	Fernando López Ursino y Orbaneja
August 9, 1681	Juan de Escalante y Mendoza
June 5, 1683	Antonio Vidal y Abarca
January 25, 1684	Cristóbal de Palma y Mesa
January 13, 1687	Francisco de Feijóo y Centellas
December 1, 1689	Juan de Somoza
July 23, 1690	José Osorio Espinosa de los Monteros
June 2, 1691	José de Miranda Villagrán
1703	José Domonte y Pinto
1706	Pedro de Malo de Villavicencio
1707	Juan Manuel de Oliván Rebolledo
1708	Diego Francisco de Castañeda
1710	Fernando de Urrutia
1710	Antonio Real y Quesada

1720	Prudencia Antonio de Palacios
1722	José Vicente Antonio de Garziga
1724	José de la Mesía de la Cerda
1726	Juan Rodríguez de Albuerne
1732	Miguel Tomás de Lugo y Arrieta
1733	José Antonio Cavallero
1733	Juan Carrillo Moreno
1740	Sebastián Calvo de la Puerta
1740	Martín de Blancas y Espeleta
1747	Francisco de López y Portilla
1748	Antonio Joaquín de Rivadeneira y Barrientos
1749	Francisco Gomez Algarín
1750	José Manuel de la Garza Falcón
1755	Francisco de Galindo Quinoñes y Barrientos
1764	Eusebio Sánchez Pareja de la Torre
1764	Ramón Joaquín González Becerra
1772	Ruperto Vicente de Luyando
1773	Antonio Equia Ramírez de Arrellano
1773	Joaquín Cabeza Enríquez
1774	Juan Antonio Mon y Velarde
1775	Modesto de Salcedo y Somodevilla
1777	Estanislao Joaquín de Andino
1777	Juan Francisco de Anda y Salazar
1778	Juan Romualdo Navarro
1779	José de Moya
1783	Manuel Silbestre
1786	Martín Santos Domínguez Hoyos
1787	Manuel del Castillo y Negrete
1788	Francisco Rafael de Monserrate y Urbina
1791	Luis Antonio de Múzquiz y Aldunate
1794	Francisco Camacho Canovas
1795	Francisco de Nava Grimón
1796	Nicolás de Mesía y Caicedo
1800	Manuel Mariano de Irigoyen de la Quintana
1800	Manuel del Campo y Rivas
1801	Juan Antonio de la Riva
1803	Cecillo Odoardo y Palma
1804	Juan José Recacho
1804	Juan Hernández de Alva
1805	Nicolás de Mesía y Caicedo
1807	Juan de Sousa Viana
1814	José Domingo Rus
1815	Mariano Mendiola Velarde
1816	José Ignacio Ortiz de Salinas
1821	José Ignacio Ansorena y Foncerrada
1821	Juan José Flores Alatorre
1821	Octaviano Obregón
1821	Angel Pinilla y Pérez

Fiscales

May 18, 1568	Bernardino Morante
1571	Vásquez
1575–1578	Alonso Martínez
June 25, 1578	Miguel de Pinedo
February 1, 1606	Gaspar de Chaves y Sotomayor

May 26, 1618	Juan de Castro
June 8, 1626	Damián Gentil de Parraga
August 17, 1629	Andrés Pardo de Lago
December 30, 1632	Pedro Lezcano de Contreras
March 23, 1637	Gerónimo de Alzate
December 25, 1652	Juan Cesati del Castelo
September 25, 1663	Gerónimo de Luna
July 10, 1669	Fernando de Haro y Monterroso
December 4, 1672	Agustín Félix Maldonado de Salazar
June 10, 1675	Diego de Acosta y Cabrera
October 11, 1678	Pedro de Barreda
August 15, 1681	Luis Martínez Hidalgo
1695	José de Miranda Villagrán
1705	Juan Picado Pacheco y Montero
1721	Fernando Dávila Madrid
1739	Agustín Jimenez Caro
1742	Juan Aparicio del Manzano
1754	Miguel José de Rojas Almansa
1763	Domingo de Armangoyti
1774	Francisco Ignacio González Maldonado
1777	Manuel de Martín Merino
1779	Antonio López Quintana
1786	Francisco Xavier Borbón y Torrijos
1792	Ignacio Ponce de León y Maroto
1795	Diego Miguel de Moya y Colón
1798	Juan Ignacio Fernández Munilla
1799	Manuel Aguado y Oquendo
1809	Vicente Alonso de Andrade
1813	Miguel López de Andreu
1821	Ignacio María Olloquí Sánchez Hidalgo

LAS CALIFORNIAS: GOBERNADORES

November 1767–July 1770	Gaspar de Portolá (Alta and Baja California)
June 1769–November 1770	Matías de Armona (Diego González, Juan Gutiérrez, Antonio López de Toledo, and Bernardino Moreno substituted)
March 1770–March 1775	Felipe de Barri (at Loreto)
March 1775–July 1782	Felipe de Neve (at Loreto and Monterrey; the teniente gobernador now in Loreto)
July 1782–April 1791	Pedro Fages
April 1791–April 1792	José Antonio Romeu
April 1792–May 1794	José Joaquín de Arillaga (interino)
May 1794–March 1800	Diego de Borica
March 1800–November 1804	José Joaquín de Arillaga (interino)

Baja California: Gobernadores

1804–1813	Felipe de Goycochea
1818–1821	José Darío Argüello
1822–1825	José Manuel Ruíz
1825–1826	José María Padrés (diputado)
1825–1829	José María de Echandía
1826–1829	Miguel Mesa (diputado)
1829–1830	Manuel Victoria

1830–1831	Mariano Monterde
1831–1833	The Territorial Deputation by Rotation
1833–1834	Mariano Monterde
1834–1835	The Territorial Deputation (interino)
1835	Miguel Martínez
1836	Miguel Conseco
1837	Fernando de la Toba
1837–1842	Luis del Castillo Negrete
1842	Francisco Padilla
1846	Coronel Francisco Palacio Miranda
1847	Mauricio Castro
1847	Manuel Pineda
1848–1849	Nicolás Lastra
1849	Coronel Rafael Espinosa
1853–1854	Coronel Juan Clímaco Rebolledo

Alta California: Gobernadores

November 1804–July 1814	José Joaquín de Arillaga
July 1814–August 1815	José Darío Argüello (interino)
August 1815–November 1822	Pablo Vicente de Solá
November 1822–November 1825	Luis Argüello
November 1825–January 1831	José María de Echeandía
January 1831–December 1831	Manuel Victoria
December 1831–January 1833	José María de Echeandía (in the south) (January-February, 1832, Pío Pico interino)
February 1832–January 1833	Agustín Vicente Zamorano (in the north)
January 1833–September 1835	José Figueroa
September 1835–January 1836	José Castro (interino)
January 1836–May 1836	Nicolás Gutiérrez (interino)
May 1836–August 1836	Mariano Chico (interino)
August 1836–November 1836	Nicolás Gutiérrez
November 1836–December 1836	José Castro
December 1836–December 1842	Juan B. Alvarado (as revolutionary governor from December 1836 to July 1837 and constitutional governor from July 1837 to December 1842)
December 1842–February 1845	Manuel Micheltorena
February 1845–August 1846	Pío Pico
October 1846–January 1847	José María Flores
January 1847	Andrés Pico

CALIFORNIA: AMERICAN GOVERNORS UNDER MILITARY RULE

July 1846	Commodore John D. Sloat
July 1846	Commodore Robert F. Stockton
January 1847–March 1847	Captain John C. Frémont
March 1847–May 1847	General Stephen Watts Kearny
May 1847–February 1849	Colonel Richard B. Mason
February 1849–April 1849	General Persifor F. Smith
April 1849–December 1849	General Bennett Riley

STATE OF CALIFORNIA: GOVERNORS

December 1849–January 1851	Peter H. Burnett
January 1851–January 1852	John McDougal

CHIHUAHUA

Provincia de Chihuahua: Jefes Políticos

August 1823	Mariano Orcasitas
November 1823	Coronel José de Urquidi
April 1824	Simón de Ochoa
May 1824	Coronel José de Urquidi

Estado de Chihuahua: Gobernadores

September 1824	Coronel José de Urquidi
September 1825	Teniente Coronel José Antonio Arce
November 1825	Coronel José de Urquidi
February 1826	Teniente Coronel José Antonio Arce
September 1826	Coronel Simón Elías González
November 1826	Teniente Coronel José Antonio Arce
March 1827	Licenciado José Antonio Ruiz de Bustamante
October 1827	Coronel Simón Elías González
January 1828	Teniente Coronel José Antonio Arce
June 1830	José Andrés Luján
June 1830	Teniente Coronel José Antonio Arce
August 1830	José Isidro Madero
May 1833	Licenciado José Rafael Revilla
July 1833	José Isidro Madero
November 1833	Licenciado José Rafael Revilla
December 1833	José María Sánchez Pareja
February 1834	José Isidro Madero
August 1834	Coronel Simón Elías González
September 1834	Coronel José Joaquín Calvo
June 1835	Licenciado José María Echavarría
August 1835	General José Joaquín Calvo
October 1835	General José Joaquín Calvo
August 1836	Licenciado José M. Bear
August 1836	General José Joaquín Calvo
April 1837	Coronel Simón Elías González
July 1838	Bernardo Revilla
July 1838	Coronel Simón Elías González
October 1838	Mariano Orcasitas
October 1838	Bernardo Revilla
January 1839	José María de Irigoyen
January 1839	Coronel Simón Elías González
April 1839	Licenciado José María Irigoyen de la O.
April 1839	Coronel Simón Elías González
May 1839	Licenciado José María Irigoyen de la O.
May 1840	Pedro Olivares
July 1840	General Francisco García Conde
September 1842	Coronel Mariano Martínez

October 1842	General Francisco García Conde
December 1842	General José Mariano Monterde
June 1843	Coronel Mariano Martínez
August 1843	General José Mariano Monterde
January 1845	Luis Zuloaga
June 1845	Joaquín de Bustamante
June 1845	Pedro Olivares
August 1845	General Angel Trías
January 1846	Coronel Mauricio Ugarte
February 1846	Coronel Cayetano Justiniani
May 1846	José María de Irigoyen
September 1846	General Angel Trías
February 1847	Licenciado Laureano Muñoz
February 1847	General Angel Trías
February 1847	Licenciado Laureano Muñoz
American Invasion:	
March–April 1847	Coronel Alexander Doniphan
April 1847	José María Sánchez Pareja
May 1847	Licenciado Laureano Muñoz
September 1847	General Angel Trías
March 1848	Licenciado Laureano Muñoz
May 1848	General Angel Trías
September 1848	Licenciado Laureano Muñoz
March 1849	General Angel Trías
November 1850	Licenciado Juan N. de Uriquidi

COAHUILA: GOBERNADORES

November 1674–October 1676	Coronel Antonio Balcarcel Rivadeneira y Sotomayor
October 1687–March 1691	General Alonso de León
March 1691–June 1698	Diego Ramón
June 1698–May 1703	Francisco Cuerbo y Valdés
May 1703–June 1705	General Matías de Aguirre
June 1705–January 1708	Sargento Mayor Martín de Alarcón
January 1708–January 1714	General Simón de Padilla y Córdova
January 1714–July 1714	General Pedro Fermín de Echeveres y Subiza
July 1714–August 1716	Juan de Valdés
August 1716–August 1717	Joseph Antonio de Ecay Múzquiz
August 1717–November 1719	General Martín de Alarcón (interino)
November 1719–October 1722	Joseph Azlor y Virto de Vera
October 1722–February 1723	Juan de Valdés
February 1723–February 1729	Blas de la Garza Falcón
February 1729–September 1733	Manuel de Sandoval
September 1733–December 1735	Blas de la Garza Falcón
1735–December 1739	Clemente de la Garza Falcón
1739	Luis García de Pruneda (never took office)
December 1739–August 1744	General Juan García de Pruneda
August 1744–June 1754	Pedro de Rábago y Terán
June 1754–February 1756	Manuel Antonio Bustillos y Caballos
February 1756–November 1757	Miguel de Sesman y Escudero
November 1757–February 1759	Angel Martos y Navarrate
February 1759–September 1762	Jacinto de Barrios y Jáuregui

September 1762–June 1764	Lorenzo Cancio Sierra y Cienfuegos (interino)
June 1764–December 1765	Coronel Diego Ortíz Parrilla
1765, 1768, 1769	Teniente Francisco Flores (as substitute, various times)
December 1765–February 1768	Jacinto de Barrios y Jáuregui
February 1768–December 1769	José Costilla y Terán
December 1769–November 1777	Jacobo de Ugarte y Loyola
November 1777–April 1783	Coronel Juan de Ugalde (José de Castillo y Terán and Francisco Javier Barrera filled in in 1778 and 1779, respectively)
April 1783–October 1788	General Pedro Fueros
October 1788–March 1790	Juan Gutiérrez de la Cueva (interino)
March 1790–October 1795	Miguel José de Emparán
July 1791–June 1793 and October 1795–March 1797	Juan Gutiérrez de la Cueva (interino)
March 1797–January 1811	Coronel Antonio Cordero y Bustamante
January–April 1811	Simón de Herrera
April 1811–1817, 1805–1810 as governor of Texas	Coronel Antonio Cordero y Bustamante (while in Texas, Juan Ignacio de Arizpe, August 1805–July 1807, and José Joaquín de Ugarte, July 1807–August 1807, substituted)
January–March 1811	Pedro Aranda
March 1811	General Ignacio López Rayón
1817–March 1818	Antonio García de Texada (substituted for Cordero y Bustamante)
March 1818–July 1819	Teniente Coronel Manuel Pardo
July 1819–November 1820	Coronel José Franco
November 1820–March 1822	Coronel Antonio Elosúa
July 1821–March 1823	Coronel Gaspar Antonio López (Comandante de las Provincias Internas (de Oriente)
March–August 1823	Antonio Crespo (como Presidente de la Junta Gubernativa)
August 1823–February 1824	Pedro Valdés (como alcalde del Ayuntamiento de Monclova)
February–August 1824	Licienciado Rafael Ecay Múzquiz (como presidente de la Diputación Provincia)
August 1824–March 1826	Teniente Coronel Rafael González
March–May 1826	José Ignacio de Arizpe
May 1826–January 1827	Victór Blanco
January–August 1827	José Ignacio de Arizpe
August 1827	José María Viesca (interino)
August–September 1827	Victór Blanco
September 1827–October 1830	José María Viesca
October 1830–January 1831	Licenciado Rafael Ecay Múzquiz
January–April 1831	José María Viesca
April 1831	Licenciado José María de Letona
April–May 1831	Licenciado Rafael Ecay Múzquiz
May 1831–September 1832	Licenciado José María de Letona
September 1832–January 1833	Licenciado Rafael Ecay Múzquiz
January 1833–January 1834	Juan Martín de Beramendi
January–July 1834	Francisco Vidaurri y Villaseñor
July 1834–March 1835	Juan José Elquézabal
March 1835	José María Cantú

March–April 1835	Marcial Borrego
April–June 1835	Agustín Viesca y Montes
July–August 1835	Miguel Falcón
August 1835	Bartolomé de Cárdenas
August 1835–March 1837	Licenciado Rafael Ecay Múzquiz
March 1837–April 1839	General Francisco García Conde
April 1839–January 1841	General Isidro Reyes
January 1841–January 1842	Ignacio de Arizpe
January 1842–March 1843	General Francisco Mejía (interino)
March–April 1843	José Juan Sánchez
April 1843–May 1844	General Antonio Vizcaíno
May 1844–January 1845	General Francisco Mejía (Constitucional)
January 1845–January 1846	Licenciado Santiago Rodríguez
February 1846–October 1846	Licenciado José María Aguirre
October 1846	Licenciado Santiago Rodríguez
October 1846–June 1847	Licenciado José María Aguirre
June 1847–February 1849	Eduardo González
March 1849–September 1850	Licenciado Santiago Rodríguez
September 1850	Licenciado Juan Vicente Campos
September–October 1850	Licenciado José María Aguirre
October 1850–September 1851	Licenciado Rafael de la Fuente
September 1851–February 1856	Licenciado Santiago Rodríguez

NUEVO MEXICO: Gobernadores

Spain

1598–1608	Juan de Oñate y Salazar
1608–1610	Cristóbal de Oñate
1610–1614	Pedro de Peralta
1614–1618	Bernardino de Ceballos
1618–1625	Juan de Eulate
1625–1629	Phelipe Sotelo Ossorio
1629–1632	Francisco Manuel de Silva Nieto
1632–1635	Francisco de la Mora y Ceballos
1635–1637	Francisco Martínez de Baeza
1637–1641	Luis de Rosas
1641	Juan Flores de Sierra y Valdés
1641–1642	Francisco Gómez
1642–1644	Alonso Pacheco de Heredia
1644–1647	Fernando de Argüello Caravajal
1647–1649	Luis de Guzmán y Figueroa
1649–1653	Hernando de Ugarte y la Concha
1653–1656	Juan de Samaniego y Xaca
1656–1659	Juan Mansso de Contreras
1659–1661	Bernardo López de Mendizábal
1661–1664	Diego Dionisio de Peñalosa Briceño y Berdugo
1664–1665	Juan Durán de Miranda
1665–1668	Fernando de Villanueva
1668–1671	Juan de Medrano y Mesía
1671–1675	Juan Durán de Miranda
1675–1677	Juan Francisco de Treviño
1677–1683	Antonio de Otermín
1683–1686	Domingo Jironza Pétriz de Cruzate
1686–1689	Pedro Reneros de Posada

1689–1691	Domingo Jironza Pétriz de Cruzate
1691–1697	Diego de Vargas Zapata Luján Ponce de León
1697–1703	Pedro Rodríguez Cubero
1703–1704	Diego de Vargas Zapata Luján Ponce de León
1704–1705	Juan Páez Hurtado
1705–1707	Francisco Cuervo y Valdés
1707–1712	Joseph Chacón Medina Salazar y Villaseñor
1712–1715	Juan Ignacio Flores Mogollón
1715–1717	Félix Martínez
1717	Juan Páez Hurtado
1717–1722	Antonio Valverde y Cossio
1722–1731	Juan Domingo de Bustamante
1731–1736	Gervasio Cruzat y Góngora
1736–1739	Henrique de Olavide y Micheleña
1739–1743	Gaspar Domingo de Mendoza
1743–1749	Joachín Codallos y Rabál
1749–1754	Tomás Veles Cachupín
1754–1760	Francisco Antonio Marín del Valle
1760	Mateo Antonio de Mendoza
1760–1762	Manuel del Portillo y Urrisola
1762–1767	Tomás Veles Cachupín
1767–1778	Pedro Fermín de Mendinueta
1778	Francisco Treból Navarro
1778–1788	Juan Bautista de Anza
1788–1794	Fernando de la Concha
1794–1805	Fernando Chacón
1805–1808	Joaquín del Real Alencaster
1808	Alberto Maynez
1808–1814	José Manrique
1814–1816	Alberto Maynez
1816–1818	Pedro María de Allande
1818–1822	Facundo Melgares

Mexico

1822	Francisco Xavier Cháves
1822–1823	José Antonio Viscarra
1823–1825	Bartolomé Baca
1825–1827	Antonio Narbona
1827–1829	Manuel Armijo
1829–1832	José Antonio Cháves
1832–1833	Santiago Abreú
1833–1835	Francisco Sarracino
1835–1837	Albino Pérez
1837–1844	Manuel Armijo
1844	Mariano Chávez
1844	Felipe Sena
1844–1845	Mariano Martínez de Lejanza
1845	José Chávez y Castillo
1845–1846	Manuel Armijo
1846	Juan Bautista Vigil y Alaríd

United States

1846	General Stephen Watts Kearny
1846–1848	Colonel Sterling Price
1846–1847	Charles Bent

1848	Donaciano Vigil
1848–1849	Colonel J.M. Washington
1849	Colonel John Munroe
1851–1852	James S. Calhoun

NUEVO LEON: GOBERNADORES

1582	Luis de Carvajal y de la Cueva
1585–1586	Diego de Montemayor, El Viejo
1610	Diego de Montemayor, El Mozo
1611–1615	Agustín de Zavala
1615	Cristóbal Curzueta e Iturreta
1615–1624	Diego Rodríguez
1624	Alonzo Lucas, El Bueno
1626	Martín de Zavala
1664	Cabildo Metropolitano
1665	General León de Arza
1667	Nicolás de Azcárraga y Montero
1676	Diego Pruñeda
1681	Domingo Videgaray y Zarza
1681	Juan de Echevarría
1683	Capitán Alonzo de León
1684	Agustín de Echéverz y Subízar
1687	Francisco Cuervo de Valdés
1688	Pedro Fernández de Ventosa
1693	Juan Pérez de Merino
1698	Francisco de Vergara y Mendoza
1703	Francisco Báez Treviño
1705	Gregorio Salinas de Verona
1707	Cipriano García de Pruneda
1708	Luis García de Pruneda
1710	Francisco de Mier y de la Torre
1714	Francisco Báez Treviño
1718	General Juan Flores Mogollón
1719	Licenciado Francisco Barbadillo y Victoria
1723	Juan José de Arriaga y Brambila
1725	Pedro de Sarabia y Cortés
1730	Pedro de la Barrera e Ebra
1730	Fernando Meneses Monroy y Mendoza
1731	José Antonio Fernández de Jáuregui y Urrutia
1740	Pedro Elizondo
1740–1746	Pedro del Barrío Junco y Espriella
1746–1752	Vicente Bueno de la Barbolla
1752	Pedro del Barrío Junco y Espriella
1757	Domingo Miguel Guajardo
1759	Juan Manuel Muñoz de Villavicencio
1762	Carlos Velasco
1764	Ignacio Wessel y Guimbarda
1772	Francisco Echegaray
1773	Melchor Vidal Llorca y Villena
1781	Vicente González de Santianes
1785	Joaquín de Mier y Noriega
1787	Manual Balamonde y Villamil
1795	Sargento Mayor Simón Herrera y Leyva

1805	Pedro Herrera y Leyva
1810	Manuel de Santa María
1811	Bernardo Wessel y Guimbarda
1811	José Santiago Villarreal
1811	Junta Gobernadora
1813	Ramón Díaz de Bustamante
1813	Pedro Manuel del Llano y Fernando Uribe
1814	Froylán Mier y Noriega
1815	Francisco Bruno de Barrera
1817	Bernardo Villarreal
1818	Francisco Bruno de Barrera
1821	Joaquín Arredondo y Mioño
1823	Rafael González Echandia y Eusebio Gutiérrez
1823	Francisco de Paula Mier y Moriega
1824	José Antonio Rodríquez
1825	José María Paras
1827	Manuel Gómez de Castro
1827	Joaquín García
1833	Manuel Gómez de Castro
1833	Manuel María del Llano
1833	Lumus y Garza Evia
1835	Juan Nepomuceno de la Garza
1836	Manuel Gómez de Castro
1836	Domingo Martínez y Gómez y Castro
1837	Joaquín García
1839	Ortega
1845	Juan Nepomuceno de la Garza
1846	Licenciado Francisco de Paula Morales Mier
1848	José María Paras
1851	Pedro José García
1851	Agapito García

NUEVA VIZCAYA

Gobernadores. 1562–1819

1562–1575	Francisco de Ibarra
1563–1564	Alonso Pacheco
1564–1565	Bartolomé de Arriola
1565–1580	Martín López de Ibarra
1575–1576	Hernando de Trejo
1576	Diego de Ibarra
1580–1583	Hernando de Trejo
1582	Alonzo Díaz
1583–1585	Hernando (Fernando) de Bazán
1586	Alonso Zúñiga
1586–1589	Antonio de Monroy
1589	Alonzo Díaz
1589–1595	Rodrigo del Río Loza y Gordijuelo
1595–1598	Diego Fernández de Velasco
1598–1600	Jaime Hernández de Arriaga (Arrillaga)
1600–1603	Rodrigo de Vivero
1603–1613	Francisco de Urdiñola
1613–1618	Gaspar de Alvear y Salazar
1618–1625	Almirante Mateo de Vezga

1618–1620	José de Rivera y Solórzano
1620	Martín de Agüero
1625–1630	Hipólito de Velasco
1629	Gabriel de Egurrola
1630	Gaspar Mendoza de Quezada Hurtado
1630–1631	Luis de Velasco
1631	Bartolomé Salvago y Ahumada
1630–1633	Gonzalo Gómez de Cervantes
1633–1638	Luis de Monsalve y Saavedra
1638	Gaspar Mendoza de Quezada Hurtado
1639–1640	Francisco Montaño de la Cueva
1640	Luis de Valdés
1640–1642	Francisco Bravo de la Serna
1640–1642	Fernando Souza de Suárez
1642–1648	Luis de Valdés
1648–1653	Diego Guajardo Fajardo
1653–1660	Enrique Dávila y Pacheco
1660–1666	Francisco de Gorráez y Beaumont
1666–1670	Antonio de Oca y Sarmiento
1670	Nicolás de Medina
1670–1671	Bartolomé de Estrada y Ramírez
1671–1674	José García de Salcedo
1674–1676	Martín de Rebollar y Cueva
1677–1678	Lope de Sierra y Osorio
1678–1679	Francisco de Agramont y Arce
1679–1684	Bartolomé de Estrada y Ramírez
1684–1688	Gabriel José de Neyra y Quiroga
1688–1693	Juan Isidro de Pardiñas
1693–1698	Gabriel del Castillo
1698–1704	Juan Bautista de Larrea y la Puente
1704	Luis Ruiz de Guadiana
1704–1708	Juan Fernández de Córdoba
1708–1712	Antonio de Deza y Ulloa
1712–1714	Juan Felipe de Orozco y Molina
1714–1720	Manuel San Juan y Santa Cruz
1720–1723	Martín de Alday
1723–1727	José Sebastián López Carbajal
1728–1733	Ignacio Francisco de Barrutia
1733–1738	Juan José Vértez y Ontañón
1738	Manuel de Uranga
October 1738	Juan Bautista de Balaunzarán
December 1742	Manuel de Laguizábal
December 1742	Antonio Gutiérrez de Noriega
July 1743	José Enrique Cosío y Campo (Marqués de Torre Campo)
January 1746	José Velarde Cosío (interino)
April 1746	José Enrique Cosío y Campo (Marqués de Torre Campo)
October 1748	Juan Francisco de la Puerta y Barrera
May 1752	Alonso de Gastesí
May 1754	Mateo Antonio de Mendoza
April 1761	José Carlos de Agiiero (Agüero)
October 1762	José de Larrea y Campo
1767	Lope de Cuéllar
1768	Juan Carlos de Agüero
May 1768	José de Fayni (Manuel de Ureta y San Juan and Manuel Antonio de Escárcega substituted frequently)

1776	Felipe de Barri
July 1778	Felipe de Yarto
May 1784	Juan Velázquez
September 1785	Manuel Muñoz
October 1785	Manuel Flon
February 1786	José de Jandiola
April 1786	Felipe Díaz de Ortega
March 1790	Pedro Plo y Alduán
May 1791	José de Barcena
January 1792	Francisco Javier Potau y Portugal
March 1794	Francisco Javier de Urrutia
March 1796	Bernardo Bonavía y Zapata
1799	Manuel Pérez Valdéz
April 1809	Angel Pinilla y Pérez
April 1814	Francisco de Espejo
April 1814	Juan José Zambrano
April 1814	Alejo García Conde
July 1818	Antonio Cordero
March 1819	Diego García Conde

Comandantes Generales (Provincias Internas), 1777–1820

1777	Coronel José Robles
August 1783	Brigadier al General Felipe Neve
August 1784	Coronel José Antonio Rengel
May 1786	Brigadier Jacobo de Ugarte y Loyola
March 1787	Coronel Juan de Ugalde
September 1788	Coronel Antonio Cordero
December 1788	Mariscal Pedro de Nava, and Coronel Ramón de Castro
November 1802	General Nemesio Salcedo
March 1813	Brigadier Joaquín de Arrendondo, and Mariscal Bernardo Bonavía y Zapata

Jefes Superiores Políticos Militares, 1820–1823

August 1821	Alejo García Conde
September 1821	Francisco Javier Trujillo
September 1821	Mariano de Urrea
July 1822	Juan Navarro del Rey
August 1822	Ignacio del Corral
March 1823	Mariano Herrera
July 1823	Luis de Uturribarría

NUEVA VIZCAYA (DURANGO) INTENDENTES

April 1786–January 1792	Felipe Díaz de Ortega
January 1792–July 1793	Francisco Javier Potau de Portugal
July 1793–March 1796	Francisco José Urrutia
March 1796–July 1813	Bernardo Bonavía y Zapata (April 1809–September 1810, Angél Pinilla y Pérez as interim)
February 1814–	
April 1814	Juan José Zambrano
April 1814–May 1814	Francisco de Espejo

May 1814–	
November 1817	Alejo García Conde
July 1818–March 1819	Antonio Cordero
March 1819–	
September 1821	Diego García Conde

OSTIMURI

Justicias Mayores

1676	Antonio Carrillo	1684	Pedro Martínez Mendívil
1678	Simón Francisco de la Herrán y Velasco	1685	Agustín García de Illescas
1680	Pedro Martínez Mendívil	1686	Francisco de Iglesias
1682	Agustín García de Illescas	1688	Juan Francisco de Gayeneche

Alcaldes Mayores

1691	Marcos Fernández de Castañeda	1714	Andrés de Búcar Fajardo
1694	Gabriel de Lizarralde	1718	Blas Gutiérrez de la Meza
1696	Augustín García de Illescas	1720	José de Ochoa y Larrea
1697	José de Zubiate	1723	Domingo Romero y Fuertes
1701	Juan Andrés de Egurrola	1724	José de Ulloa
1704	Felipe de Bustamante	1725	Francisco Vásquez y Samaniego
1705	Pedro Martínez Mendívil	1727	Francisco Javier Valenzuela
1706	Felipe de Bustamante	1728	Miguel de Lucenilla
1707	Blas de Esquér	1730	Ildefonso Pomar y Burgos
1710	Domingo Romero y Fuertes	1731–1733	Juan Antonio del Rey
1712	Ignacio Morsillo		

SINALOA

Alcaldes Mayores

1563	Pedro Ochoa de Lárraga	1632	Francisco Enríquez Pimental
1583	Pedro de Montoya	1634	Andrés de Cárdenas
1584	Juan López Quijada	1635	Alonso Contreras
1585	Melchor de Téllez	1636	Bernabé Pérez de Lugo
1586	Pedro de Tovar	1636	Francisco de Bustamante
1587	Bartolomé de Mondragón	1637	Luis Cestín de Cañas
1594	Miguel Ortiz Maldonado	1641	Diego Bergonza y Preciado
1596	Alonso Díaz	1645	Juan de Peralta
1600	Diego Martínez de Hurdaide	1646	Pedro Portel y Casanate
1626	Pedro de Perea	1648	Alonso Ramírez de Prado
1630	Francisco Enríquez Pimental	1649	Diego de Alarcón Fajardo
1631	Leonardo de Argüello	1651	Gaspar Quezada y Hurtado de Mendoza

Capitanes Vitalicios del Presidio de Sinaloa

1660	Capitán Juan de Salazar	1687	Diego de Quirós
1665	Miguel de Calderón	1692	Manuel de Agramont y Arce
1671	Mateo de Castro	1696	General Andrés de Rezábal
1680	Alonso Hurtado de Castilla	1723	General Manuel Bernal de Huidobro
1682–1686	Isidro de Atondo y Antillón		

Gobernadores

March 14, 1831–June 13, 1831	Francisco Iriarte
March 14, 1831–June 18, 1831	Agustín Martínez de Castro
June 18, 1831–June 20, 1832	Fernando Escudero
July 20, 1832–March 24, 1834	Manuel María Bandera
March 24, 1834–July 7, 1834	José Palao, Manuel de la Herrán y Agustín Martínez de Castro
July 7, 1834–August 2, 1834	José Felipe Gómez
August 2, 1834–November 20, 1834	José Antonio Jorganes
November 20, 1834–January 22, 1835	José Blas de Guevara
January 22, 1835–October 26, 1835	Manuel María de la Vega y Rabago
September 28, 1836–June 3, 1837	Pedro Sánchez
June 3, 1837–1838	José Francisco Orrantia y Antelo
June 18, 1838–1842	Luís Martínez de Vea
September 7, 1843–December 19, 1843	General Francisco Ponce de León
December 19, 1843–March 6, 1844	General Juan J. Andrade
March 6, 1844–May 7, 1844	General Francisco Ponce de León
May 7, 1844–May 15, 1844	General José Antonio Mozo
May 15, 1844–June 8, 1844	Agustín Martínez de Castro
June 8, 1844–October 30, 1844	General José Antonio Mozo
October 20, 1844–November 7, 1844	Coronel José Ruíz de Tejeda
November 7, 1844–November 9, 1844	Teniente Coronel Juan Ignacio Brambila
November 9, 1844–December 1, 1844	Agustín Martínez de Castro
December 1, 1844–April 24, 1845	General Francisco Duque
April 24, 1845–January 22, 1846	Rafael de la Vega
January 22, 1846–February 5, 1846	Teniente Coronel Angel Miramón
February 5, 1846–February 5, 1846	Pomposo Verdugo
February 6, 1846–February 12, 1846	Teniente Coronel Angel Miramón
February 12, 1846–March 1, 1846	Rafael de la Vega
March 1, 1846–May 11, 1846	Agustín Martínez de Castro
May 11, 1846–July 13, 1846	Rafael de la Vega
July 13, 1846–August 6, 1846	Pomposo Verdugo
August 6, 1846–September 5, 1846	Rafael de la Vega
September 5, 1846–November 21, 1846	Licenciado Gumersindo Laija
November 21, 1846–July 1, 1847	Rafael de la Vega
June 1, 1847–July 2, 1847	Coronel Rafael Téllez
June 2, 1847–February 29, 1848	Rafael de la Vega
February 20, 1847–March 1, 1848	José Esquerro
March 1, 1848–April 2, 1848	José María Visavilbaso
April 2, 1848–May 7, 1848	José Rojo y Eseverri
May 7, 1848–January 9, 1851	Pomposo Verdugo
January 9, 1851–July 19, 1851	Licenciado José María Gaxiola

SONORA-SINALOA: GOBERNADORES

In 1734 Sonora and Sinaloa became a separate unit, detached from Nueva Vizcaya.

1732–1741	Manuel Bernal de Huidobro
1737 and 1740	Miguel Nicolás de Mena
1741–1748	Agustín de Vildósola
1748–1749	José Rafael Rodríguez Gallardo
June 1749–1753	Diego Ortíz Parrilla

January 1753–1755	Pablo de Arce y Arroyo
1755	Juan Antonio de Mendoza
November 27, 1760	Bernardo de Urrea
June 10, 1761–1762	José Tienda de Cuervo
December 9, 1762	Bernardo de Urrea
May 28, 1763–1770	Juan Claudio Pineda
July 18, 1770	Pedro Corbalán
January 20, 1772	Mateo Sastré
March 15, 1773	Manuel de la Azuela
May 1773	Bernardo de Urrea
August 1773	Francisco Antonio Crespo
February 21, 1777	Pedro Corbalán
October 30, 1787	Pedro Garrido y Durán
June 6, 1789	Agustín de la Cuenta y Zaejas
1790	Enrique Grimarest
1793	Alonso Tresierra y Cano
November 1796	Alejo García Conde
October 1, 1813	Ignacio Bustamante
November 1813	Alonso Tresierra y Cano
May 1814	Antonio Cordero
1817	Esteban Echeagaráy
January 1818	Ignacio Bustamante
August 1, 1818	Manuel Fernando Rojo
December 1818	Ignacio Bustamante
June 27, 1819	Juan José Lombán
October 1819	Antonio Cordero
September 7, 1821	Ignacio Bustamante
July 23, 1822	Antonio Narbona
March 1823	Rafael Morales
June 1823	Antonio Narbona
July 31, 1823	Mariano de Urrea
September 12, 1824	Juan Miguel Riesgo
October 7, 1824	Francisco Iriarte
April 27, 1825	Simón Elías Gonzáles
October 25, 1825	Nicolás M. Gaxiola
February 3, 1826	Simón Elías Gonzáles
August 28, 1826	Nicolás M. Gaxiola
November 25, 1826	Francisco Iriarte, briefly substituted for Francisco Orrantia
November 29, 1827	José María Gaxiola
August 1828	José María Almada
September 30, 1828	José María Gaxiola
August 29, 1829	José María Almada
October 22, 1829	Francisco Iriarte
April 1, 1830	Leonardo Escalante
April 14, 1830	Francisco Escobosa
May 27, 1830–March 15, 1831	Leonardo Escalante

SONORA-SINALOA (ARIZPE): INTENDENTES

July 1770–October 1787	Pedro de Corbalán, as intendente of Sonora and gobernador of the province of Sonora y Sinaloa
October 1787–June 1789	Licenciado Pedro Garrido y Durán (gobernador-intendente)

1787–1789	Agustín de las Cuentas Zayas, intendente of Sinaloa
June 1789–November 1793	Enrique Grimarest, gobernador-intendente of Sonora y Sinaloa
November 1793–1796	Alsonso Tresierra y Cano
August 1796–October 1813	Alejo García Conde
October 1813–November 1813	Ignacio Bustamante
November 1813–May 1814	Alonso Tresierra y Cano
May 1814–1817	Antonio Cordero
1817–January 1818	Esteban Echeagaráy
January 1818–August 1818	Ignacio Bustamante
August 1818–December 1818	Licenciado Manuel Fernández Rojo
December 1818–June 1819	Ignacio Bustamante
June 1819–October 1819	Teniente Coronel Juan José Lombán
October 1819–September 1821	Antonio Cordero
September 1821–July 1822	Coronel Antonio Narbona

SONORA

Alcaldes Mayores

1637	Pedro de Perea		Domingo Martínez de Arenal,
1644	Francisco Granillo Salazar		Juan de Encinas
1645	Juan de Peralta	1679	Gaspar Fernández de la Concha
1648	Simón Lazo de la Vega	1680	Lázaro de Verdugo y Chávez
1650	Juan Fernández Morales	1681	Francisco Cuervo y Valdez,
1651	Diego de Lara y Trujillo		Antonio de Chacón
1652	Juan Munguía Villela	1684	Antonio Barba y Figueroa
1654	Andrés Pérez de Lara	1686	Francisco Pacheco Cevallos
1656	Francisco de Coto	1688	Blas del Castillo
1658	García de Castro y Vela	1689	Lázaro de Verdugo y Chávez
1660	Francisco de Coto	1690	Melchor Ruiz
April 1661	Francisco de la Rocha	1692	Isidro Ruiz de Avechuco
September 1661	Matías de Cerralvo	1693	Domingo Jironza Petris de Cruzat
1663	Matías de Pereyra y Lobo	1698	Isidro Ruiz de Avechuco
1664	Pedro Francisco de Sartillón	1701	Juan Mateo Manje
1665	Andrés Montemayor	1703	Miguel de Abajo
1665	Andrés de Almagro	1706	Manuel de Hugues y San Martín
1666	Pedro Francisco de Sartillón	1708	Juan Francisco de Bustamante
1667	García de Castro y Vela,	1711	Pedro Téllez de Carbajal
	Francisco Fuentes y Sierra,	1712	Gregorio Alvarez Tuñón Quirós
	Francisco Alvarez Lavandera	1713	Luis Antonio Cevallos Ortega
1668	Juan Martín Bernal,	1714	Francisco Pacheco Cevallos
	Carlos Gago de Mendoza,	1715	José de Aguirre
	Melchor de la Peña	1717	Manuel de Hugues y San Martín
1669	Pedro Manzo y Valdez	1719	Gregorio Alvarez Tuñón Quirós
1670	Pedro Alvarez Castillón	1720	Rafael Pacheco Cevallos,
1672	Gregorio López Dicastillo		José Joaquín Rivera,
1673	Domingo del Hoyo Santillana		Francisco Pacheco Cevallos
1675	Alonso de Rascón y Sandoval,	1723	Antonio Díaz de Valdez
	Diego Gómez de Silva	1724	Miguel Alvarez Lavandera
1676	Juan Bautista de Escorza,	1725	José Garro
	Luis de Morales	1727–1733	Gabriel de Prudhom, Butrón y Mújica, Barón de Heijder
1677	Francisco Sigler de Rebollar		
1678	Francisco Fuertes de Sierra,		

Gobernadores

March 1831–May 1832	Leonardo Escalante y Mazón (teniente gobernador, Tomás Escalante y Corella, acted as governor for most of this term)
1832–1836	Manuel Escalante y Arvizu
1835–1838	Manuel Escalante y Arvizu (Rafael Elías González y Romo de Vivar served most of this term while Escalante y Arvizu became the chief military officer of the state)
1837–1842	Manuel María Gándara y Gortari, José Urrea, Rafael Elías González y Romo de Vivar, Leonardo Escalante y Mazón, José Lucas Pico y Encinas (At one time or another during this four year period, each of these men acted as governor, as the centralists and federalists fought for control of the state government.)
April 1842–June 1842	Pedro Bautista Aguaryo y Cázares
April 1842–April 1845	José Urrea
April 1845–June 1845	Francisco Andrade y Félix
June 1845–February 1846	José María Gaxiola
February 1846–January 1847	Fernando Cuesta
January 1847–May 1847	Luis Redondo
May 1847–February 1849	Manuel María Gándara y Gortari
February 1849–May 1849	Juan Bautista Gándara y Gortari
May 1849–November 1851	José de Aguilar y Escoboza
November 1851–January 1853	Fernando Cubillas Iñigo

TEXAS

Gobernadores

1717–1719	Martín de Alarcón
1719–1722	Marques de San Miguel de Aguayo
1722–1727	Fernando Pérez de Almazán
1727–1730	Melchor Media Villa y Ascona
1730–1734	Juan Bustillos Zevallos
1734–1736	Manuel de Sandoval
1736–1737	Carlos Benites Franquis de Lugo
1737–1741	Prudencio de Orobio Bazterra
1741–1743	Tomás Felipe Wintuisen
1743–1744	Justo Boneo y Morales
1744–1748	Francisco García Larios
1748–1751	Pedro del Barrío Junco y Espriella
1751–1759	Jacinto de Barrios y Jáuregui
1759–1766	Angel Martos y Navarrete
1767–1770	Hugo Oconór
1770–1778	Juan María de Ripperdá
1778–1786	Domingo Cabello
1786–1790	Rafael Martínez Pacheco
1790–1798	Manuel Muñoz
1798–1800	Josef Irigoyen
1800–1805	Juan Bautista de Elguezábal

1805–1808	Manuel Antonio Cordero y Bustamante
1808–1813	Manuel María de Salcedo
1813–1815	Cristóbal Domínguez
1815	Benito Armiñán and Mariano Varela (provisional)
1815–1817	Ignacio Pérez
1817	Manuel Pardo (provisional)
1817–1822	Antonio María Martínez
1822–1823	José Félix Trespalacios
1823	Luciano García

Gobernadores of Coahuila and Texas

1824–1826	Rafael González
1826	José Ignacio de Arizpe
1826–1827	Victor Blanco
1827	José Ignacio de Arizpe and Victor Blanco
1827–1831	José María Viesca
1831–1832	José María Letona
1832–1833	Rafael Eca y Músquiz
1833	Juan Martín de Veramendi
1833–1834	Francisco Vidaurri y Villaseñor

| 1834–1835 | Juan José Elguezábal |
| 1835 | Agustín Viesca, José María Falcón, and Rafael Eca y Músquiz |

Presidents of the Republic of Texas

1836	David G. Burnet
1836–1838	Sam Houston
1838–1841	Mirabeau Bonaparte Lamar
1841–1844	Sam Houston
1844–1846	Anson Jones

Governors of the State of Texas

1846–1847	J. Pinckney Henderson
1847–1849	George T. Wood
1849–1853	P. Hansborough Bell

BISHOPS

Durango

Founded 1620

1621	Gonzalo de Hermosillo
1632	Alonso Franco y Luna
1639	Francisco Diego de Hevía y Valdés
1655	Pedro de Barrientos Lomelín
1660	Juan de Gorozpe y Aguirre
1674	Juan de Ortega y Montáñez
1677	Bartolomé de Escañuela
1686	Manuel de Herrera
1689	García de Legazpi Velasco
1699	Manuel de Escalante Colombres y Mendoza
1705	Ignacio Díez de Berrera
1712	Pedro Tápiz
1723	Benito Crespo y Monroy
1736	Martín Elizacoechea
1749	Anselmo Pedro Sánchez de Tagle
1758	Pedro Tamarón y Romeral
1769	José Vicente Díaz Bravo
1773	Antonio Mascarayuca
1783	Esteban Lorenzo de Tristán
1794	José Joaquín Granados
1796	Francisco Gabriel de Olivares y Benito
1815	Juan Francisco Márquez de Castaniza
1831	José Antonio Laureani de Zurbiría

Guadalajara

Founded July 13, 1548

1547	Pedro Gómez Maraver
1562	Pedro de Ayala
1574	Francisco Gómez de Mendiola
1580	Juan de Trujillo
1583	Domingo de Alzola
1591	Alonso Fernández de Bonilla
1592	Francisco Santos García de Ontiveros

1597	Alonso de la Mota y Escobar
1607	Juan del Valle
1618	Francisco de Ribera
1630	Leonel de Cervantes Carvajal
1636	Juan Sánchez, Duque de Estrada
1646	Juan Ruíz Colmenero
1665	Francisco Verdín y Molina
1674	Manuel Fernández de Sahagún y Santacruz
1677	Juan de Santiago de León Garabito
1695	Felipe Galindo y Chávez
1706	Diego Camacho y Avila
1714	Manuel de Mimbela
1723	Juan Bautista Alvarez de Toledo
1727	Nicolás Carlos Gómez de Cervantes
1736	Juan Gómez de Parada
1751	Francisco Díez de Velasco
1762	Diego Rodríguez de Velasco
1771	Antonio de Alcalde
1794	Esteban Lorenzo de Tristán
1795	Juan Ruíz de Cabañas

México

Bishopric founded September 2, 1530
Archbishopric founded November 16, 1547

1527	Juan de Zumárraga
1551	Alonso de Montúfar
1573	Pedro Moya de Contreras
1592	Alonso Fernández de Bonilla
1600	García de Santamaría y Mendoza
1608	García de Guerra
1613	Juan Pérez de la Serna
1627	Francisco Manso de Zúñiga
1637	Francisco Verdugo
1639	Feliciano de Vega
1642	Juan de Palafox y Mendoza
1644	Juan de Mañosca y Zamora
1652	Marcelo López de Azcona
1656	Mateo Saga de Bugueiro
1662	Diego Osorio de Escobar y Llamas
1664	Alonso de Cuevas y Dávalos
1667	Marcos Ramírez de Prado
1668	Payo Enríquez de Rivera
1668	Juan de Aguirre
1680	Francisco de Aguilar y Seijas
1700	Juan de Ortega Montáñez
1711	José Lanziego y Equilaz
1728	Manuel Hendaya y Haro
1730	Juan Antonio de Vizarrón y Equiarreta
1748	Manuel Rubio y Salinas
1765	Francisco A. de Lorenzana
1771	Alonso Núñez de Haro y Peralta
1802	Francisco Javier de Lizana y Beaumont
1812	Antonio Bergesa y Jordan
1815	Pedro José Fonte
1840	Manuel Posada y Garduño

Monterrey/Linares

Founded 1777

1778	Antonio de Jesús Sacedón
1783	Rafael José Verger
1792	Andrés Ambrosio de Llanos y Valdez
1802	Primo Feliciano Marín de Porras
1818	Ignacio de Arancibia y Hormaegui
1831	José María de Jesús Belaúnzaran y Urena
1843	Salvador Apodaca y Loreto
1844	Ignacio Sánchez Navarro

Sonora

Founded May 1779

1780	Antonio de los Reyes
1788	José Joaquín Granados
1794	Damián Martínez Galisonga
1796	Francisco Rouset
1817	Bernardo del Espíritu Santo
1832	Angel Mariano Morales
1837	Lázaro de la Garza
1852	Pedro Loza

FRANCISCAN COMISARIOS GENERALES OF NUEVA ESPANA

1531	Alonso de Rojas
1533	Juan de Granada
1535	Francisco de Ossuna (never took office)
1535–1540	Juan de Granada (died in office)
1540–1542	Jacobo de Testera (died in office)
1542–1547	Martín Sarmiento de Hojacastro
1547–1553	Francisco de Bustamante
1553–1559	Francisco de Mena
1559–1561	vacant
1561–1563	Francisco de Bustamante
1563	Juan de San Miguel (never took office)
1563–1568	vacant
1568–1569	Diego de Olarte
1569–1572	Francisco de Rivera
1573–1574	Miguel Navarro
1575–1582	Rodrigo de Sequera (Zequera)
1582–1583	Pedro de Oroz
1584–1588	Alonso Ponce
1588–1593	Bernardino de San Cebrián
1593	Antonio Victoria (never took office)
1593	Pedro de Pila
1593–1599	Bernardino de San Cebrián
1599–1602	Diego Muñoz
1602–1603	Diego Caro (died in office)
1603–1604	Miguel López
1604–1610	Juan de la Cieza
1610–1612	Juan Zurita
1612–1617	Christóbal Ramírez
1617–1618	Juan López

1618–1622	Diego de Otalora
1622–1627	Alonso Montemayor
1627–1633	Francisco de Apodaca
1633–1640	Luis Flores
1640–1646	Juan de Prada
1646–1653	Buenaventura de Salinas
1653–1659	Juan de la Torre y Castro
1660–1667	Diego Zapata
1667–1671	Fernando de la Rúa
1671	Alonso Guerrero
1671–1677	Francisco Triviño
1677	Lucas de la Carrera (never took office)
1677–1682	Domingo de Noriega
1682–1688	Juan de Luzurriaga
1688–1695	Juan Capistrano
1695–1698	Miguel de Monzábal
1698–1703	Bartholomé Guier
1703–1706	Joseph de la Llana
1706–1711	Juan de la Cruz
1712–1715	Luiz Morote
1715–1717	Joseph Pedraya
1717–1723	Agustín de Messones
1723–1734	Fernando Alonso Gonsález (died in office)
1736–1744	Pedro Navarrete
1744–1747	Juan Fogueras
1747–1748	Gregorio López Hernáez
1748–1755	Juan Antonio Abasolo
1755–1761	Joseph Antonio de Oliva
1761	Manuel de Nájera

FRANCISCAN PROVINCIALS
Provincia de Santo Evangelio (Mexico)

1524	Martín de Valencia
1527	Luis de Fuensalida
1530	Martín de Valencia
1533	Jacobo de Testera
1535	García de Cisneros
1537	Antonio Ciudad Rodrigo
1540	Marcos de Niza
1543	Francisco de Soto
1546	Alonso Rangel
1548	Toribio de Benavente (Motolinía)
1551	Juan de Gasna
1552	Juan de San Francisco
1555	Francisco Bustamante
1558	Francisco de Toral
1561	Francisco Bustamante
1562	Luis Rodríguez
1564	Diego de Olarte
1567	Miguel Navarro
1570	Alonso de Escalona
1573	Antonio Roldán
1576	Pedro Oroz

1578	Domingo de Areyzaga
1581	Miguel Navarro
1583	Pedro de San Sebastián
1589	Domingo de Areyzaga
1592	Rodrigo Santillán
1595	Esteban de Alzúa
1598	Juan de Lascano
1600	Buenaventura de Paredes
1602	Pedro de la Cruz
1605	Juan de Salas
1608	Juan de Elormendi
1611	Hernando Durán Poblano
1614	Juan de Torquemada
1617	Juan López
1620	Juan Marques Maldonado
1623	Domingo del Portu
1626	Miguel de la Cruz Céspedes
1629	Francisco Velasco
1634	Francisco Rodríguez
1637	Andrés de Possada
1640	Lucas Benítez
1643	Andrés de Arteaga
1646	Hilario de Ibarra
1648	Alonso Ruiz Lima
1652	Francisco de Guzmán
1655	Tomás Manzo
1656	Augustín de Amézaga
1658	Bartholomé de Tapia
1661	Antonio Meléndez
1664	Martín del Castillo
1667	Domingo Cardoso
1668	Diego de Silva
1670	Domingo Martínez
1671	Juan Gutiérrez
1673	Pedro de Iguren
1676	Miguel de Aguilera
1679	Bernabé de Vergara
1682	Francisco Pérez Muñoz
1682	Francisco de Avila
1685	Joseph de la Llana
1688	Joseph Sánchez
1691	Diego Trujillo
1694	Clemente Ledesma
1696	Alonso de León
1699	Luis Morote
1702	Manuel de Argüello
1705	Pablo Padilla
1705	Juan Antonio Noriega
1708	Manuel Vigil
1710	Martín de Aguirre
1711	Luis de Céspedes
1714	Juan Antonio Noriega
1714	Joseph Cillero
1717	Alonso de León
1718	Manuel Aranda Saabedra
1720	Antonio Mancilla

1723	Pedro Navarrete
1726	Antonio Harison
1727	Buenaventura de Caleza
1729	Juan de Estrada
1731	Pedro Navarrete
1735	Diego Suárez
1735	Juan Domingo
1737	Antonio Joseph Pérez
1740	Diego Suárez
1743	Manuel de Enciso y Tejada
1745	Bernardo de Arratia
1749	Joseph Ximeno
1752	Joseph de la Vallina
1755	Juan Joseph de Moreyra
1758	Juan Bravo
1760	Pedro Serrano
1763	Joseph Leyza
1767	Juan Antonio Barros
1769	Pablo Antonio Pérez
1771	Fernando Gómez
1772	Francisco García Figueroa
1775	Isidoro Urillo
1778	Juan B. Dosal
1781	Antonio Ordóñez
1785	Juan Bravo
1787	Joaquín de Llazarve
1790	Francisco García Figueroa
1793	Francisco Martín de Cruzalegui
1796	Joaquín de Llazarve
1798	Antonio López Murto
1799	José Angel Dorrego
1802	Antonio Crespo
1805	Diego Antonio de las Piedras
1808	José Angel Dorrego
1811	Antonio Crespo
1812	Diego Antonio de las Piedras
1817	José Antonio Guisper
1820	Diego Meneses
1823	Agustín Bustamante
1826	Diego Meneses
1829	José Antonio Guisper
1832	Manuel Aromir y Bustamante
1835	José Antonio Guisper
1838	Juan B. Machorro
1841	Miguel Orellana
1844	Miguel Ruiz
1847	Buenaventura Omedes
1850	Mariano de la Peña

Provincia de Jalisco

1763	Miguel Naranjo
1766	Blas Villarejo
1769	Juan José de Aguiar
1772	Alonso Domínguez Muñoz
1775	Manuel Riezu
1778	Juan de Prestamero

1781	Miguel María Valcárcel
1784	Bartolomé Maceres
1787	Agustín José de Morán
1788	José Emanuel de Andrade
1790	Vicente Dávila
1790	Vicente Pau
	Francisco Miralles
1805	Pedro Partida y Rojas
1808	Francisco Vicente Olivares
1811	Diego Durón
1815	Antonio Olivares
1818	Francisco Antonio Padilla
1821	Juan Bautista Zaragosa
1823	Diego Durón
1824	José Durón
1827	Antonio Olivares
1830	José Rafael de Andrade
1833	Antonio de Jesús Galindo
1836	Rafael Torres
1838	Antonio de Jesús Galindo

Provincia de Zacatecas

1604	Alonso Caro
1605	Gabriel Arías
1608	Diego Maestro
1610	Gerónimo de la Peña
1613	Antonio de Alexos
1616	Ignacio Gómez
1619	Antonio Mondragón
1621	Francisco López Aragones
	Francisco Rodríguez
1625	Ignacio de Vergara
1628	Ignacio de Aroza
1631	Alonzo Rebollo
1633	Martín de Valenzuela
1636	Ignacio Gutiérrez
1639	Andrés de Ocampo
1642	Francisco Correa
1645	Francisco Godoy
1648	Christóbal Palomino
1651	Ambrosio Vigil
1654	Francisco Ancia
1656	Juan de Echevarría
1659	Domingo Leytón
1662	Juan Gutiérrez
1665	Antonio Valdes
1668	Ignacio de Echevarría
1671	Phelipe de Arvestain
1674	Antonio de Salas
1677	Antonio Valdes
1680	Juan de Salas
1683	Bartholomé Ramírez
1686	Juan de Lascano
1689	Martín de Urizar
1692	Francisco de Zamora
1694	Gerónimo Martínez

1697	Andrés Sánchez
1700	Luis Hermoso
1704	Lucas del Castillo
1707	Luis Athanasio
1710	Juan de San Miguel
1713	Joseph Fernández
1717	Antonio de Salazar
1719	Antonio de Mendiqutia
1722	Diego Valdes
1725	Joseph Arlegui
1728	Joseph de la Torre
1730	Diego de Halconta
1733	Antonio Rizo
1736	Pedro Beltrán
1739	Joseph Antonio de Oliva
1742	Antonio de Briones
1745	Antonio Rizo

THE FRANCISCAN COLLEGE OF THE HOLY CROSS OF QUERETARO, SUPERIORS, 1766-1843

1766	Sebastián Flores
1769	José Miguel Araujo
1722	Romualdo Cartagena
1775	Diego Ximénez Pérez
1778	Sebastián Flores
1782	Esteban de Salazar
1785	Juan José Sáenz de Gumiel
1788	Juan Alias
1791	Juan José Sáenz de Gumiel
1794	Juan Rivera
1797	Sebastián Ramis
1799	Francisco Miralles
1801	Juan Bautista de Cevallos
1804	Sebastián Ramis
1807	José Ximeno
1810	Angel Alonso del Prado
1813	Francisco Iturralde
1813	Diego Miguel Bringas
1816	Angel Alonso del Prado
1819	Buenaventura Tuny
1822	José Ximeno
1825	Mariano Llobet
1828	Agustín Reig
1833	José Cardoso
1839	José María Pérez Llera
1849	Francisco Muñoz

JESUIT PROVINCIALS OF NUEVA ESPANA

July 15, 1571	Pedro Sánchez
January 31, 1579	Juan de la Plaza
1585	Antonio Mendoza
1590	Diego de Avellaneda
February 1591	Pedro Díaz

February 1594	Esteban Páez
October 10, 1597	Francisco Báez
March 15, 1602	Ildefonso de Castro
January 23, 1608	Martín Peláez
June 30, 1609	Rodrigo de Cabredo (Visitor)
April 26, 1611	Rodrigo de Cabredo
April 8, 1616	Nicolás de Arnaya
April 18, 1622	Augustín Quiroz (Visitor)
April 18, 1622	Juan Laurencio
March 28, 1628	Diego de Sosa (Visitor)
March 28, 1628	Gerónimo Díez
April 25, 1631	Florián de Ayerve
November 30, 1634	Luis Bonifaz
October 30, 1637	Andrés Pérez de Rivas
February 1641	Luis Bonifaz
March 16, 1644	Francisco Calderón
1646	Juan de Bueras
February 21, 1646	Pedro de Velasco
February 19, 1649	Andrés de Rada
January 3, 1653	Francisco Calderón
November 3, 1653	Diego de Molina
July 4, 1654	Juan de Real
July 4, 1657	Alonso Bonifacio
1660	Pedro Antonio Díaz
1661	Hernando Cavero (Visitor)
July 3, 1664	Hernando Cavero
April 25, 1665	Francisco Carboneli
April 25, 1668	Pedro de Valencia
April 25, 1671	Andrés Cobián
June 4, 1673	Manuel de Arteaga
August 22, 1674	Francisco Jiménez
July 20, 1676	Tomás Altamirano
February 2, 1680	Antonio Núñez de Miranda
September 20, 1680	Bernardo Pardo
September 11, 1683	Luis del Canto
1686	Bernabé de Soto
October 23, 1689	Ambrosio Odón
January 8, 1693	Diego de Almonacir
January 8, 1696	Juan Palacios
January 8, 1699	Francisco Arteaga
January 8, 1702	Ambrosio Odón
1703	Manuel Piñeiro
October 21, 1704	Juan María de Salvatierra
September 17, 1706	Bernardo Rolandegui
November 4, 1707	Juan de Estrada
April 17, 1708	Antonio Jardón
April 1711	Alonso de Arrevillaga
August 1711	Andrés Luque (Visitor)
October 14, 1715	Ignacio Loyola
November 21, 1715	Gaspar Rodero
January 7, 1719	Alejandro Romano
1722	José de Arjó
1725	Gaspar Rodero
June 13, 1726	Andrés Nieto
November 4, 1729	Juan Antonio de Oviedo
November 4, 1732	José Barba

February 24, 1736	Antonio de Peralta
November 3, 1736	Juan Antonio de Oviedo
June 25, 1739	Mateo Ansaldo
1743 (beginning)	Christóbal Escobar y Llamas
1747 (beginning)	Juan María Casati
March 1747	Andrés Javier García
August 31, 1750	Juan Antonio Baltazar
August 31, 1753	Juan Ignacio Calderón
January 1755	Augustín Carta
1760 (beginning)	Pedro Reales
May 19, 1763	Francisco Ceballos
May 19, 1766	Salvador Gándara
1769	José Utrera
1772	Ignacio Lizoazoáin

JESUIT VISITORS: NORTHERN MISSIONS

1615	Martín Pérez
1616	Vicente del Aguila
1620	Cristóbal Villalta
1622	Hernando Villafañe
1621–1627	Luis Bonifaz
1628	Diego de Guzmán
1628–1629	Juan Varela
1634	Tomás Basilio
1636–1637	Vicente Aguila
1639	Leonardo Játino
1640	Luis Bonifaz
1641–1646	Pedro Pantoja
1646–1650	Juan de Bueras
1647–1650	Manuel Trujillo
1647	Francisco de Ibarra
1650	Jacinto Cortés
1653–1658	Manuel Benavides
1658–1661	Francisco Turices
1661–1664	Hernando Cavero
1667–1671	Bernardo Francisco Gutiérrez
1669–1675	Daniel Angelo Marras
1671–1673	Alvaro Flores de la Sierra
1674–1677	Gonsalo Navarro
1677	Juan de Almonacir
1678	Juan Ortiz Zapata
1678	Gerónimo Pistoya
1678	Tomás Hidalgo
1679	Bartolomé de Escañuela
1681–1684	Juan Bautista Ancieta
1684–1687	Juan de Almonacir
1686–1687	Francisco de Celada
1687–1690	Manuel González
1690–1693	Juan María de Salvatierra
1693–1696	Gerónimo Pistoya
1694–1701	Marcos de Loyola
1694–1696	Juan Muñoz de Burgos
1696	Horacio Póllice
1697	Melchor Bartiromo
1697–1705	Antonio Leal

1698–1701	Francisco de Celada	1727–1732	Cristóbal de Cañas
1699	Juan Bautista Ancieta	1732–1739	José Echeverría
1701–1705	Francisco María Píccolo	1735–1737	Ignacio Xavier Aguado
1702	Horacio Póllice	1735–1742	Luis María Marciano
1704	Manuel Piñeiro	1736–1737	José Toral
1705–1708	Antonio Leal	1737–1740	Andrés Xavier García
1705–1709	Francisco María Píccolo	1737–1744	Juan Bautista Duquesney
1707–1708	Nicolás Villafañe	1740–1741	José Xavier Molina
1708	José Pallares	1741–1744	Ignacio Xavier Duque
1709	Horacio Póllice	1742–1748	Lucas Luis Alvarez
1712–1718	Francisco Xavier Mora	1744–1747	Juan Antonio Baltazar
	Andrés Luque	1744	Gregorio Hernández
1714	Luis Mancuso	1746	Juan María Casati
1714	José Xavier Molina	1748–1767	Carlos de Rojas
1716	Marcos Antonio Kappus	1751	Agustín Carta
1716–1726	Fernando Bayerca	1751–1753	Philip Ségesser
1718–1722	José María Genovesi	1754–1755	José Utrera
1722–1723	Daniel Januske	1755–1767	Juan Lorenzo Salgado
1723	Bernardo Garfias	1757–1760	José Cabrera Roldán
1723–1724	Miguel Xavier de Almanza	1760–1763	José Antonio Garrucho
1725–1728	Juan de Guendulain	1761–1763	Lucas Atanasio Merino
1726–1729	Nicolás de Oro	1763–1767	Manuel Aguirre

MAPS

The maps in this section are designed to fulfill two purposes. First is to provide locator maps for the computer access Geofile and the system of site designation employed by the Arizona State Museum and the Documentary Relations of the Southwest. Initiated in 1928 by the Gila Pueblo Archaeological Foundation, this mapping system was continued by the Arizona State Museum and through the years has been widely adopted in the Southwest for the identification and location of sites. Recently, the Instituto Nacional de Antropología e Historia (INAH) of Mexico decided to adopt it for northern Mexico and to convert its existing system to it. The attraction of this method is its applicability to any country or state, and its logical and uniform reliance upon longitude and latitude. The system is easy to grasp and its standardization makes it possible for someone in one area to have a precise notion of the location of a site in another.

A geopolitical region, in this case states of the U.S. and Mexico, is divided into quadrants along lines of longitude and latitude. Each quadrant is an even one degree of longitude wide and one degree of latitude high. The quadrant belongs to that state which occupies the largest proportion of it. Thus, if one-quarter of a particular quadrant lies in Texas, one-quarter in Coahuila, and one-half lies in Chihuahua, it will be designated as Chihuahua. Once quadrants are attributed to states, they are given letter identifications. Beginning with "A" for the most northerly and westerly quadrant to fall within the category of any state, they are lettered in sequence from west to east, skipping down a degree when the row leaves the state. States with more quadrants than letters in the alphabet are given double and triple letter designations. Each quadrant is then further divided into sections of fifteen minutes on a side, giving sixteen per quadrant. These are numbered 1–16 in the same manner as the quadrants were lettered. An area is identified by state, a letter giving the quadrant location in the state, and a number indicating the fifteen-minute section in the quadrant. To this is simply added a final number corresponding to each site identified in that section. This last arabic number is also sequential, and sites can be added as they are located. A typical site identification might be: *Chih: K: 12: 43*. This identifies it as the 43rd site recorded in Chih: K: 12:, and Chih: K: 12: is the same for everybody.

Following are maps of the states within the greater Southwest showing one-degree grid lines and the correct state and letter designation for all quadrants. Much of Mexico has never had this system applied to it before, and the maps are offered as a base of reference to avoid confusion and potential errors in the assignment of quadrants. Only those parts of the southwestern United States having significant Spanish occupation are included.

The second group of maps serves as a kind of mini-historical atlas. They are provided solely as a general geographical framework for northern New Spain and are intended more to remind the user rather than teach him. The maps show changing indigenous concentrations, and the advance of Spanish mining, mission, and administrative centers. Four time periods are represented; the first, circa 1575, when Spain was only just beginning to tap the resources of the North, and the last, circa 1800, after the settlement of Alta California and near the end of the colonial era. Others at 1650 and 1725 are glimpses of the region after considerable Spanish penetration had altered economics and native culture patterns and demography. The northern frontier areas are emphasized, and the later maps indicate approximate limits of effective Spanish control. The indigenous groups and Spanish population centers that appear reflect their relative contemporary size and importance.

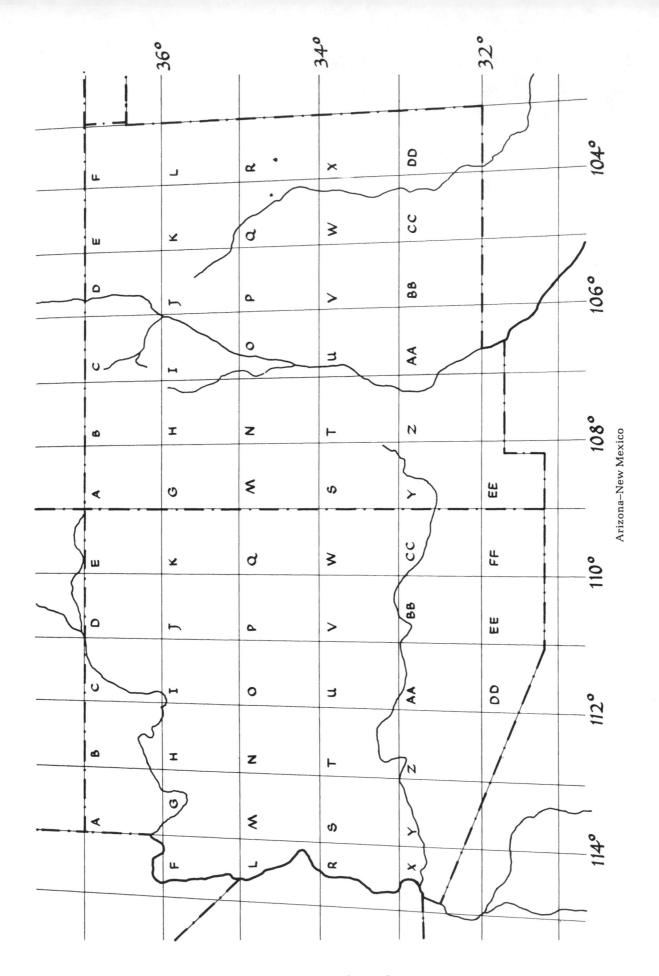

Arizona–New Mexico

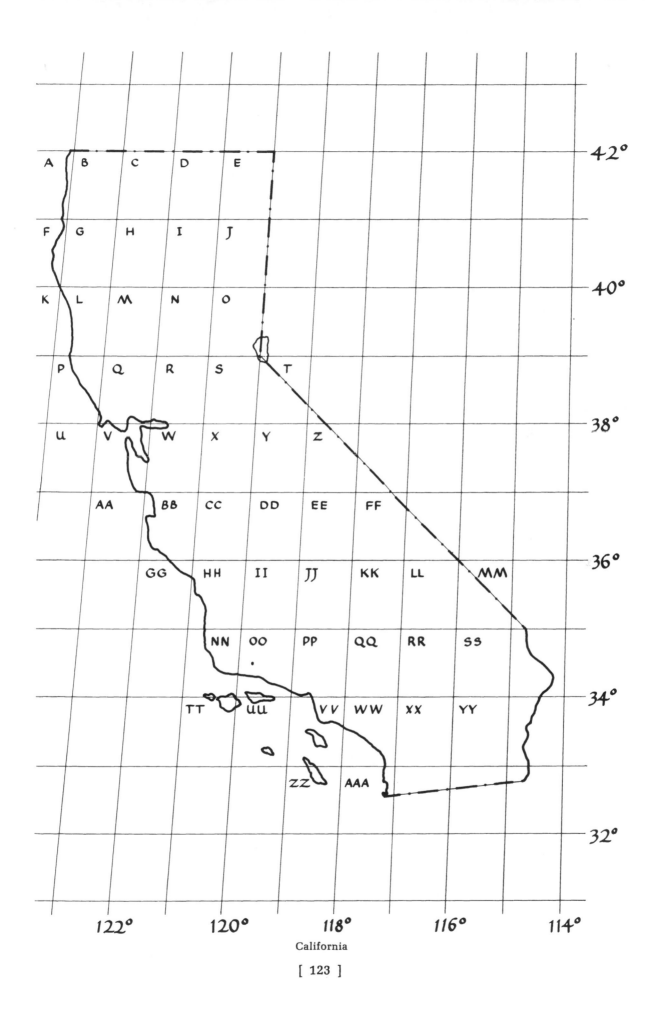

California

[123]

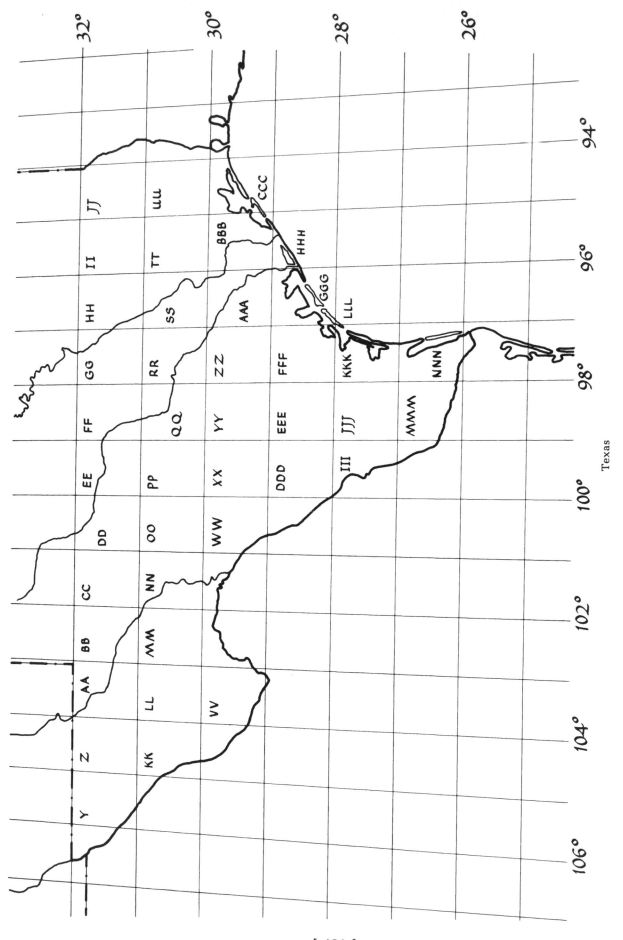

Texas

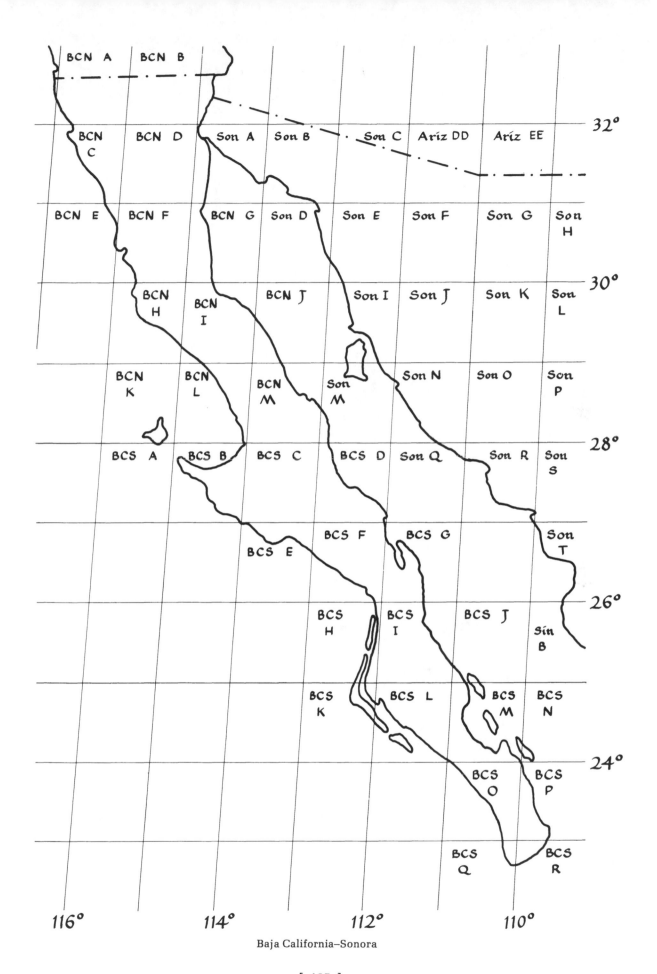

Baja California–Sonora

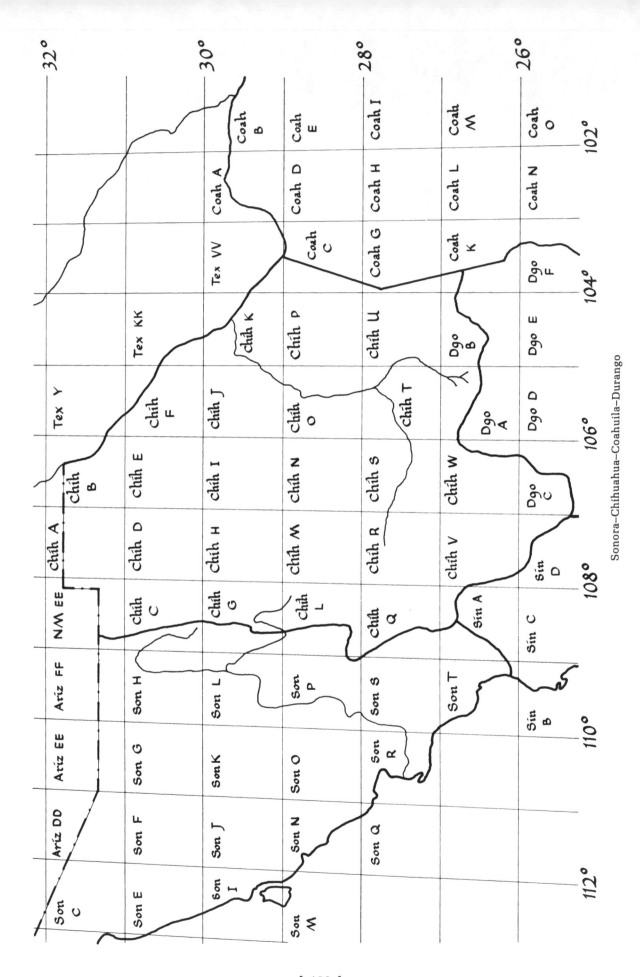

Sonora–Chihuahua–Coahuila–Durango

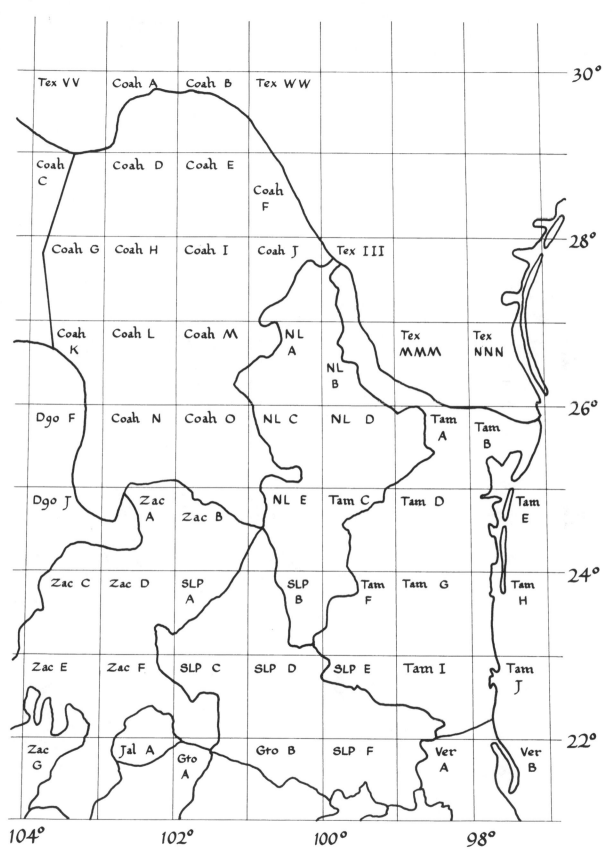

Coahuila–Nuevo León–Tamaulipas–Zacatecas–San Luis Potosí

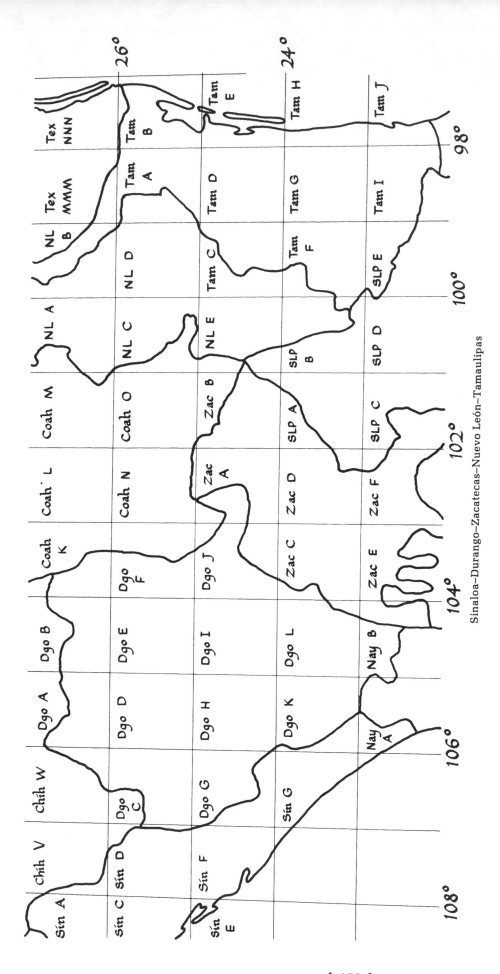

Sinaloa–Durango–Zacatecas–Nuevo León–Tamaulipas

Greater Southwest ca. 1575

Greater Southwest ca. 1725

[129]

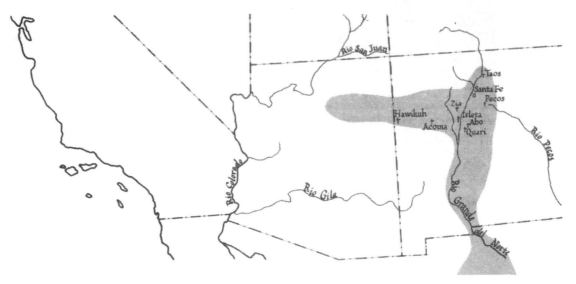

Northern New Spain Borderlands ca. 1650

Northern New Spain Borderlands ca. 1725

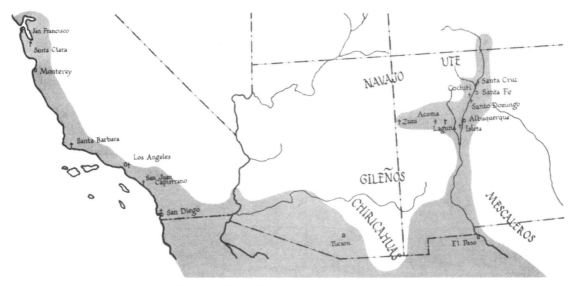

Northern New Spain Borderlands ca. 1800

GLOSSARY

a maquilas. Custom milling and refining of ore.

abogado. Lawyer, attorney.

acequia. Canal or ditch.

acordada. Rural police force established in New Spain in the early years of the eighteenth century. A revival of the Santa Hermandad of sixteenth century Spain, this tribunal employed some two to three thousand agents, who, under the auspices of a supreme judge called the *juez* or *capitán de la acordada,* served without pay for the honor and privileges this service entailed. Criminals apprehended by the *acordada* were swiftly tried and punished without the time and expense of the usual judicial system.

acordado. Nonpromulgated decision reached by a governing body, usually an *audiencia* or the Council of the Indies.

acuerdo (real acuerdo). A meeting of the *audiencia* or its senior members, usually with its respective executive in attendance, to deliberate on political administrative matters. *Acuerdo* also indicated the decision arrived at in these meetings. See *auto acordado.*

actuario. Scribe or notary.

adelantado. The individual responsible for the conquest or opening of a new area. The office of *adelantado* dates back to medieval Castile, where the office was mainly judicial. During the reconquest the *adelantado* became a military and administrative office in frontier or Moslem-held areas. The office fell into obscurity toward the end of the reconquest but found use in the frontiers of the New World.

The granting of the title in the New World meant special privileges and honors for the individual concerned. In return, the crown expected and often received new lands, new subjects and converts, and different forms of wealth. The office and its privileges were usually granted for one or two lifetimes and sometimes in perpetuity.

In return for the expense of outfitting an expedition, transporting settlers, conquering an area if necessary, and establishing two or more permanent towns or forts, the *adelantado* became the governor of the land, received title to a large amount of property, was assigned a certain percentage of the income generated in the province, received monopolies in trade, and was exempted from certain taxes. Being the chief executive officer of a new area or province, he could nominate certain civil and ecclesiastical officers. He could distribute land and water rights to those who had accompanied him and had power to parcel out *encomiendas* of Indians.

Even though the *adelantado* received these privileges for at least his own lifetime and often for that of his children, most individuals of this rank had limited success. If they did not meet a violent death, the crown often moved to weaken them, appointing royal governors and putting restrictive limits on the use of original privileges. By 1650, *adelantados* no longer played a role in the Spanish New World empire.

admenes. Wooden support system used in mines (crib-lathing).

admenes de cajón. Crib-lathing used on all four sides of a weak portion of a shaft (*cajón marqueado*).

aduana. Public office of export and import taxes. Also refers to the tax itself.

agravio. Injury or offense.

albacea. Executor of a will or estate.

alcabala. A sales tax. Not effectively levied in the New World colonies until the last quarter of the sixteenth century. This tax of 2 percent was levied on most sales and exchanges. The rate of 2 percent remained stable until ca, 1630 when it was doubled in New Spain; thereafter, it fluctuated upward depending on the needs of Spain.

alcalde. Municipal officer with administrative and judicial functions. The office has roots in both Islamic and Roman occupations of the Iberian peninsula. See section on Colonial Government.

alcalde de crimen. Oidor in the criminal chamber of an *audiencia.* A criminal judge.

alcalde de la hermandad (alcalde de la mesta or

alcalde de la santa hermandad). Of medieval Spanish origin. Served as local police force in rural areas with police and judicial powers. Transplanted to New Spain in 1552. This in turn evolved into the *acordada.* See *acordada.* The *alcalde de la hermandad* was an official within the organization.

alcalde de indios. Indian communities under Spanish authority had the same governmental structure as Spanish municipalities. Thus, these native communities had *alcaldes,* as well as other officials common to Spanish urban settlements.

alcalde mayor. Chief executive officer in a town or a district composed of several towns. He had political authority and could be the judge of appeal in cases heard by the *alcaldes ordinarios* of the *cabildo.* In rank he stood equal to the *corregidor,* and just below the *gobernador,* although the duties of all three were nearly identical in their respective jurisdictions. Because of distance from superiors or sources of appeal, his power might approach dictatorial levels. See section on Colonial Government.

Alcalde ordinario. A member of the *cabildo.* In small municipalities there were generally two; they were the local court of first instance. Cases appealed might go to the *alcalde mayor* or to the *gobernador* or to the respective *audiencia.* The *alcalde ordinarios* were chosen by the *regidores* of the *cabildos.* See section on Colonial Government.

alcaldía. Geographical jurisdiction of an *alcalde mayor.*

aldeano. Local resident. Resident of a community (aldea).

alférez (mayor, real). First or second lieutenant in the army. In this case, often referred to as a *teniente.* Also, a municipal official, attached to the cabildo as a herald or standard bearer who ranked as a superior *regidor* and who could replace an absent *alcalde ordinario.*

alguacil (mayor). Chief constable, usually on a municipal level.

alhóndiga. Public market for the selling of grains. Designed to control price and quality. Also, stores established to sell necessities and other goods to Indians working in mines or on haciendas at fair prices.

amojonamiento. Action of marking with stones the boundaries of a piece of land.

amparo. Concept of amnesty or forgiveness. Associated with judicial cases where the presiding judge finds the defendant in violation of the law but decides that this particular case merits exception. Literally, "assistance."

apoderado. Person with the power of attorney (legally acting for another).

arbitrios. Irregular taxes or contributions collected at a local level for specific local purposes.

armero. Armorer, gunsmith.

arrastra. Process or tool used to grind ore into powder-like fineness.

arriero. Driver of pack animals.

arroba. Common unit of weight equal to 25 libras. See section on Weights and Measures.

asesor (general). Legal counsel attached to official government offices.

asiento de salinas. Contract granted by the crown to an individual for the purpose of exploiting salt deposits for eventual sale to miners.

asiento and libro de asientos. Asiento is generally associated with the contract let out by the crown for the transport and sale of negroes in the New World. *Libro de asientos* was a commercial or military record listing different items or people.

atestación. Deposition or testimony.

audiencia. A judicial and legislative council administering royal affairs over a substantial geographic area in the New World. Judicially, it was subordinate only to the Council of the Indies. In a legislative role, it acted in conjunction with the viceroy. For the composition, function, and different levels of *audiencias,* see the section on Colonial Government.

autillo. An order issued by the Inquisition pertaining to a patricular case.

auto. Judicial or administrative decree. Common general title for documents sent from a higher body or jurisdiction to a lower level outlining a new law, program, or regulation.

auto acordado. The results of a meeting of an *audiencia* with its respective executive officer (viceroy, president, governor). Also refers to conclusions reached in deliberations of the Council of Castile and the Council of the Indies. Technically these *autos acordados* had the force or standing of law but usually stressed existing practice, sometimes in the form of commanding obedience. However, as the environment of the New World toyed with custom, *autos acordados* issued in the colonies at times contained new material with demands for compliance, thereby making them effective as law.

auto de fe. The decree of judgment and sentence of a tribunal of the Inquisition.

auto definitivo. An *auto* with the force of law or sentence rendered by a judicial authority.

avidor. A supplier of goods to miners. He might supply goods on credit if necessary or extend credit in cash.

avio. Mining supplies: goods or cash credit.

aviso. Official announcement or document of advice.

ayuntamiento. The municipal corporation in charge of administering and governing a town. More commonly known as a cabildo in Spain's New World colonies. See *cabildo.*

bachiller. The lowest academic degree. Followed by *licenciado* and doctor.

badanas. Sheepskin-lined boxes used to transport mercury.

baldio. Public lands.

bando. Executive documents indicating certain points in laws or regulations pertinent or peculiar to a specific incident or issue, which, because of the character of the incident or issue, needed emphasis. Therefore, *bandos,* in their limited scope, often demanded immediate and complete obedience because of some particular urgency. A *bando* differs from an *edicto* in that the former is an order and the latter an announcement, similar to an *aviso.*

barranca. A deep ravine or canyon.

barras de mina. Share(s) in a mine. Also referred to the actual bars of metal.

barretero. A mine laborer employed in cutting ores with a *barra,* or crowbar.

barriles, barriletes. Small barrels used to transport mercury.

batea. Large wooden bowl used for mining gold in stream deposits. Also refers to similar wooden bowls for household purposes.

beneficio. Purchase of a position from the government.

beneficio de patio. The open-air amalgamation process.

beneficio eclesiastico (simple). Church position held by one who has no parish duties. An endowed church office.

bienes. In general usage, property.

bienes de comunidad. In a town, public property.

bienes de difuntos. In the widest sense, those goods or the estate left on the death of a person. More exactly, the goods or belongings left by death to which, in the colonies, there were no heirs. In such a case, the royal exchequer in Spain took charge, probating the estate or will.

bienes raíces. Property. Specifically, land, buildings, roads, mines, and other forms of property considered permanent. Legal or natural right considered to be inherent and irrevocable.

buscador. Prospector.

caballería. Usually the amount of land given to soldiers for services rendered in the opening of new or hostile land. See section on Weights and Measures.

caballero. Gentleman or knight of a military order.

cabecera. Administrative head of a province or mission district. Geographic head.

cabildo. The municipal corporation or town council charged with local municipal government. See *ayuntamiento.* See also section on Colonial Government.

cabildo abierto. Meeting of the cabildo to which certain local residents were invited. These people were important citizens of property and churchmen for the most part. Such meetings were not frequent and usually entailed discussion of an issue with wide-ranging impact.

cabo. A corporal in the military.

cacique. Traditional Indian headman or chief of an Indian town or tribe.

cámara. Chamber, court, or cabinet.

Capa y espada. Used in reference to officials in government who did not possess the formal qualifications for the position they held. This usually meant that such a person was not a lawyer but, owing to circumstances, filled the position anyway.

capellán. Chaplain or priest often associated with the saying of a private mass. See *capellanía.*

capellanía. Provision made by individuals for the saying of a certain number of masses annually for the person who established the *capellanía.*

capilla. Chapel.

capitán-general. Chief military officer. In the colonies the title belonged to the viceroy, although in a province the superior military commander was often so called. The provincial commander technically was a lieutenant *capitán-general.* In frontier areas this rank was often filled by the governor of the province. As necessity dictated, the rank became a brevet type, with a lower ranking officer or enlisted man holding the position.

capitán a guerra. Head of military operations in an area smaller than a province—usually on a frontier beset with unfriendly Indians.

carabinero. Soldier armed with a carbine.

carbonero. Charcoal maker. Charcoal burners.

carga. A load of varying capacity and weight. See section on Weights and Measures.

carpeta. File or folder of documents. See *legajo; expediente.*

carreta. A two-wheeled cart.

carro. A wagon.

carta. General title found at the head of a wide variety of documents. Because of its general application, the contents of the documents have to be determined by a close reading.

carta annua. Annual letter or report, especially of Jesuit provincials. See section on Types and Structure of Documents.

casa de afinación. Assay office (an institution of the Royal Treasury).

casa de contratación. Official body in Spain concerned with the economic and commercial matters of Spain's colonies.

casa de fundición. The royal smelter. By law, all new mines and their owners had to bring their bullion to the *casa* to be assayed and taxed.

cazuela. Crock or pan.

cédula. General title attached to a variety of documents. Decree. *Cédula Real.* Royal decree issued by Council of the Indies over the king's signature.

cédula real. A law or measure passed through the Council of the Indies with the authority of the king.

cendrada. Hearth lead.

Chino. Commonly, a person from the Philippine Islands. See section on Racial Terminology.

cofradía. Brotherhood. Group formed for religious purposes at a lay level.

cohete. Blasting cartridge; rocket; fireworks.

colorados. Silver ore with a high content of iron oxide.

comandancia. The office or area of a commander. Most often referred to during the years of the Provincias Internas and the military reorganization of northern New Spain, 1776–1823.

compadrazgo. God-parentage. A very important social institution establishing ties between parents of a baptized child and the child's godparents. Especially important in Indian communities.

consejo. Council. Such as *Consejo de Indias,* or *consejo de guerra.*

consumido. The manner by which a miner's stock of mercury was maintained. On registering silver with the treasury, he was issued the amount of mercury it was calculated he had consumed in producing that silver.

contador. Accountant.

consultores, asesores. In the widest sense, individuals of legal training.

conversión. An Indian mission in a primitive state, the natives not having been converted or educated in the faith.

conversor. Priest in charge of a *conversión.*

corregidor. Local political official. In most cases, the same as an *alcalde mayor.* See *alcalde mayor.* See section on Colonial Government.

corregidor de indios. Official placed in charge of Indian towns paying tribute to the crown. In addition to duties of a *corregidor* and *alcalde mayor,* the *corregidor de indios* was to protect and encourage Indian welfare. This office was subject to a great deal of abuse.

corregimiento. Administrative area governed by a *corregidor.*

correspondencia. The ratio of silver produced to mercury consumed in the amalgamation process of silver refining. The normally accepted ratio was 100 marks of silver to one *quintal* of mercury; but, depending on the quality of silver ore, the ratio could vary from 80 to more than 120 marks to a quintal.

crestón. The exposed part of a vein on the surface of the earth.

criollo. Person of Spanish blood born in the New World. A white person.

cuadrilla. A miner's labor force, generally living in his *hacienda de minas* and working his plant and his mines.

cubos. Leather buckets used to carry water to the surface in the process of draining a mine.

cura. Priest in charge of a secular church (curato).

curato. A full-fledged parish composed of Catholics, that is, neither pagans nor recent converts. A secular parish.

custodia. Franciscan ecclesiastical subdivision. An incipient province.

denuncia. A statement (denunciation) bringing to the attention of a judge the intention to act against another party who in some way has fallen short of a requirement in a certain situation or who is in violation of a law.

denuncio. A legal declaration stating the existence of a newly discovered mine and the intention to lay claim to it. Also, a claim to a mine previously worked but since abandoned.

depositario general. Public trustee. Official attached to the cabildo.

depósito. A miner's stock of mercury.

diezmo. A tithe (tenth).

diligencias. General title of, or category of documents. Usually, a communication counseling caution. It could be both administrative or judicial.

doctrina. An ecclesiastical district served by a missionary, generally a regular cleric. A group or pueblo of Indians not yet advanced to the status of a parish.

doctrinero. The priest charged with teaching doctrine to native peoples.

donativo. Contribution, gift, or forced loan.

dote. Dowry. Usually found in documents as "*carta de dote.*"

edicto. Order issued by an authority demanding obedience to certain laws or regulations.

ejido. Municipal common lands, usually associated with Indian towns.

encomienda. The granting of Indians and land to an *encomendero.* In return for their labor the encomendero was to provide for the welfare and civilization of the Indians and their instruction in Christianity.

ensayador. Assayer who recorded, assayed, and stamped refined bars with an identity number and a figure indicating fineness.

entrada. Expedition into unknown or unsettled areas. Usually associated with the military, as the purpose was often to confront Indians, or the military acted as an escort for settlers or missionaries. It could also be the exploration of a single individual.

escribano. Secretary or notary.

escrituras. General category for documents containing a variety of material. Writings.

estancia. Large landed estate usually devoted to raising livestock.

estatutos. Generally, rules or regulations within a corporation having enough autonomy to govern its internal affairs.

expediente. A group of papers or documents pertaining to a specific issue or event.

fanega. Common unit of weight. Also a land measure See section on Weights and Measures.

fiel. In a municipality, the inspector of weights and measures. He was also in charge of market prices and the supply of food stuffs. Often known as *fiel ejecutor.* See section on Colonial Government.

firma. Commonly seen as "*firma,*" also indicating "signed by." Signature. Regularly abbreviated as "*f.*"

fiscal. Generally an attorney for the state. Also an official of lower rank in a native settlement. See section on Colonial Government.

fuelles. Bellows.

fuero. Privileges granted to a place, group or person, such as the *fuero militar* or *fuero eclesiastico,* which left to the church or military the power to decide upon civil and ecclesiastical crimes pertaining to them.

ganaderia. Cattle ranch. Also, stock raising, livestock.

ganado mayor, ganado menor (estancia or hacienda de). *Ganado mayor,* refers to cattle and *ganado menor* to sheep and goats. An *estancia* of either one would mean, respectively, a cattle or sheep/goat ranch.

gente de razón. Literally, people of reason. Term denoting social and economic superiority. In most cases reserved for persons of European blood.

gobernación. Area governed by a governor (*gobernador*).

granja. Farm.

greta. Litharge (lead in a variety of forms used for flux in smelting).

hacienda. Large landed estate. Also, a treasury or an enterprise. See section on Colonial Government and Weights and Measures.

hacienda de beneficio. A reduction works for mineral ore.

hacienda de carbón. A facility where charcoal was manufactured.

hacienda de minas. A silver refining plant. More correctly and fully termed "*hacienda de sacar plata para el beneficio de azoque,*" or "*de fundición*" if a smelter.

hornos castellanos. Rectangular blast furnaces made of stone or adobe.

incorporadero. The yard of a *hacienda de minas* in which amalgamation took place.

informe. General title for a variety of documents, most of which carried information as opposed to orders or laws.

intendencia. Administrative unit introduced in the New World between 1764 and 1790. Designed to centralize colonial administration for the purposes of efficiency, the production of more revenue, and protection against Spain's enemies, particularly the English. The *gobernador, corregidor,* and the *alcalde mayor* disappeared, as the *intendente* assumed their duties and reported to the respective audiencia and viceroy. See section on Colonial Government.

Intendente. Also "*gobernador intendente,*" the individual appointed by the King to govern an *intendencia.*

inventario: Inventory.

jacal. Hut; crude dwelling.

jornada. A day's work 'or march.

jornal. wage(s).

juez. A judge.

juez de residencia. The individual charged with carrying out the residencia. He asked the questions, determined the facts and passed judgment or sentence.

justicia mayor. An individual in each *cabildo* appointed by the governor to serve as his deputy.

junta. A gathering of people for a specific purpose.

junta de guerra. Council of war. A meeting of local civil and military officials in response to hostilities. A *junta de guerra* was held at all levels of colonial government. At the viceregal level it consisted of the viceroy, his top military commanders and certain members of the *virreinal audiencia.*

juzgado de Indios. A special court created in New Spain in 1573 to handle affairs dealing with the abuse of Indians. Technically, the viceroy was the protector of the Indians and his lawyers represented him in this function. This special tribunal expedited matters and its decisions carried considerable weight.

lavadero. The part of an *hacienda de minas* in which the crude mixture of amalgam and waste earth and rock material was washed.

legajo. File, bundle of papers or documents.

legua. Unit of measure for distance. See section on Weights and Measures.

letrado. A person with university training in law or with a legal degree.

libra. Common unit of weight. See section on Weights and Measures.

libro. Literally, book. Often found in such forms as "*libro de asientos,*" "*libros de escrituras,*" meaning a book or sheaf of documents pertaining to a certain topic or period of time.

libros de raya. Wage books.

licenciado. A higher degree in a Spanish or Spanish-American university. The person with such a degree. A lawyer.

magistral. Copper sulphate used in the amalgamation process.

malacate. Mule-operated whim used to drain mines. The mules turned a spindle which had two long ropes attached to it. At the end of each rope was a bucket which was alternately lowered and raised by the revolving motion of the spindle. A vertical winch.

manantiales y esteros. Artesian well (fresh water). Salt springs.

mandamiento. Written order dispatched by a judge demanding the execution of a certain action.

maravedí. Since the eleventh century, the basis of the Spanish monetary system. See section on Money and Currency.

marca del diezmo. A mark placed on a bar of silver showing that it was *plata del diezmo.*

marco. Common unit of weight. See section on Weights and Measures.

masa. Water-soaked ore.

mayordomo. Municipal official attached to the *cabildo.* He served as the custodian of civic property. Also, foreman of a *hacienda.*

mayorazgo. Almost the same as the English "entail." Any individual above the status of peasant could create a *mayorazgo* and many did so in order to acquire the privileges and status which went with it.

memoria. List of items to be ordered or supplied; want list.

memorial. Advisement, usually written, of some event or events which have already taken place.

mercader de plata. A large-volume dealer in silver. Usually based in Mexico City, he bought refined silver for minting; he acted through agents—*aviadores* and *rescatadores*—in mining towns.

metal. The usual term for ore.

milpa. Plot of land; cornfield.

molino. A stamp mill in a *hacienda de minas.*

multa. A fine.

naborio. Free labor in mines.

negros. Silver ore with a high lead-sulphide content.

noria. Commonly, a chain of buckets for raising water from a well, though more properly, a waterwheel with the same function. A hand-operated windlass.

notario. Secretary or scribe, solicitor or attorney.

obraje. Work or workshops conducted by slaves, involuntary Indian labor, or criminals sentenced to a period of hard labor.

oidor. Member of an *audiencia* who served as a judge. An *oidor* often performed other duties, the most important being the administration of *residencias.* See section on Colonial Government.

orden. Literally, order. Often a group following a set rule or pattern of life, such as the *Orden de San Francisco.*

ordenanza. An ordinance.

padrón. Census. Often taken to determine the number of people in a certain area eligible for the payment of tribute, or the number already paying.

papel sellado. Official paper. Used for official communications and marked with the royal seal.

parada de fuelles. Small furnace for smelting silver ores usually operated by men who were not recognized miners (*hornos de afinación*).

parecer. An opinion, usually filed prior to making a policy decision.

parroquia. Parish.

patio. Rock-floored area where reagents were mixed with water-soaked ore.

patronato (real). Patronage. In the New World, the prerogative of the King to appoint religious officials.

pella. Washed amalgam of mercury and silver.

peninsular. Denotes a person of Spanish blood born in Spain.

pepenas. An indeterminate quantity of ore which laborers were permitted to extract from mines for their own use and profit.

petate. Woven fiber mat.

plata del diezmo. Silver recovered by a licensed miner, generally from ores at his own mine and in his own *hacienda de minas;* therefore, assessable at a tax rate of one-tenth (*diezmo*).

plata del rescate. In general, silver produced from purchased or stolen ores, and refined by men who were not recognized miners. It was taxable at a full fifth (*quinto*).

plata dezmada. Silver that had been taxed at one-tenth.

plata quintada. Any silver that had been taxed (see *quintar*).

plomillos. Slag with high lead content.

poder. In legal documents a person assigns power or authority to another person to act as his legal agent—power of attorney.

pozo. Shallow vertical shafts. Shaft used to ventilate upper levels of a mine (*lumbreras*); well.

presidio. Official military establishment, especially in frontier areas. A permanent location, staffed by regular army personnel for the defense of a certain area.

probanza. Affidavit of services rendered presented to crown for compensation.

procurador. Attorney. Generally, the city or municipal attorney. In religious orders, the person charged with financial and temporal care.

própios. Municipal properties, the revenues of which go to the local treasury.

presidente. Usually the chief officer of an *audiencia.*

protocolo (also *registro*). An official register kept by a scribe or notary of all transactions.

provincia. The largest and most important political unit in colonial government next to the kingdom, presided over by a governor. See section on Colonial Government.

provincias internas. Administrative unit established in 1776 in the northern frontier of New Spain. Designed to improve royal administration and the production of revenue and to enhance Spanish presence to counter French, Russian, and English intrusions.

pueblo de visita. Chapel or locality attached to a mission attended to by non-resident clergy.

puntales. Wooden props used to sustain walls in mines.

quinceno. A fifteenth: The fraction of a miner's current silver production normally taken by the treasury in payment for mercury and salt issued to him on credit.

quintar. Common term for "to tax," with reference to silver. Its meaning was not restricted to taxing at the rate of a fifth.

quinto. A fifth: the tax levied by the royal treasury on mining.

rancho. Settlement, ranch.

ranchería. An Indian settlement where dwellings are not permanent and are scattered some distance from each other.

real caja. Any local branch office of the royal treasury.

real de minas. Town specialized in mining; a mining district.

real hacienda. Royal treasury.

Real orden. Royal order. Measure adopted by the king without the intervention of the Council of the Indies.

reducción. An area into which Indians were collected for intensive missionary effort.

regidor. Member of a cabildo. See section on Colonial Government.

relación. Documents containing information, often in the form of a response to questions from higher officials concerning a certain subject or area.

repartimiento. Labor draft used to employ Indians in various forms of agriculture, mining, and ranching. An individual requested a number of Indians for a certain job for a definite period of time, guaranteeing to treat them well and pay them fairly. Although an Indian was required to participate in the labor draft, ideally he could choose his employer. Abuse of rules and regulations was frequent.

requerimiento. Formal decree claiming title and control over newly discovered lands; occasionally used by citizenry as a form of ultimatum.

rescatador. A man who bought unfinished silver, in order to refine it himself; or one who bought finished silver from a miner, for minting coins, at a discount.

rescate. Purchase, either of finished silver or of ore.

residencia. A review held at the time when a person resigned or otherwise came to the end of his term in office. From the lowest officials to the viceroy, they were held accountable for any wrongdoing uncovered by the judge of the residencia *(juez de residencia).*

salinas. Playas of impervious clay with salt crusts on the surface.

saltierra. Deposits of impure salt found on the surface of dry lake beds *(playas).*

sargento mayor. Strictly speaking a major, the third in command of a regiment. In frontier areas, often filled by a nonprofessional and often in command of local forces under the lieutenant captain-general.

síndico. Municipal attorney.

socavón. In a mine, a conduit for drainage or ventilation; or simply for access to workings *(contaminas).*

sol a sol. A twelve-hour working shift in the mines.

tahona. Device for grinding ores very finely, by means of heavy stones slung under a rotating arm. Also refers to a device for grinding flour, usually from wheat *(tauna).*

tameme. A bearer, usually Indian.

temporalidades. Properties, movable and unmovable, owned by religious orders.

tenatero. Carrier or bearer, usually on Indian or negro. Climbing notched logs, the mine laborer carried ore to the surface in hide bags which weighed up to 350 pounds.

tenates. Hide bag used for carrying ore *(costales).*

tequío. Amount of ore to be extracted in a given time by a laborer under contract to a miner; the contract itself.

tesorero. Treasurer.

testamento. Last will or testament.

testimonio. Testimony, deposition.

tina. A washing vat for separating amalgam from crushed rock and earth.

vecino. Citizen of good standing; usually a property owner.

visita. An inspection or review performed by an official for the purpose of gathering information. See sections on Colonial Government and Types and Structures of Documents.

visitador. Person in charge of a *visita.*

visitas de minas. Periodic inspections of mines by government officials to insure adherence to regulations.

zapatillas. Sills used to support wooden props in a mine or mine shaft.

BIBLIOGRAPHY

GENERAL HISTORICAL

Aguado Bleye, Pedro. *Manual de historia de América*. Bilbao: Eléxpuru Hermanos, S.A., 1927.

Aguirre Beltrán, Gonzalo. *La población negra de Mexico, 1519–1810*. 2d ed. Mexico, D.F.: Fondo de Cultura Economica, 1972.

Alamán, Lucas. *Obras*. México, D.F.: V. Agueros, 1889–1911.

Alegre, Francisco Javier. *Historia de la Compañía de Jesús en Nueva España*. 4 vols. E.J. Burrus, S.J. and F. Zubillaga, S.J., editors. Rome: Institutum Historicum, S.J., 1956–1960.

Bancroft, Hubert Howe, *History of Mexico*. 6 vols. San Francisco: The History Company, 1883–1888.

Bannon, John Francis, S.J. *The Spanish Borderlands Frontier, 1513–1821*. New York: Holt, Rinehart and Winston, 1970.

Benavente o Motolinía, Fray Toribio de. *Historia de los indios de la Nueva España*. Edited by Edmundo O'Gorman. 2d ed. México, D.F.: Editorial Porrúa, S.A., 1973.

Blackmar, Frank W. *Spanish Institutions of the Southwest*. Glorieta, New Mexico: The Rio Grande Press, Inc., 1976.

Bobb, Bernard E. *The Viceregency of Antonio María Bucareli in New Spain, 1771–1779*. Austin: University of Texas Press, 1962.

Bolton, Herbert E. *Coronado: Knight of Pueblos and Plains*. Albuquerque: University of New Mexico Press, 1964.

————. *Kino's Historical Memoir of Pimería Alta*. Berkeley: University of California Press, 1948.

————. *Rim of Christendom: A Biography of Eusebio Francisco Kino, Pacific Coast Pioneer*. New York: Russell and Russell, 1960.

Borah, Woodrow W., and Sherburne F. Cook. *The Aboriginal Population of Central Mexico on the Eve of the Spanish Conquest*. Berkeley: University of California Press, 1963. *(Iberoamericana*, No. 45).

Brand, Donald D. "The Early History of the Range Cattle Industry in Northern Mexico." *Agricultural History*, July 1961.

Bravo Ugarte, José. *Instituciones políticas de la Nueva España*. México, D.F.: Editorial JUS, 1968.

Calderón Quijano, José Antonio. *Los virreyes Hispano-Americanos en el reinado de Carlos III*. 2 vols. Sevilla: Escuela de Estudios Hispano-Americanos de Sevilla, 1967.

Castañeda, Carlos E. *Our Catholic Heritage in Texas, 1519–1936*. 7 vols. Austin: Von Boeckmann-Jones Co., 1936.

Chevalier, François. *Land and Society in Colonial Mexico: The Great Hacienda*. Berkeley: University of California Press, 1966.

Cook, Sherburne F., and W. Wilson Borah. *The Indian Population of Central Mexico, 1531–1610*. Berkeley: University of California Press, 1960. *(Iberoamericana*, No. 44).

Corle, Edwin. *The Royal Highway*. New York: The Bobbs-Merrill Co., Inc., 1949.

Decorme, Gerard, S.J. *La obra de los Jesuitas Mexicanos durante la época colonial, 1572–1767*. 2 vols. México, D.F.: Antigua Librería Robredo de José Porrúa e Hijos, 1941.

Donohue, John Augustine, S.J. *After Kino: Jesuit Missions in Northwestern New Spain, 1711–1767*. Rome: Jesuit Historical Institute, and St. Louis, Missouri: St. Louis University Press, 1969.

Dunne, Peter Masten, S.J. *Andrés Pérez de Ribas: Pioneer Black Robe of the West Coast, Administrator, Historian*. New York: The United States Catholic Historical Society, 1951.

————. *Pioneer Black Robes on the West Coast*. Berkeley: University of California Press, 1940.

————. *Pioneer Jesuits in Northern Mexico*. Berkeley: University of California Press, 1944.

Forbes, Jack D. *Apache, Navajo and Spaniard*. Norman, Oklahoma: The University of Oklahoma Press, 1960.

Galvan, G. *Ordenanzas de tierras y aguas*. Paris: 1855.

García Carraffa, Alberto y Antonio. *Diccionario heráldico y genealógico de apellidos españoles y americanos*. 88 vols. Madrid: Nueva Imprenta Radio, S.A., 1955.

Gerhard, Peter. *A Guide to the Historical Geography of New Spain.* Cambridge: Cambridge University Press, 1972.

González Obregón, Luis. *Rebeliones indígenas y precursores de la independencia mexicana en los siglos XVI, XVII y XVIII.* 2d Ed. México: Ediciones Fuente Cultural, 1952.

Greenleaf, Richard E., and Michael C. Meyer, eds. *Research in Mexican History: Topics, Methodology, Sources, and a Practical Guide to Field Research.* Lincoln, Nebraska: University of Nebraska Press, 1973.

Griffen, William B. *Culture Change and Shifting Populations in Central Northern Mexico.* Anthropological Papers of the University of Arizona, No. 13. Tucson: University of Arizona Press, 1969.

Hackett, Charles W., ed. *Historical Documents Relating to New Mexico, Nueva Vizcaya, and Approaches Thereto, Collected by Adolph F.A. Bandelier and Fanny R. Bandelier.* 3 vols. Washington, D.C.: Carnegie Institution, No. 330, 1923–1937.

Haggard, J. Villasana. *Handbook for Translators of Spanish Historical Documents.* Austin: University of Texas Press, 1941.

Hanke, Lewis, and Celso Rodríguez. *Los virreyes españoles en América durante el gobierno de la Casa de Austria.* Madrid: Atlas, 1976. (7 vols.)

Hedrick, Basil C. *The North Mexican Frontier: Readings in Archaeology, Ethnohistory and Ethnography.* Carbondale, Illinois: 1971.

Hernández Sánchez-Barba, Mario. *La última expansión española en América.* Madrid: Instituto de Estudios Políticos, 1957.

Hodge, Frederick Webb., ed. *Handbook of American Indians North of Mexico.* 2 vols. Totowa, New Jersey: Rowman and Littlefield, 1975.

Icaza, Francisco de. *Conquistadores y pobladores de Nueva España, diccionario autobiográfico sacado de los textos originales.* 2 vols. Madrid: El Adelantado de Segovia, 1923.

Jones, Oakah L., Jr. *Pueblo Warriors and Spanish Conquest.* Norman: University of Oklahoma Press, 1966.

————. *Los Paisanos: Spanish Settlers on the Northern Frontier of New Spain.* Norman: University of Oklahoma Press, 1979.

Lafora, Nicolás de. *Relación del viaje que hizo a los presidios internos situados en la frontera de la América septentrional.* Edited by Vito Alessio Robles. México, D.F.: Editorial Pedro Robredo, 1939.

Lange, Charles H. and Carroll L. Riley, eds. *The Southwestern Journals of Adolph F. Bandelier, 1880–1882.* Albuquerque: University of New Mexico Press, 1966.

Lohmann Villena, Guillermo. *Los americanos en las ordenes nobiliarios, 1529–1900.* 2 vols. Madrid: Consejo Superior de Investigaciones Científicas Instituto "Gonzalo Fernández de Oviedo," 1947.

Mayer, Vincent Villanueva, Jr. *The Black Slave on New Spain's Northern Frontier: San José del Parral, 1632–1676.* Salt Lake City: Unpublished Ph. D. dissertation, University of Utah, 1975.

Menéndez y Pidal, Ramón, and Juan Manzano Manzano, eds. *Recopilación de leyes de los Reynos de las Indias.* Madrid: Ediciones Cultura Hispánica, 1973.

Mirafuentes Galván, José Luis. *Movimientos de resistencia y rebeliones indígenas en el norte de México, 1680–1821.* México, D.F.: Talleres de Impresión de Estampillas y Valores, 1975.

Moorhead, Max L. *The Presidio: Bastion of the Spanish Borderlands.* Norman: University of Oklahoma Press, 1975.

Mota y Escobar, Alonso de la. *Descripción geográfica de los reynos de Nueva Galicia, Nueva Vizcaya y Nuevo León.* 2d ed. México, D.F.: Editorial Pedro Robredo, 1940.

Nasatir, Abraham P. *Borderland in Retreat: From Spanish Louisiana to the Far Southwest.* Albuquerque: University of New Mexico Press, 1976.

Navarro García, Luis. *Don José de Gálvez y la comandancia general de las Provincias Internas del norte de Nueva España.* Sevilla: Publicaciones de la Escuela de Estudios Hispano-Americanos de Sevilla, 1964.

Ocaranza, Fernando. *Capítulos de la historia franciscana.* 2 vols. México, D.F.: el autor, 1933–1934.

————. *Crónicas y relaciones del occidente de México.* 2 vols. México, D.F.: Antigua Librería, Robredo de José Porrúa e Hijos, 1939.

O'Gorman, Edmundo. *Historia de las divisiones territoriales de México.* 3d ed. México, D.F.: Editorial Porrúa, S.A., 1966.

Orozco y Berra, Manuel. *Apuntes para la historia de la geografía en México.* México, D.F.: Imprenta de Francisco Díaz de León, 1881.

Pacheco, Joaquín F., and Francisco de Cárdenas, eds. *Colección de documentos inéditos, relativos a descubrimiento, conquista, y organización de las antiguas posesiones españoles de América y Oceanía, sacadas de los archivos del de Indias.* 42 vols. Madrid: Imprenta de Manuel B. de Quirós, 1864–1884.

Parry, J. H. *The Spanish Theory of Empire in the Sixteenth Century.* Cambridge: The University Press, 1940.

Pérez de Ribas, Andrés. *My Life Among the Savage Nations of New Spain.* Translated by Tomás

Antonio Robertson. Los Angeles: The Ward Ritchie Press, 1968.

Porrúa e Hijos. *Diccionario Porrúa de historia, biografía y geografía de México.* 2 vols. 4th ed. México, D.F.: Editorial Porrúa, S.A., 1976.

Powell, Philip Wayne. *Soldiers, Indians and Silver: The Northward Advance of New Spain, 1550–1600.* Berkeley: University of California Press, 1952.

Priestly, Herbert I. *José de Gálvez, Visitor-General of New Spain.* Berkeley: University of California Press, 1916.

Schurz, William Lytle. *The Manila Galleon.* New York: E.P. Dutton and Co., Inc., 1959.

Spicer, Edward H. *Cycles of Conquest: The Impact of Spain, Mexico, and the United States on the Indians of the Southwest, 1533–1960.* Tucson: University of Arizona Press, 1962.

Surville, Luis de. *Descripción de la situación de los puertos, ensenadas, caletas, y sondas . . . situado en la América meridional.* Folio, ms. book. In, *The Sea Chart,* Derek Howse and Michael Sanderson, New York: McGraw-Hill Book Co., 1973.

Vicens Vives, Jaime, ed. *Historia de España y América.* 5 vols. Barcelona: Editorial Vicens-Vives, 1961.

Wauchope, Robert, ed. *Handbook of Middle American Indians.* Austin: University of Texas Press, 1964.

Wormington, H.M. *Prehistoric Indians of the Southwest.* Denver: The Denver Museum of Natural History, 1969.

Zambrano, Francisco, S.J. *Diccionario bio-bibliográfico de la Compañia de Jesús en México.* 14 vols. México, D.F.: Editorial JUS, S.A., 1961.

REGIONAL AND LOCAL HISTORICAL

Acosta, Roberto. *Apuntes históricos sonorenses: la conquista temporal y espiritual del Yaqui y del Mayo.* México, D.F.: Imprenta Aldina Rosell y Sordo Noriega, 1941.

Alessio Robles, Vito. *Coahuila y Texas; desde la consumación de la independencia hasta el tratado de paz de Guadalupe Hidalgo.* 2 vols. México, D.F.: Talleras Gráficos de la Nación 1946.

Almada, Francisco R. *Diccionario de historia, geografía y biografía chihuahuenses.* Chihuahua: Impresora de Juárez, 1968.

———. *Diccionario de historia, geografía y biografía sonorenses.* Chihuahua: Ruíz Sandoval, S. de R.L., 1952.

———. *Resumen de historia del estado de Chihuahua.* México, D.F.: Libros Mexicanos, 1955.

Archer, Christon. "The Making of Spanish Indian Policy on the Northwest Coast." *New Mexico Historical Review,* January 1977.

Bancroft, Hubert Howe. *History of Arizona and New Mexico, 1520–1888.* Albuquerque: Horn and Wallace, 1962.

———. *History of the North Mexican States and Texas.* 2 vols. San Francisco: The History Company, 1884–1889.

Bannon, John Francis, S.J. *The Mission Frontier in Sonora, 1620–1687.* New York: The United States Catholic Historical Society, 1955.

Barco, Miguel del. *Historia natural y crónica de la antigua California.* Edited by Miguel Léon-Portilla. México, D.F.: Universidad Nacional Autónoma de México, 1973.

Bloom, Lansing B. "The Governors of New Mexico," *The New Mexico Historical Review,* Vol. 10 (1935), 152–157.

Burrus, Ernest J., S.J. *Kino and Manje, Explorers of Sonora and Arizona: Their Vision of the Future. A Study of Their Expeditions and Plans, with an Appendix of Thirty Documents.* Rome: Jesuit Historical Institute, and St. Louis, Missouri: St. Louis University Press, 1971.

Castillo, José Mena. *Historia compendiada del estado de Sinaloa.* México, 1942. Private edition with aid of Rodolfo T. Loaiza, gobernador del estado de Sinaloa.

Clavijero, Francisco Xavier, S.J. *Historia de la antigua Baja California.* Estudio preliminar por Miguel León-Portilla. México, D.F.: Editorial Porrúa, S.A., 1970.

Corbala Acuña, Manuel. *Sonora y sus constituciones.* México, D.F.: Editorial Libras de México, S.A., 1972.

Dabdoub, Claudio. *Historia del Valle del Yaqui.* México, D.F.: Librería Manuel Porrúa, S.A., 1964.

Dobyns, Henry F. *Spanish Colonial Tucson: a Demographic History.* Tucson: University of Arizona Press, 1976.

Dunne, Peter Masten, S.J. *Black Robes in Lower California.* Berkeley: University of California Press, 1952.

———. *Early Jesuit Missions in Tarahumara.* Berkeley: University of California Press, 1948.

Engelhardt, Zephyrin, O.F.M. *The Missions and Missionaries of California.* 2 vols. 2d ed. Santa Barbara, California: Mission of Santa Barbara, 1929.

Galavíz de Capdevielle, María Elena. *Rebeliones indígenas en el norte del reino de la Nueva España, siglos XVI y XVII.* México, D.F.: Editorial Campesina, 1967.

Horgan, Paul. *Lamy of Santa Fe: His Life and Times.* New York: Farrar, Straus and Giroux, 1975.

Hoyo, Eugenio del. *Historia del Nuevo Reino de León.* 2 vols. Monterrey: Instituto Tecnológico y de Estudios Superiores de Monterrey, 1972.

Hunt, Rockwell D., and Nellie Van De Grift Sánchez. *A Short History of California.* New York: Thomas Y. Crowell Co., 1929.

John, Elizabeth A. H. *Storms Brewed in Other Men's Worlds: The Confrontation of Indians, Spanish, and French in the Southwest. 1540–1795.* College Station, Texas: Texas A and M Press, 1975.

Kessell, John L. *Friars, Soldiers, and Reformers: Hispanic Arizona and the Sonora Mission Frontier, 1767–1856.* Tucson: University of Arizona Press, 1976.

————. *Mission of Sorrows: Jesuit Guevavi and the Pimas, 1691–1767.* Tucson: University of Arizona Press, 1970.

Ladrón de Guevara, Antonio. *Noticias de los poblados de que se componen el Nuevo Reino de León, provincia de Coahuila, Nueva Extremadura, y la de Téxas.* Monterrey: Edición de Andrés Montemayor Hernández, 1969.

Lister, Florence C., and Robert H. Lister. *Chihuahua: Storehouse of Storms.* Albuquerque: University of New Mexico Press, 1966.

López-Velarde López, Benito. *Expansión geografíca franciscana en el hoy norte central y oriental de México.* México, D.F.: Editorial Progreso, S.A., 1964.

McCarty, Kieran, O.F.M. *Desert Documentary: The Spanish Years, 1767–1821.* Tucson: The Arizona Historical Society, 1976.

Mecham, J. Lloyd. *Francisco Ibarra and Nueva Viscaya.* Durham, North Carolina: Duke University Press, 1927.

"Memorial sobre las misiones de Sonora, 1772" *Boletín del Archivo General de la Nación.* 9:2 (1938), 276–320.

Mendizábal, Miguel Othón de. *La evolución del noreste de México.* México, D.F.: Publicaciones del Departamento de la Estadistica Nacional, 1930.

Moorhead, Max L. *The Apache Frontier: Jacobo Ugarte and Spanish-Indian Relations in Northern New Spain, 1769–1791.* Norman: University of Oklahoma Press, 1968.

Morales Gómez, Antonio. *Cronología de Nuevo León, 1527–1955.* México, D.F.: Editorial Benito Juárez, 1955.

Navarro García, Luis. *Sonora y Sinaloa en el siglo XVII.* Sevilla: Escuela de Estudios Hispano-Americanos de Sevilla, 1967.

Nentvig, Juan. *Descripción geográfica . . . de Sonora.* Edited by Germán Viveros. México, D.F.: Archivo General de la Nación, 1971.

Nentvig, Juan. *Rudo Ensayo: A Description of Sonora and Arizona in 1764.* Translated and annotated by Alberto Francisco Pradeau and Robert R. Rasmussen. Tucson: University of Arizona Press, 1980.

Ocaranza, Fernando. *Los franciscanos en las provincias internas de Sonora y Ostímuri.* México, D.F.: Propiedad del autor, 1933.

————. *Parva crónica de la sierra madre y las pimerías.* México, D.F.: Instituto Panamericano de Geografía e Historia, No. 64, Editorial Stylo, 1942.

Ochoa Reyna, Arnulfo. *Historia del estado de Durango.* México, D.F.: Editorial del Magisterio, 1958.

Palóu, Francisco, O.F.M. *Vida de Fr. Junípero Serra.* Estudio preliminar por Miguel León-Portilla. México, D.F.: Editorial Porrúa, S.A., 1970.

Pfefferkorn, Ignaz, S.J. *Sonora: A Description of the Province.* Translated and annotated by Theodore E. Treutlein. Albuquerque: University of New Mexico Press, 1949.

Piccolo, Francisco María, S.J. *Informe del estado de la nueva cristiandad de California, 1702.* Edited by Ernest J. Burrus, S.J. Madrid: Ediciones José Porrúa Turanzas, 1962.

Polzer, Charles W., S.J. *Rules and Precepts of the Jesuit Missions of Northwestern New Spain.* Tucson: University of Arizona Press, 1976.

Polzer, Charles W., S.J., and Ernest J. Burrus, S.J. *Kino's Biography of Francisco Javier Saeta, S.J.* Rome: Jesuit Historical Institute, 1971.

Portillo, Diez de Sollano, Alvaro de. *Descubrimientos y exploraciones en las costas de California.* Madrid: Publicaciones de la Escuela de Estudios Hispano-Americanos de Sevilla, 1947.

Richman, Irving B. *California Under Spain and Mexico.* Boston: Houghton Mifflin Co., 1911.

Rodríguez Gallardo, J. Rafael. *Informe sobre Sinaloa y Sonora, año de 1750.* Germán Viveros, ed. México, D.F.: Archivo General de la Nación, 1975.

Rouaix, Pastor. *Diccionario geográfico, histórico y biográfico del estado del Durango.* México, D.F.: Instituto Panamericano de Geografía e Historia, No. 80, 1946.

Sheridan, Thomas E., and Thomas H. Naylor. *Rarámuri: A Tarahumara Chronicle, 1607–1791.* Flagstaff, Arizona: Northland Press, 1979.

Simmons, Marc. *Spanish Government in New Mexico.* Albuquerque: University of New Mexico Press, 1968.

Spicer, Edward H. *The Yaquis, A Cultural History.* Tucson: University of Arizona Press, 1980.

Stagg, Albert. *The First Bishop of Sonora, Antonio de los Reyes, O.F.M.* Tucson: University of Arizona Press, 1976.

Thomas, Alfred B. *Forgotten Frontiers: A Study of the Spanish Indian Policy of Don Juan Bautista* de Anza, *Governor of New Mexico, 1777–1787.* Norman: University of Oklahoma Press, 1932.

_____. *After Coronado: Spanish Exploration Northeast of New Mexico, 1696–1727.* Norman: University of Oklahoma Press, 1935.

_____. *Teodoro de Croix and the Northern Frontier of New Spain, 1776–1783.* Norman: University of Oklahoma Press, 1941.

Tjarks, Alicia V. "Demographic, Ethnic and Occupational Structure of New Mexico, 1790," *The Americas,* Vol. 35, No. 1 (July 1978), 45–88.

Treutlcin, Theodore E., ed. and trans. *Missionary in Sonora: The Travel Reports of Joseph Och. S.J., 1755–1767.* San Francisco: California Historical Society, 1965.

Tuthill, Franklin. *The History of California.* San Francisco: H. H. Bancroft and Co., 1866.

Van De Griff Sánchez, Nellie. *Spanish Arcadia.* San Francisco: Powell Publishing Co., 1929.

Venegas, Miguel, S.J. *Noticia de la California y de su conquista temporal y espiritual.* 3 volumes. México, D.F.: Editorial LAYAC, 1943.

West Robert C. *The Mining Community in Northern New Spain. The Parral Mining District.* Berkeley: University of California Press, 1949. (*Iberoamericana,* No. 30).

Zorrilla, Juan Fidel. *El poder colonial en Nuevo Santander.* México, D.F.: Manuel Porrúa, S.A., 1976.

PALEOGRAPHY

Arribas Arranz, Filemón. *Estudios sobre diplomática castellana de los siglos XV y XVI.* Valladolid: Sever-Cuesta, 1959.

Bently, Harold W. *A Dictionary of Spanish Terms in English, with Special Reference to the American Southwest.* New York: Octagon Books, 1973.

Bribiesca Sumano, Ma. Elena. *Manual de paleografía: Apuntes para un curso de paleografía.* México, D.F.: Archivo General de la Nación, Guías y Catalogos, 24, 1978.

Cappelli, Adriano. *Dizionario Di Abbreviature Latine ed Italiane.* 5th ed. Milan: Ulrico Hoepli, 1954.

Cuervo, José Rufino. *El castellano en América.* Bogotá: Editorial Minerva, 1935.

Floriano Cumbreño, Antonio C. *Curso general de paleografía y diplomático españolas.* Oviedo: La Cruz, 1946.

Garcés, Jorge A. *Paleografía diplomática española y sus peculiaridades en América.* Quito: Publicaciones del Archivo de la Ciudad, Vol. 25, 1949.

Haggard, J. Villasana. *Handbook for Translators of Spanish Historical Documents.* Austin: University of Texas Press, 1941.

Islas Escarcega, Leovigildo. *Diccionario rural de México.* México, D.F.: Editorial Comaval, S.A., 1961.

_____. *Vocabulario campesino nacional.* México, D.F.: Beatríz de Silva, 1945.

Lerner, Isaís. *Arcaismos lexicos del español de América.* Madrid: INSULA, 1974.

López de Toro, José. *Abreviaturas hispánicas.* Madrid: Dirección General de Archivos y Bibliotecas, 1957.

Millares Carlo, Agustín. *Tratado de paleografía española.* Madrid: Hernando S.A., 1932.

Millares Carlo, Agustín, and José Ignacio Mantecón. *Album de paleografía Hispanoamericana de los siglos XVI y XVII.* México, D.F.: Instituto Panamericano de Geografía e Historia, 1955.

Muñoz y Rivero, Jesús. *Manual de paleografía diplomática española de los siglos XII al XVII; método teórica-práctico para aprender a leer los documentos españoles de los siglos XII al XVII.* 2d ed. Madrid: Viuda de Hernando, 1889.

Neves, Alfredo N. *Diccionario de americanismos.* 2d ed. Buenos Aires: Editorial Sopena Argentina, S.A., 1975.

Paluzie y Cantalozella, Esteban. *Paleografía española.* Barcelona: del autor, 1846.

Peñalosa, Joaquín Antonio. *Vocabulario y refranero religioso de México.* México, D.F.: Editorial Jus, 1965.

Rodríguez, Cristobál. *Bibliotheca universal de la polygraphía española.* Madrid: A. Marín, 1738.

Sobarzo, Horacio. *Vocabulario sonorense.* México, D.F.: Editorial Porrúa, S.A., 1966.

Terreros y Pando, Estéban. *Paleografía española.* Barcelona: Autografía del autor, 1846.

COLONIAL GOVERNMENT

Altamira y Crevea, Rafael. *Autonomía y decentralización legislativa en el régimen colonial español: legislación metropolitana y legislación propiamente indiana, siglos XVI a XVII.* Madrid: Coimbra Editora, Ltd., 1945.

_____. *Plan y documentación de la historia de las municipalidades en las Indias españolas, siglos XVI–XVIII.* México, D.F.: Editorial Cultura, S.A., 1950.

Bayle, Constantino, S.J. *Los cabildos seculares en la América Española.* Madrid: Sapientia, S.A., 1952.

Blackmar, Frank W. *Spanish Institutions of the Southwest.* Glorieta, New Mexico: The Rio Grande Press, 1976.

Bravo Ugarte José. *Instituciones, políticas de la Nueva España.* México, D.F.: Editorial, JUS, 1968.

Burkholder, Mark A., and D.D. Chandler. *From Impotence to Authority: The Spanish Crown and the American Audiencias, 1687–1808.* Columbia, Missouri: University of Missouri Press, 1977.

Carrancá y Trujillo, Raul. *La evolución política de Iberoamérica.* Madrid: J. Pérez, 1925.

Chapman, Charles E. *Colonial Hispanic America: A History.* New York: The Macmillan Co., 1933.

Cunningham. Charles H. "The Institutional Background of Spanish American History," *Hispanic American Historical Review,* Vol. 1, No. 1 (February, 1918), 24–39.

————. *The Audiencia in the Spanish Colonies as Illustrated by the Audiencia of Manila, 1583–1800.* Berkeley: University of California Press, 1919.

Diffie, Bailey W. *Latin-American Civilization, Colonial Period.* New York: Octagon Books, 1967.

Gibson, Charles. *The Aztecs Under Spanish Rule: A History of the Indians of the Valley of Mexico, 1519–1810.* Stanford: Stanford University Press, 1964.

————. *Spain in America.* New York: Harper and Row, Harper Torchbacks, 1966.

Haring, Clarence H. *The Spanish Empire in America.* New York: Harcourt Brace and World, Inc., A Harbinger Book, 1963.

Henige, David P. *Colonial Governors: A Comprehensive List, 15th Century to Present.* Madison: University of Wisconsin Press, 1970.

MacLachlan, Colin M. *Criminal Justice in Eighteenth Century Mexico: A Study of the Tribunal of the Acordada.* Berkeley: University of California Press, 1974.

Martínez Peñalosa, Teresa María. *Vocabulario: Explicación de algunos términos y conceptos usados en documentos históricos.* México, D.F.: El Archio General de la Nación, 1977.

Mecham, J.L. "The Real de Minas as a Political Institution," *Hispanic American Historical Review,* Vol. 7, No. 1 (February, 1927), 45–83.

————. "Francisco de Urdiñola, Governor of Nueva Viscaya," *New Spain and the Anglo-American West.* 2 vols. Vol. 1 (1932), 39–66. Los Angeles: Private printer, 1932.

Menéndez-Pidal, Ramón, ed. *Recopilación de leyes de los Reynos de las Indias.* Madrid: Ediciones Cultura Hispánica, 1973.

Navarro García, Luis. *Intendencias en Indias.* Sevilla: Escuela de Estudios Hispano-Americanos de Sevilla, 1959.

O'Gorman, Edmundo. *Historia de las divisiones territoriales de México.* 5th ed. México, D.F.: Editorial Porrúa, S.A., 1973.

Ots Capdequí, José María. *Instituciones.* Madrid: Salvat Editores, S.A., 1959.

————. *El estado español en las Indias.* 3d ed. Buenos Aires: Fondo de Cultura e Económica, 1957.

Parry, J.H. *The Audiencia of New Galicia in the Sixteenth Century.* Cambridge: The University Press, 1948.

Rubio Mañé, Jorge Ignacio. *Introducción al estudio de los virreyes de Nueva España.* México, D.F.: Universidad de México, 1957.

Schäfer, Ernesto. *El consejo real y supremo de las Indias.* 2 vols. Sevilla: M Carmone, 1935, 1947.

Simmons, Marc. *Spanish Government in New Mexico.* Albuquerque: University of New Mexico Press, 1968.

MONEY AND CURRENCY

Argüello, Vicente. *Memoria sobre el valor de las monedas de D. Alfonso El Sabio: mencionadas en las leyes del espéculo, fuero real y partidas.* Madrid: Real Academia de la historia, N.D.

Barrio Lorenzot, Francisco del. *Ordenanzas de gremios de la Nueva España.* Published and compiled by la Secretaría de Industria, Comercio y Trabajo. Introduction by Genaro Estrada. México, D.F.: Secretaría de Gobernación, 1920.

Cantos Benítez, Pedro de. *Escritorio de maravedises, y monedas de oro antiguas, su valor, reducción, y cambio a las monedas corrientes.* Madrid: Lo Imprimio, A. Marín, 1763.

Carrera Stampa, Manuel. "The Evolution of Weights and Measures in New Spain," *Hispanic American Historical Review,* Vol. 29, No. 1 (February) 1949, 2–24.

Elhuyar, Fausto de. *Indagaciones sobre la amonedación en Nueva España . . .* Madrid: Imprenta de la Calle de la Greda, 1810.

Florescano, Enrique, and Isabel Gil. *Descripciones económicas generales de Nueva España, 1784–1817.* México, D.F.: Instituto Nacional de Antropología e Historia, 1973.

Hamilton, Earl J. *American Treasure and the Price Revolution in Spain, 1501–1650.* Cambridge: Harvard University Press, 1934.

————. *Money, Prices, and Wages in Valencia, Aragon and Navarre, 1351–1500.* Cambridge: Harvard University Press, 1936.

Haring, Clarence H. *Trade and Navigation Between Spain and the Indies in the Time of the Hapsburgs.* Cambridge: Harvard University Press, 1918.

————. "American Gold and Silver Production in the First Half of the Sixteenth Century," *The Quarterly Journal of Economics,* Vol. 29 (May) 1915, 433–74.

Mateu y Llopis, Felipe. *Glosario hispanese de numismática.* Barcelona: Consejo Superior de Investigaciones Científicas, 1946.

. *La moneda española (breve historia monetaria de España)*. Barcelona: Editorial Alberto Martín, 1946.

Meek, Wilbur T. *The Exchange Media of Colonial Mexico*. New York: King's Crown Press, Columbia University, 1948.

Nesmith, Robert I. *The Coinage of the First Mint of the Americas at Mexico City, 1536–1572*. New York: The American Numismatic Society, 1955.

Paz-Soldán, Moreyra. "La técnica de la moneda colonial; unidades, pesos, medidas y relaciones," *Revista de Historia de América*. No. 20 (1945), 347–69.

Pradeau, Alberto Francisco. *Numismatic History of Mexico, from the Pre-Columbian Epoch to 1823*. Los Angeles: Western Printing Company, 1938.

Sentenach, Narciso. "El maravedí: su grandeza y decadencia," *Revista de Archivos, Bibliotecas y Museos*. 3rd ser. Vol. 12 (January–June) 1905, 180–220.

. "Monedas de oro castellanas: la dobla, el excelente o ducado, el escudo," *Revista de Archivos, Bibliotecas y Museos*. 3rd ser. Vol. 13 (Julio-Diciembre, 1905), 180–99.

. "Monedas de plata y de vellón castellanas," *Revista de Archivos, Bibliotecas y Museos*. 3rd ser. Vol. 14 (January–June) 1906, 329–45.

Shaw, W.A. *The History of Currency, 1252–1894*. New York: Burt Franklin, 1896.

WEIGHTS AND MEASURES

Alexander, J.H. *Universal Dictionary of Weights and Measures*. New York: 1867.

Amiran, D.H.K., and A.P. Schick. *Geographical Conversion Tables*. Zurich: Aschmann and Scheller, A.G., 1961.

Carrera Stampa, Manuel. "The Evolution of Weights and Measures in New Spain," *Hispanic American Historical Review*, Vol. 29, No. 1 (February, 1949), 2–24.

Florescano, Enrique, and Isabel Gil. *Descripciones económicas generales de Nueva España, 1784–1817*. México, D.F.: Instituto Nacional Antropología e Historia, 1973.

García de Palacio, Diego. *Instrucción nautica para navegar (1587)*. In *Colección de incunables Americanos*, Siglo XVI, Volume VIII. Madrid: Ediciones Cultura Hispánica, 1944.

García Franco, Salvador. *Historia del arte y ciencia de navegar*. 2 vols. Madrid: Instituto Histórico de Marina, 1947.

. *La legua náutica en la edad media*. Madrid: Instituto Histórico de Marina, 1957.

Kennelly, A.E. *Vestiges of Pre-Metric Weights and Measures*. New York: The Macmillan Co., 1928.

Kisch, Bruno. *Scales and Weights: A Historical Outline*. New Haven: Yale University Press, 1965.

McCann, Ferdinand. *Guía minera para ingenieros y prácticos*. México, D.F.: Tipografía de Bouligny y Schmidt Sucesos, 1910.

Naft, Stephen E.E., and Ralph DeSola. *International Conversion Tables*. New York: Duell, Sloan and Pearce, 1961.

O'Scanlan, Timoteo. *Diccionario marítimo español*. Madrid: Museo Naval, 1974.

Páez Courvel, Luis E. *Historia de las medidas agrarias antiguas: legislación colonial y republicana y el proceso de su aplicación en las titulaciones de tierras*. Bogotá: Editorial Librería Voluntad, S.A., 1940.

Rodríguez, G. *Pesos y medias del mundo*. Habana: Instituto de Agricultura, 1922.

Santa Cruz, Alonso de. *Libro de las longitudines*. Sevilla: Tip. Zarzuela, 1921.

Spain. Instituto Geográfico y Estadístico. *Equivalencias entre las pesas y medias usadas antiguamente en las diversas provincias de España y las legales del sistema métrico-decimal*. Madrid: Imp. de la Dirección General del Instituto Geográfico y Estadístico, 1886.

NATIVE GROUPS

Bancroft, Hubert H. *The Native Races of the Pacific States*. San Francisco: A.L. Bancroft and Company, 1883.

Barco, Miguel del. *Historia natural y crónica de la antigua California*. Edited by Miguel León-Portilla. México, D.F.: Universidad Nacional Autónoma de México, 1973.

Bolton, Herbert E. *Font's Complete Diary: Anza's California Expedition, 1774–1776*. Berkeley: University of California Press, 1931.

Brugge, David M. "Some Plains Indians in the Church Records of New México," *Plains Anthropologist*, Vol. 10 (29), 181, 1965.

Campbell, T.N. *Ethnohistoric Notes on Indian Groups Associated with Three Spanish Missions at Guerrero, Coahuila*. Center for Archaeological Research. The University of Texas at San Antonio, Archaeology and History of the San Juan Bautista Mission Area, Coahuila and Texas, Report No. 3, 1979.

Cones, Elliot. *On the Trail of a Spanish Pioneer: Diary of Gárces*. New York: F.P. Harper, 1900.

Decorme, Gerard, S.J. *La obra de los Jesuitas mexicanos durante la época colonial, 1572–1767*. Tomo II., *Las Misiones*. México, D.F.: Antigua Librería Robredo de José Porrúa e Hijos, 1941.

Documentary Relations of the Southwest, Master Index. Computer Access Bibliography. Tucson: Arizona State Museum, 1979.

Engelhardt, Zephyrin, O.F.M. *The Missions and Missionaries of California*. 2 vols. 2nd ed. Santa Barbara, California: Mission of Santa Barbara, 1929.

Forbes, Jack D. *Apache, Navaho and Spaniard*. Norman: University of Oklahoma Press, 1960.

Galaviz de Capdevielle, María Elena de. *Rebeliones Indígenas en el Norte del Reino de la Nueva España, Siglos XVI y XVII*. México, D.F.: Editorial Campesina, 1967.

Geiger, Maynard and Clement W. Meighan. *As the Padres Saw Them: California Indian Life and Customs as Reported by the Franciscan Missionaries, 1813–1815*. Santa Barbara Mission Archive/Library, Arthur H. Clark Company, 1976.

Gómez Canedo, Lino. *Primeras exploraciones y poblamiento de Texas (1686–1694)*. Monterrey: Publicaciones del Instituto Tecnológico y Estudios.

Griffen, William B. "Changing Indian Societies in North Central Colonial Mexico," (Unpublished Ph.D. dissertation, 2 vols., University of Arizona, 1965).

————. "Franciscan Missions and Indian Assimilation in Nueva Vizcaya," (Unpublished ms., Arizona State Museum, 1968).

————. *Culture Change and Shifting Populations in Central Northern Mexico*. Anthropological Papers of the University of Arizona, No. 13. Tucson: University of Arizona Press, 1969.

————. *Indian Assimilation in the Franciscan Area of Nueva Vizcaya*. Anthropological Papers of the University of Arizona, No. 33. Tucson: University of Arizona Press, 1979.

Heizer, Robert F. (volume editor). *Handbook of North American Indians*. Vol. 8, *California*. Washington: Smithsonian Institution, 1978.

Hoyo, Eugenio del. *Historia del Nuevo León (1577–1723)*. Monterrey: Instituto Tecnológia y Estudios Superiores de Monterrey, 1972.

John, Elizabeth A.H. *Storms Brewed in Other Men's Worlds*. College Station: Texas A&M University Press, 1975.

Kroeber, A.L. *Handbook of the Indians of California*. Washington, D.C.: Bureau of American Ethnology, 1925.

Mirafuente Galván, José Luis. *Movimientos de resistencia y rebeliones indigenas en el norte de México (1680–1821)*. México: Archivo General de la Nación, 1975.

Morfi, Fray Augustín de. *History of Texas, 1673–1779*. Translated by Carlos Eduardo Castañeda. Albuquerque: Quivira Society, 1935.

Navarro García, Luis. *Sonora y Sinaloa en el Siglo XVII*. Sevilla: Escuela de Estudios Hispano-Americanos de Sevilla, 1967.

Pérez de Ribas, Andrés. *Historia de los triunfos de nuestra Santa Fe entre gentes las mas bárbaras y fieras del Nuevo Orbe* . . . México, D.F.: Editorial Layac, 1944.

Powers, Stephen. "Tribes of California." *Contributions to North American Ethnology*, Vol. III. Washington, D.C.: U.S. Government Printing Office, 1887.

Preciado, María Teresa Huerta. *Rebeliones indigenas en el Noroeste de México en la época colonial*. México: Instituto Nacional de Antropología e Historia, 1966.

Schuetz, Mardith Keithly. The Indians of the San Antonio Missions 1718–1821, (Unpublished Ph.D. dissertation, University of Texas, Austin, 1980).

RACIAL TERMINOLOGY

Aguirre Beltrán, Gonzalo. *La población negra de México, 1519–1810*. México, D.F.: Ediciones Fuente Cultural, 1946.

Echánove Trujillo, Carlos. "Sociologia Mexicana," in *La estructura social y cultural de Mexico*, by José E. Iturriaga. 4th ed. México, D.F.: Editorial Porrúa, 1972.

Keen, Benjamin, ed. *Readings in Latin American Civilization, 1492 to the Present*. "Noticias Secretas," by Jorge Juan and Antonio de Ulloa. 2d ed. Boston: Houghton Mifflin, 1967.

Pérez de Barradas, J. *Los mestizos de América*. Madrid: Cultura Clasica y Moderna, 1948.

Real Academia Español. *Diccionario de la Lengua Española*. 16th ed. Madrid: Espasa-Calpe, 1939.

Roncal, Joaquín. "The Negro Race in Mexico," *Hispanic American Historical Review*. Vol. 24 (August, 1944), 530–40.

Santamaría, Francisco J. *Diccionario de mejicanismos*. 2d ed. México, D.F.: Editorial Porrúa, S.A., 1974.

ECONOMIC

Aguirre, Beltrán G. "Slave Trade in Mexico," *Hispanic American Historical Review*, Vol. 24 (1944), 412–31.

Borah, Woodrow. *New Spain's Century of Depression*. Berkeley: University of California Press, 1951 (*Iberoamericana*, No. 35).

Borah, Woodrow, and Sherburne F. Cook. *Price Trends of Some Basic Commodities in Central Mexico, 1531–1570*. Berkeley: University of California Press, 1958. (*Iberoamericana*, No. 40).

Brading, D.A. *Miners and Merchants in Bourbon Mexico, 1763–1810*. Cambridge: University Press, 1971.

Chávez Orozco, L., ed. *Documentos para la historia económica de México. Vol. IV; Dictamen del Virrey Revillagigedo sobre la ordenanza de intendentes de la Nueva España.* México, D.F.: Publicaciones de la Secretaría de la Economía Nacional, 1934.

————. *Documentos para la historia económica de México, Vol. III; Los salarios y el trabajo en México, 1708–1810.* México, D.F.: Publicaciones de la Secretaría de la Economía Nacional, 1934.

Colmeiro, Manuel. *Historia de la economía política en España,* 2 vols. Madrid: Taurus Ediciones, S.A., 1965.

Florescano, Enrique. *Precios del maíz y crisis agrícolas en México, 1708–1810.* México, D.F.: El Colegio de México, 1969.

Florescano, Enrique, y Isabel Gil. *Descripciones económicas generales de Nueva España, 1784–1817.* México, D.F.: Instituto Nacional de Antropología e Historia, 1973.

Gómez de Cervantes, Gonzalo. *La vida económica y social de Nueva España al Finalizar del Siglo XVI.* Edited by Alberto María Carreño. México, D.F.: Antigua Librería Robredo de J. Porrúa e Hijos, 1944.

Haring, Clarence H. *The Spanish Empire in America.* New York: Oxford University Press, 1947.

Klein, Julius. *The Mesta: A Study in Spanish Economic History, 1273–1836.* Cambridge: Harvard University Press, 1920.

Ots Capdequí, José María. *España en América; el régimen de tierras en la época colonial.* México, D.F.: Fondo de Cultura Económica, 1959.

Roncal, Joaquín. "The Negro Race in Mexico," *Hispanic American Historical Review,* Vol. 24 (1944), 530–40.

Scholes, France. "Supply Service of the New Mexican Missions in the Seventeenth Century," *New Mexican Historical Review,* Vol. 5 (1930), 93–115, 186–210, 286–404.

Simpson, Lesley Byrd. *The Encomienda in New Spain: Forced Native Labor in the Spanish Colonies, 1492–1550.* Berkeley: University of California Publications, History, Vol. 19, 1929.

Velarde, Carlos E. *Historia del derecho de minería hispano-americano.* Buenos Aires: N.P., 1919.

Zavala, Silvio. *La encomienda indiana.* 2nd ed. México, D.F.: Editorial Porrúa, 1973.

Zavala, Silvio, and María Castello, ed. *Fuentes para la historia del trabajo en Nueva España.* 8 vols. México, D.F.: N.P., 1939–1946.

LEGAL

Altamira y Crevea, Rafael. *Diccionario castellano de palabras jurídicas y técnicas tomadas de la legislación indiana.* México, D.F.: Instituto Pan-americano de Geografía e Historia, No. 112, 1951.

————. *Autonomía y decentralización legislativa en el régimen colonial español; legislación metropolitana y legislación propiamente indiana.* Madrid: Coimbra Editora, Ltd., 1945.

————. *Manual de investigación de la historia del derecho Indiano.* México, D.F.: Instituto Panamericano de Geografía e Historia, 1948.

Cabanellas, Guillermo. *Diccionario de derecho usual.* 3 vols. Buenos Aires: Ediciones ARAYU, 1953.

Escriche y Martín, Joaquín. *Diccionario razonado de legislación civil, penal, comercial y forense.* 2nd ed. Madrid: Librería de Calleja e Hijos, 1832.

————. *Elementos del derecho español.* 3rd ed. Paris: Librería de Salva, 1840.

Menéndez-Pidal, Ramón, ed. *Recopilación de leyes de los Reynos de las Indias.* Madrid: Ediciones Cultura Hispanica, 1973.

Ossorio y Floret, Manuel, et. al. *Enciclopedia jurida omeba.* 25 vols. Buenos Aires: Editorial Bibliografía Argentina, 1954—.

Ots Capdequí, José María. *Estudios de historia del derecho español en las indias.* Bogotá: Editorial Minerva, S.A., 1940.

Ots Capdequí, José María. *Instituciones.* Barcelona: Salvat Editores, S.A., 1959.

Palleres, Eduardo. *Diccionario de derecho procesal civil.* México, D.F.: El Caballitón, 1975.

Pedret y Torres, Rodríguez, et al. *Enciclopedia jurídica española.* Barcelona: Francisco Seix, 1910. 30 vols. with annual appendix.

Pina, Rafael. *Diccionario de derecho.* 4th ed. México, D.F.: Porrúa, 1975.

Real Academia Española. *Diccionario de la lengua española.* Madrid: Editorial Espasa-Calpe, S.A., 1974.

Real Díaz, José Joaquín. *Estudio diplomático del documento indiano.* Sevilla: Escuela de Estudios Hispanamericanos, 1970.

Rodríguez de San Miguel, Juan. *Pandectas Hispano-Megicanas.* México, D.F.: Mariano Galván Rivera, 1840. 3 vols.

Santamaría, Francisco J. *Diccionario de Mejicanismos.* México, D.F.: Editorial Porrúa, S.A., 1974.

Solórzano Pereira, Juan. *Política Indiana.* Madrid: 1736.

Vance, John T. *The Background of Hispanic American Law: Legal Sources and Juridical Literature of Spain.* Washington, D.C.: Catholic University of America Press, 1937.

Zavala, Silvio. *Las instituciones jurídicas en la conquista de América.* 2nd ed. México, D.F.: Editorial Porrúa, S.A., 1971.

**Books of Related Interest from
The University of Arizona Press**

Friar Bringas Reports to the King:
Methods of Indoctrination on the Frontier of New Spain, 1796–97
(Documentary Relations of the Southwest series)

Daniel S. Matson and Bernard L. Fontana, translators and editors

Rules and Precepts of the Jesuit Missions
of Northwestern New Spain
(Documentary Relations of the Southwest series)

Charles W. Polzer

Juan Nentvig's Rudo Ensayo:
A Description of Sonora and Arizona in 1764

Alberto F. Pradeau and Robert R. Rasmussen, translators and editors

Spanish and Mexican Records of the American Southwest:
A Bibliographic Guide to Archive and Manuscript Sources

Henry P. Beers
